S0-ASX-474

THE SOVIET UNION
AND THE PACIFIC

The Royal Institute of International Affairs is an independent body which promotes the rigorous study of international questions and does not express opinions of its own. The opinions expressed in this publication are the responsibility of the author.

THE SOVIET UNION
AND
THE PACIFIC

GERALD SEGAL

THE ROYAL INSTITUTE OF
INTERNATIONAL AFFAIRS · London

UNWIN HYMAN · Boston
London · Sydney · Wellington

ARCHBISHOP ALEMANY LIBRARY
DOMINICAN COLLEGE
SAN RAFAEL, CALIFORNIA

DS
518.7
.S44
1990

© 1990 by Royal Institute of International Affairs.
This book is copyright under the Berne Convention. No reproduction
without permission. All rights reserved.

Unwin Hyman, Inc.
955 Massachusetts Avenue, Cambridge, Mass. 02139, USA

Published by the Academic Division of
Unwin Hyman Ltd
15/17 Broadwick Street, London W1V 1FP, UK

Allen & Unwin (Australia) Ltd,
8 Napier Street, North Sydney, NSW 2060, Australia

Allen & Unwin (New Zealand) Ltd in association with the
Port Nicholson Press Ltd,
Compusales Building, 75 Ghuznee Street, Wellington 1, New Zealand

First published in 1990

Library of Congress Cataloging in Publication Data

Segal, Gerald, 1953–
  The Soviet Union and the Pacific/Gerald Segal.
    p.   cm.
Includes bibliographical references.
ISBN 0-04-445813-4. — ISBN 0-04-445814-2 (pbk.)
1. East Asia—Relations—Soviet Union. 2. Soviet Union—Relations—
East Asia. 3. Asia, Southeastern—Relations—Soviet Union.
4. Soviet Union—Relations—Asia, Southeastern.   I. Title.
DS518.7.S44   1990   90-32193
303.48′24705—dc20   CIP

British Library Cataloguing in Publication Data

Segal, Gerald, *1953–*
  The Soviet Union and the Pacific.
  1. Pacific region. Foreign relations with Soviet Union
  2. Soviet Union. Foreign relations with Pacific region
  I. Title
  327.091823
  ISBN 0-04-445813-4
  ISBN 0-04-445814-2 pbk

Typeset in 10 on 12 point Bembo by Fotographics (Bedford) Ltd
and printed in Great Britain by Billing and Sons Ltd, London and Worcester

For J.M.L.

Contents

List of Figures

Acknowledgments

You have to bring your own computer to Chatham House, and the food in the canteen leaves a great deal to be desired, but otherwise it is the perfect place to research and write. This book was undertaken as part of the Soviet foreign policy programme, directed by Alex Pravda and supported by the Economic and Social Science Research Council (grant no. E 00 22 2011). The East Asia programme, directed by Brian Bridges, ensured that I never became too Soviet-centred. Other members of the Chatham House staff helped me understand aspects of the Pacific economy as well as the strategic balances in the region. John Roper, Jon Stern and Lenny Geron laboured through earlier drafts, and Pauline Wickham wielded her savage, but effective, green editorial pen. I am also grateful to Wolf Mendl, Edwina Moreton and other members of the Chatham House study group who read drafts at various stages. Several research trips to East Asia were undertaken in 1988–9, most notably to the Soviet Far East, Japan, China and Hong Kong. The entire project was made possible by funding from the Sasakawa Peace Foundation.

G.S.

1
Introduction

Time-worn standards and stereotypes are particularly tenacious in politics, to say nothing of political thinking. It seems to us that with regard to many problems of the Asian Pacific region mass perceptions and consciousness are dominated by views and approaches whose roots lie in the experience gained by us in European and Soviet-U.S. affairs. . . . It would evidently be premature to claim that the Asian Pacific region has already taken up a proper place in Soviet foreign policy. We have unquestionably begun to concern ourselves with the region, but unfortunately this is not enough.[1]

The Soviet Union may not be a natural East Asian power, but it is very much a natural Pacific power. Yet with all the fashionable speculation about an impending Pacific century, it is striking just how little attention is paid to the Soviet factor. To be sure, only in recent years has the Soviet Union itself begun to consider the Pacific as anything more than an arena of naval competition. Mikhail Gorbachev has clearly placed parts of the Pacific very high on his agenda for foreign policy reform, and he has already engineered major foreign policy triumphs in the region. Thus, the two central questions to be answered are, what does the Soviet Union now want from the Pacific region, and how has Soviet policy towards the Pacific been reformed?

Although there have been earlier studies of Soviet policy in Asia or even East Asia, it is in keeping with the Soviet Union's own blinkered past that there have been few attempts to understand Soviet policy towards the somewhat different region called the Pacific.[2] The Pacific-wide perspective adopted in this study is essential not only because of the trend of Pacific-chic in other Western studies, but also because the Soviet Union itself has begun to take the Pacific region seriously.[3]

However, this study of international relations provides a more fully regional analysis rather than only a simple look at the Pacific through a Soviet lens. In order to tackle the diverse and difficult subject of the international relations of the Pacific from the Soviet perspective, it is essential to train the binoculars in the opposite direction, too, and assess how the states of the region see the Soviet Union. One of the most striking features of the new Soviet policies in the Pacific is the extent to which these policies are being shaped by its neighbours' criticisms of Soviet policy.

This study focuses on changes in several major dimensions of Soviet regional foreign policy, rather than adopting the conventional strategy of taking each country or subregion in turn—an approach that would fail to show how Soviet policy increasingly concerns groups of states rather than individual nations. What is more, the analysis, in keeping with its focus on international relations, draws on somewhat unusual sources, at least from the point of view of the more orthodox Soviet specialist. As we now know from Soviet sources, much of what previously appeared in the Soviet media and journals was biased and untruthful. Contemporary Soviet policy makers are quick to admit that policy is changing so fast these days that they must read their own press as well as that of the outside world to discover the latest trends. Given such rapid change, it is essential to be eclectic about sources.

The study gives weight to historical factors. Although Soviet policy towards the Pacific has changed significantly in recent years, many of the Gorbachev reforms draw on old traditions. The reasons for the past rise and fall of Russian power in the Pacific are still relevant to contemporary discussions.

The Soviet Union is likely to become a different and perhaps, in the long term, a more important power in the Pacific. Moscow has recognized that if it is to succeed at all in its objective, it will have to re-order drastically its priorities in the region. It has discovered, as the United States has, that military power gives only an illusion of influence. There is always a danger of imperial overstretch in the vast and increasingly vibrant Pacific region. Economic and political influence must also be developed. The process of arranging priorities is already underway. As a result, the international politics of the Pacific are being transformed and the balance of power shifted.

These changes in Soviet foreign policy and in the Pacific region are both affected by, and in turn reshaping, Soviet domestic politics. A constant subtheme of the analysis is that the key to the success of the new Soviet policy in the Pacific lies in domestic reform, especially in the reform of the politics and economics of the Soviet Pacific territory. With so much uncertainty surrounding the great experiment in *perestroika*, some uncertainty must also remain about the prospects for continuing reform of Soviet policy in the Pacific. Yet, in the short term, reform there must be; the Soviet Union has no option. Because domestic reform is directly related to the planned foreign policy reform, this analysis must begin with a detailed look at the Soviet Union's home base in the Pacific.

2

The Soviet Pacific Setting

Russia's Eurasian view of the Pacific is unique. From the continental heartland of the vast Russian territory, leaders in Moscow rarely see beyond East Asia to the wider Pacific. In contrast to their view of Europe, where a belt of buffer states protected them from the hostile world, in the Pacific they see only Mongolia between them and the outside world. In fact, Mongolia itself seems to call out for protection from the vastness of China—that great civilization of Asia that appears to stand in the way of every Soviet advance into East Asia.

Well beyond China, and almost invisible in its shadow, lies Southeast Asia. Even farther away are the islands of the Pacific. The larger islands, such as Australia and New Zealand, are more distant from Soviet territory than nearly anywhere in the world except Latin America. From Moscow, the tinier specks of the South Pacific are virtually invisible.

As Russians look eastward, they also focus on Japan and Korea, which block Soviet access to much of the waters of the Pacific. In its search for outlets to the great ocean, Russia retreats to the Arctic wastes, and it becomes aware of its rivals in the rear—the United States and Canada. If one is in a paranoid state of mind, the image of the Pacific from Russia is disorienting and disquieting.

Geographic realities

The most obvious geographic reality about the Pacific is the sheer distance involved. The 6,500 km from Moscow to Vladivostok (which is on the same latitude as Boston and Marseilles) is a bit more than the distance from Moscow to Lagos or Montreal. When day breaks in Moscow, the working day is drawing to a close in

Vladivostok. Residents of Vladivostok were the first in the world regularly to watch their television transmitted by satellite.[1]

The heartland of the Soviet Union is far from the Soviet Pacific, but then most other places are even more distant. The American travelling from Los Angeles—the so-called gateway to the Pacific century—has longer to travel to Tokyo than does the Russian flying from Moscow to the Soviet Pacific capital in Vladivostok. Even the trip from Vladivostok to Hong Kong (much like the one from Moscow to Cairo), is similar to the Tokyo–Hong Kong trip and less than half the distance between Sydney and Hong Kong. Yes, the Soviet Pacific is a long way from European Russia; but because of its relative closeness to the East Asian centres of population, the Soviet Union has more geographic claim to being a natural Pacific power than do any of the Americans or the inhabitants of the South Pacific.

Russia's claim to be a natural Pacific power as well as (unlike the United States) a natural European one, is, of course, derived from the great swathe of Eurasia that is the Soviet Union. The distance between Yokohama and Rotterdam via the Soviet Union is 13,770 km, but via the Panama Canal it is 23,240 km. Cargo is 25 percent cheaper to send on the Trans-Siberian railway line than via the 27,000 km journey around Africa. Russia as *the* Eurasian power clearly has economic importance as well as strategic symbolism.

But deciding what is the European part of the Soviet Union and what is the Asian portion has not always been easy. The Ural mountains, extending to the Soviet frontier with Iran and Afghanistan, is the most generally accepted demarcation of Europe from Asia. By this measure, the Soviet Union is clearly the largest state in Asia.

Yet part of that Soviet Asia is so-called Central Asia, including most of the former Khanates in the south, and it is distinct from what has often been called Siberian Asia. When discussing the Soviet Union and East Asia, it would seem most logical to include the 2.4m sq km of West Siberia, with the 4.1m sq km of East Siberia and the 6.2m sq km of the Soviet Far East. But impressive arguments have been adduced as to why West Siberia is not part of East Asia and why, in fact, not even all of East Siberia should properly be included, despite the Soviet Union's administrative arrangements.[2] The terms 'East Asian Siberia' and 'Pacific Siberia' from previous analyses are not the same, nor indeed has the Soviet government been consistent in dividing up its Asian regions.

For the purposes of our analysis, and without any more justifications than those of previous analyses, the part of the Soviet Union that is included in the current administrative regions of East Siberia and the Far East (together making up 60 percent of the land of the Russian Republic) is defined as Soviet Pacific territory.[3] With an area of 10.3m sq km, this region would be the largest country in the world, just ahead of Canada, China and the United States. The Soviet Pacific would then be the largest country in the Pacific as well. Its coastline along the Pacific is the second longest (after Indonesia's).

In terms of population, however (16.4 million people in 1986, and an average population density of 1.6 per sq km), the Soviet Pacific territory comes out just ahead of Mongolia and is second from the bottom among Pacific states. Even the Maritime Krai of the Soviet Far East, with a population of 2.2 million (similar to Mongolia or Singapore) and the most densely populated part of the Soviet Pacific, has a population density of 6.2 people per sq km, comparable to that of Papua New Guinea or the Solomon Islands and three times that of Australia.

More than three-quarters of the peoples of the Soviet Pacific are of Russian origin. As occurred in the settlement of North America, the indigenous population is now a tiny minority. In the mid-1930s, as many as 500,000 ethnic Koreans were in the area around Vladivostok, but in 1938 they were dispersed, mostly to Central Asia. The 1979 census showed about 34,000 Koreans in Sakhalin, 163,000 in the Uzbek SSR and 91,000 in the Kazakh SSR. Only 55 percent of these ethnic Koreans thought of Korean as their mother tongue.[4]

Also like the North Americans, most people (nearly 80 percent) in the Soviet Pacific region are urban, and this population is spread out along rail lines and the southern frontier. The three largest cities are modern and growing, with 800,000 in Krasnoyarsk, and 600,000 in Vladivostok and also in Khabarovsk.[5] With the people so heavily concentrated and the lines of communication so vulnerably stretched, there is a natural sense of living on the frontiers in a hostile environment. The Soviet Pacific looks remarkably like Canada—a vast, mostly cold territory with few people.

Even more so than the Canadians, the people live on the edge of a climate not really fit for human habitation. More than half the land is subject to permafrost, and ice fog hangs over the cities and towns.[6] Building factories and bridges under these conditions, let alone living an outdoor life, is difficult. Metals become brittle, lubricants freeze and skin sears in the cold. The psychological stresses of such life are a serious problem.[7]

In summer heavy rains cause the rivers to flood, marshes to spread and mosquitos with legendary appetites for human blood to flourish. It is not surprising that the population is more mobile than is the norm in the rest of the Soviet Union, and also is both younger and more fertile. Those people who brave the elements are also said to be a tougher, more individualistic breed. Nevertheless, a shortage of labour is a perennial problem. Although wages are two or three times the national average, living costs can also be high and cultural life is poorer.[8]

Of course, the climate is not all bad. Visitors to Vladivostok are pleasantly surprised to find a 'Black Sea resort' feel to the town—the climate is milder than Moscow and people bathe in the Amur basin well into September. As in Canada, the population of the Soviet Far East is concentrated in the most southerly parts. The growing of rice and grapevines suggests there is plenty of scope for a pleasant life in the area. The citizens enjoy the rough-and-ready romantic image of their region. As one Soviet observer enthused,

> Where else do grapevines wrap themselves around fir trees? Where else do tigers hunt arctic reindeer? Ginseng, geysers, volcanoes, king crabs and salmon—in our country these are found only in the Far East. . . . The very symbol of Far Eastern fauna is the Ussuri tiger. Despite an awesome appearance, this lord of the taiga rarely attacks humans unless provoked.[9]

The psychology of the Ussuri tiger, if not the romantic spirit of the Soviet Pacific, is a vital dimension of the Soviet Union's perspective on the Pacific.

Transportation

The problems of distance are in part also problems of politics. Distances from European Russia may be long, but the distances to other Pacific neighbours are not. Yet, for political reasons, most attempts at developing the Soviet Pacific have come from European Russia and not from the local region. The sense of the Soviet Pacific as a lonely outpost in a hostile world is enhanced.

Historically, waterways have provided the chief transportation routes. The magnificent rivers of the region carried the first explorers to the great ocean, but they no longer play so vital a part. The major exception today could be the Amur river, which forms part of the eastern frontier with China. As a communication route for trade with China, or as a source of hydroelectricity, the Amur could be transformed into an artery of great economic activity.

Of course, the need for water links is much reduced because of faster air travel as well as railroads, which carry most of the bulk cargo to the region. But water routes, even across the roof of Asia to Murmansk, are still crucial. The Murmansk run from Vladivostok is a bit longer than the trip from Los Angeles to Yokohama, but it is shorter than that from Los Angeles to Sydney. The big difference is one of climate rather than distance. The Arctic route is icebound for 6 to 9 months a year, with narrow and shallow channels that make it vulnerable in time of war. But major investment has been made in extending the number and types of ports, including Nakhodka, Vrangel and Sovetskaya Gavan. These ports offer the best prospects for extending contacts with other states of the Pacific.[10]

The most reliable link is the famed 'big red train'—the Trans-Siberian railway. Since its completion in 1904 it has carried the burden of supply and, unlike its Canadian counterpart, is not supplemented by transcontinental roads.[11] The Trans-Siberian railway, one of the most heavily used railways in the world, clearly needed to be supplemented by the Baikal-Amur Mainline (BAM).[12] However, despite its official opening in 1984, the BAM is still not fully operational, and the Soviet desire to develop a reliable 'land bridge' across Eurasia remains unfulfilled. Equally, the prospect of developing entrepôt trade at the Pacific terminals of the rail lines depends on much greater success in the development of the rail links. The BAM eases some of the problems of congestion and strategic vulnerability of the old line, but the Soviet Pacific remains seriously vulnerable at the end of a long, thin line of communication. The economics of the Soviet Pacific argue for closer links with Pacific neighbours and more autonomy from European Russia as the only effective long-term solutions to transportation bottlenecks and high costs.

The most rapidly growing sector of the transportation economy is the pipelines.[13] Most of the pipelines are in Western Siberia, however, and hopes of connecting Japan and the entrepôt ports to the pipelines have not yet materialized. As with many of the economic plans for the development of the Soviet Pacific, the hyperbole of planners has rarely been realized in fact.

Resources and the economy

The hyperbole about the Soviet Pacific—incomparable, inexhaustible, immeasurable—is also aptly applied to many of its resources. New discoveries occur regularly, but even the surveys of the Khrushchev era claimed that Siberia as a whole contained 90 percent of the Soviet Union's coal, 67 percent of its iron ore, 80 percent of its timber, the largest gas deposits in the world, enormous water potential and rich reserves of gold, tin, copper, and other nonferrous and precious metals.[14] Certainly the hyperbole concerning Siberia is not always applicable to the Soviet Pacific, for the largest part of the oil and gas reserves is found in Western Siberia, outside the area we have defined as the Soviet Pacific. Nevertheless, it is only a mild exaggeration to suggest that the Soviet Union might not be a superpower were it not for the Pacific region's mineral wealth and territory.

Yet many of these riches either have been squandered or have yet to be exploited. The reasons are geographic as well as political. Successive Soviet leaders regularly promise new plans to explore and exploit the resources of Siberia. Industry still constitutes the core of the Soviet Pacific's economy, with nonferrous metals, fishing and forestry accounting for 50 percent of industrial production. This imbalance in emphasis on extractive industries has been aggravated by an often perverse planning system and the associated political culture. Lack of transportation and investment have also contributed to the failure to turn the treasure trove into wealth, prosperity and power.[15]

Academician Abel Aganbegyan has pointed to deep-rooted failings of the economic system, chronically wasteful techniques and the failure to create reasonable living conditions for the workforce.[16] Indeed, the problems in the Soviet Pacific region have been so serious that some of the Gorbachev leadership's new ideas on reform were actually first developed in Siberia.[17] By the time Gorbachev came to power, growth rates in the Soviet Pacific had fallen well below national averages. To that extent, at least, the freer spirit of the Soviet Pacific, combined with the deeper problems, provided some of the newer ideas for Soviet reform.

This book is not the place to explore the specific problems of local industries.[18] Suffice it to say that vast potential exists for a more active Soviet economic role in the Pacific based on the area's resources. Energy and mineral exports are obvious examples.[19] Processed minerals or timber are equally needed by the other Pacific economies, and, of course, the success of the Soviet fishing industry has Pacific-wide appeal. Soviet sources even speak of the potential of a tourist industry as a way of developing the service sector in the Far East.

The main question has been how best to exploit the potential. Past plans and investment strategies have included an injection of 70 billion roubles in the 15 years to 1985.[20] Although these strategies produced some improvements in the first stages, and although the population increased especially quickly in the Soviet Far East, growth rates declined by the mid-1980s, so that the region was even falling behind national rates of growth. For example, despite the vast lumber industry, in recent years more than 50 million roubles worth of furniture is shipped to the Soviet Far East from elsewhere in Russia. The average per capita living space was 15 percent below the Russian average in 1986—so much for the wide-open spaces creating a better standard of life.[21] During the past decade, 85 percent of the able-bodied population coming to the Soviet Far East did not settle for long.

The most persistent of the old strategies adopted to develop the region can be described as little Russian—that is, the belief that development will come from internal investment and that the pace can be slower depending on the needs of the main population back in Europe. Foreign investment might be useful, but it need not be actively sought. The region can be treated as a 'mine or aquarium', and little processing need be done in the Soviet Far East.

Another clearly more adventurous route can be described as that of Pacific promise. This promise is based on the belief that the Soviet Pacific will have to make itself a more autonomous region by enticing foreign investment and joint ventures in order to exploit its own resources. This is not to say that the region's people will become mere hewers of wood and drawers of water for the developed economies of the region. Rather, the area itself can serve as a processing zone for the region's resources. Thus, value would be added at home and the profits earned within the Soviet Pacific.

In 1987, a major plan for the Soviet Far East was announced following Gorbachev's visit to Vladivostok in the summer of 1986. The plan was to make the Soviet Pacific self-sufficient in energy and agriculture by the year 2000. Industrial commodities and energy production were to double, while petroleum extraction was to rise threefold and natural gas production ninefold. Large-scale construction was to include processing industries and major investment in better living conditions. The task was daunting.[22]

However, this plan fudged the choice between old and new thinking. The volume of industrial production was to increase by 2.4 or 2.5 times, but regional exports were expected to triple. As Soviet officials publicly admitted, 'the foreign economic part of the program . . . was not worked out quite adequately'. Unofficial comments included such words as 'rubbish' and 'incomplete' to describe the plan.[23] Although some provisions were included for internal investment (reportedly more than $300 billion by the year 2000), it was considered vital that other Pacific states, whether socialist or capitalist, take part in joint ventures and investment. Thus, China and Vietnam are seen alongside Singapore and Japan as main potential investors. It is not clear how much of the investment would come from the Pacific region and how much would have to be coaxed out of Moscow.

Until such issues are decided, the host of more detailed questions regarding the convertibility of the rouble, the rules on joint ventures and the prospects for special export processing zones cannot be answered. All these issues depend on the broader debate in Moscow on the pace and direction of reform and on Soviet willingness to tolerate a relatively separate development strategy for the Soviet Pacific. Clearly the past strategy of 'European Russia first' will not provide a useful basis for Soviet efforts in the wider Pacific region.

Thus, the answers to many questions underlying the assessments of Soviet Pacific prospects hang on the fate of the more general Gorbachev reforms. These answers depend on greater decentralization of the economy and on more freedom for local trade as well as on convincing the outside world of the success of the reforms and the political stability of the reformers. In a sense, nearly all problems can be overcome with greater investment, newer technology and more people. All of these can come from abroad, but they are unlikely to do so if the success of earlier reforms is not evident. Like the Chinese reforms, letting certain regions prosper before others, with greater freedom to select a specific path of development, is one option. But this option still depends on the success of the central reforms and on continued political stability.

Pacific promise?

The images of the Soviet Pacific are extreme. If it were autonomous, it would be the largest country in the Pacific, yet one of the least densely populated. Its people are younger and more individualistic than is the norm in the Soviet Union. The territory and fauna are unusual and the climate is harsh. Of course, these are the usual features of a frontier region, and the challenges they pose have, in the similar cases of Canada and Alaska, already been much more successfully tamed.

The main reason for the continued frontier feel of the Soviet Pacific lies in the political system of the Soviet Union. Despite the various reforms proposed during the past decades, the stagnation of the early 1980s shows the limitations of previous efforts. Under Mikhail Gorbachev, new ideas for restructuring have again emerged. As with the nationwide campaign for reforms, it is still too early to judge the success of the changes. But it is clear that the domestic reform process, more than any other single variable, will determine the state of the Soviet base in the Pacific.

Clearly, the specific character of the Soviet Pacific will determine the role the Soviet Union can play in the Pacific century. Unlike many of the newly industrializing countries (NICs), the Soviet Pacific will not prosper by using low labour rates, because labour is always likely to be in short supply. Unlike many other states in the Pacific, the Soviet Pacific will always be hampered by its ties to a much bigger entity, the Soviet Union, which is, predominantly European in character. Whereas many Pacific states realize that they must survive on their own in the region or not at all, the Soviet Pacific is in an ambiguous position. As this book went to press in early 1990, the major changes in Eastern Europe, along with the domestic difficulties in the Soviet Union, were clearly absorbing most of the attention of Soviet policy makers. Following the May 1989 Sino–Soviet summit, the Soviet Union appears to be distracted from its search for a successful policy in the Pacific.

The domestic reform programme, however, must include a change in policy towards its far eastern lands. The Soviet Pacific needs to be integrated much more closely into the wider Pacific region and perhaps less into the Soviet Union. The Soviet Pacific region does seem to have a niche in the Pacific economy. As a provider of raw materials or, better still, of processed raw materials, it can prosper as Canada and Australia have done. Given its need for agricultural products and consumer goods, a Soviet Pacific market certainly exists for the exports of those Pacific states that need primary Soviet goods. Thus, to some extent, there is a paradoxical situation of, on the one hand, the hyperbole with respect to the Soviet Pacific's economic potential and on the other hand, its failure to live up to its potential. Development of the Soviet Pacific is both a Soviet domestic problem and, to date, an unfulfilled foreign policy. Nevertheless the potential for growth is certainly there.

3
The Historical Background

The historical pattern of Russian interest in, and later neglect of, the Pacific illustrates the ambivalence as well as the advantages that the modern-day Soviet Union brings to its policies towards the region. As Mikhail Gorbachev attempts to bring the Soviet Union back to the Pacific as a natural member, it is important to understand the extent to which he is working with, and against, history.

Shaping the Pacific

The early history of the Pacific is one of unconnected empires around the ocean rim. Few of these empires had any contact with each other, and certainly none were in touch across the vast expanse of the world's largest ocean. The greatest of these civilizations was China's, but unlike other great civilizations of the time, China had no rivals and thus established itself with ease as the predominant power in the Pacific. The advantage of its isolation bred in China a sense of superiority and a blasé attitude to international trade.[1] To be sure, overland routes existed between China and the Roman empire in Europe and the Middle East, but the territory of modern Russia was untrampled except by scattered tribes and wildlife. But the predominance of China in the Far East also meant that any prospective rival would first have to face Chinese power. When Russia did expand across the top of Eurasia, it had to deal with the Chinese empire first.

The forbidding climate of Siberia tended to keep the Russians from investigating very far eastwards. In the south, monsoons and trade winds controlled sea travel. The locations of plateaux and river deltas were important factors as civilization developed and as a consequence also kept the Pacific region divided.[2] Thus, whereas a consciousness about East Asia as an entity was formed early, the concept of the Pacific ocean as a geographic or a political region is relatively recent. The inhabitants of its shores and islands had no idea where they fitted into the pan-Pacific picture until the coming of the Europeans. Although Russia was by no means the first European power to reach the Pacific, it was the only one to come by land and was one of the few that attempted to build bridges of trade and politics across its waters. Russia may not have been a genuine East Asian power in the sense that its population was always weighted towards Europe, but it was certainly a genuine Pacific power in the sense that it was one of the first to think Pacific and to explore both sides of the northern Pacific—although the idea of thinking Pacific remained undeveloped.

This situation contrasted with the more crowded and conflictive pattern of relations around the Mediterranean. The Pacific was not only fragmented, but its component parts were also far from equal. In the Mediterranean case, however, it was the very rivalry of roughly equal European states that sparked competition, exploration and expansion.

The European impact on the Pacific developed slowly, but the lure of the orient was powerful and Europeans began to approach from all sides. The northern routes were dominated by the north European powers, Russia, Britain and, to some extent, France. Russia was the only one to come by land across Eurasia.

With the disintegration of the Mongol's Golden Horde in the late fifteenth century, independent Khanates were established. By the early sixteenth century, the Khanate of Sibir was paying tribute to Moscow, and in 1582 Moscow sent Yermak to impose control in the region. This soldier-cum-explorer, sometimes called the Cortez of Russia, spearheaded the first major Russian thrust across Eurasia. The main drive, as with the Hudson's Bay Company in the similar climate of North America, was for furs. But in Russia, the newcomers were in a sense the inheritors of an already existing Mongol empire and thus their passage could be swifter. The added incentive of exploiting mineral resources (especially salt), and the compelling need to establish firm military control, spread Russian control across the top of Eurasia at a remarkable rate.[3] Yet even though economic motives were primary in drawing Russians to the Pacific, the vast majority of settlers were military personnel, mainly cossacks of European descent.[4] Equally remarkable, little attention was paid to these Russian adventurers until much later in Pacific history.

The first route to the east was actually established further south, and the initial European influence came from the south Europeans. In fact, the name 'Pacific ocean' derives from the optimism of the commander of the most heroic voyages of all times—Magellan.[5]

Meanwhile in Russia in 1619, the tsar had tried to limit Russian expansion because the rapid pace of recent explorations was leading to a loss of control over the revenues from the fur trade.[6] Nevertheless, as early as 1639, Ivan Moskvitin took tsarist rule to Pacific waters and the sea of Okhotsk. Russia's first Pacific port, at Okhotsk, was established in 1647. In 1648 a cossak explorer reached the Pacific at the northeast tip of Siberia and proved that Eurasia was divided from North America at the top of the Pacific.[7] Later in the seventeenth century, Russian explorers survived the forbidding wastes of Kamchatka and moved down towards Japan from the Kuriles. During the reign of Peter the Great, Russia became obsessed with sea power and the need to establish a Pacific, as well as a European, naval presence.

Russia's expansion was remarkably swift, taking advantage of rivers and open country to reach the Pacific 250 years before Russia explored Central Asia. While Russians were already gazing across Pacific waters, British settlers in North America were still struggling to cross the Allegheny mountains. The race by Europeans to the north Pacific was clearly won by Russia.

By the late seventeenth century, up to one-third of total Russian state revenue came from the Far East fur trade.[8] Not surprisingly, this expanding Russian empire eventually came into contact with China. For the first time, China had to contend in the Pacific with a power that was large, confident, land-based and therefore likely to stay. Russia-China relations can be said to begin with the Russian exploration of the Amur river basin by Khabarov in the 1640s. In 1651 Khabarov established his first fort on the Amur, and a year later he reached the banks of the Ussuri river. China could no longer ignore the threat.

By the Treaty of Nerchinsk in 1689, the Russians were excluded from the Amur area. Russia had to step back from initial confrontation with China, in part because it had failed to establish a grain base in the Amur region and therefore could not support full-scale colonization.[9] The early lesson for Russia in the Pacific was the need to establish a firm economic base before taking on better-placed rivals.

Russia's early gains in the seventeenth century were made possible by the transition in China from the Ming to the Qing dynasty. By 1652, most of China was subdued by these Mongol invaders, thus creating a vacuum in the north that Russia was able to fill. By the 1660s, Chinese autonomy had been restored to such an extent that by 1662 China even controlled Taiwan; but the age of Chinese power was nevertheless rapidly coming to an end.

The other great Confucian state, Japan, had been reunified under Hideyoshi in the late sixteenth century. However, the Japanese tendency towards self-imposed isolation was already apparent as the seventeenth century drew to a close. From the perspective of other north Pacific powers, especially Russia, these two factors—the weakening of China and Japan's isolation—presented a golden opportunity for expansion.

Thus, by the end of the seventeenth century, important changes had occurred. The traditional Southeast Asian empires had been destroyed and trade was now controlled by Europeans. Russia had reached the Pacific and challenged Chinese dominance. Spain had linked its empire across the Pacific and integrated parts of Latin America into Pacific trade patterns.

In the decades that followed, a meticulous series of voyages of discovery and charting took place.[10] Exploration not only defined the extent of the Pacific basin, but it also made the often treacherous waters safer for business. Although Russia came to the Pacific by land, it, too, played a vital part in this process. In the 150 years from the dawn of the eighteenth century to the so-called opening of Japan, nearly the full extent of the Pacific and the distribution of its people became known. In the north, Vitus Bering, a Dane in the service of the tsar, sailed from Kamchatka between 1725 and 1743 and discovered that a strait separated the Americas from Eurasia. The northern tip of the Pacific had been found.

Britain was by this time the dominant empire in the world. Despite their small island base, and in contrast to the Russians, the British managed eventually to create and then leave a number of successful independent states with close cultural links to their European home. Russian imperialism left few settlers, although huge areas were incorporated into the motherland.

By far the most dramatic shifts in Pacific politics during this period took place in the northern latitudes. Peter the Great had set the tone for Russian achievement with his determination to establish a naval presence. In 1714 he sent a mission to gain control in the sea of Okhotsk, and because contact by land was so arduous, the search was begun for a northern sea route to the Russian Far East. The Bering missions were part of that vain effort to navigate through the Arctic ice floes.

Following a brief decline in naval strength after Peter's death in 1725, Catherine the Great (1762–96) drove Russian interests into direct confrontation with Spain and Britain in Pacific waters.[11] The main attraction for the rival empires was the trade of fur for gold, silver and silk in China. Russia had an advantage over other European empires in that it controlled vast regions adjacent to the Pacific with few unruly natives. While other Europeans were manoeuvering to find suitable coastal trading bases with China, Russia was already permanently and menacingly established in the north. From 1727, a new system of Sino-Russian trade at Kiakhta was established that by 1760 accounted for 60 percent of all Russian trade in the Pacific—7 percent of Russia's total trade.[12]

At the same time, Russia was embarking on adventures further afield. It tried to grab a share of the lucrative North American trade in sea otters, often termed the soft gold of Pacific waters. In 1784, G.I. Shelikhov established the first permanent Russian settlement in Alaska. This so-called Russian Columbus remains a legend for his grandiose ideas about a Russian presence along the Pacific coast of North America. His exploration of the northeastern sections of the Pacific coastline remains a powerful testament to Russia's early role in the first serious efforts to develop cross-Pacific links.[13]

In 1799 a charter was granted to the Russian-American Company to hunt for pelts along the American coast and into Spanish territory and to establish a series of forts to support that trade. This was the first systematic Russian attempt to develop a North American presence. Fort Ross, in present-day California, was established in 1811 to provide food and supplies for Russian trade. However, this southernmost point of expansion was clearly well beyond the capacity of Russia to sustain.

Having found the northern sea route blocked by ice and the land route too slow, Russia looked for other means to strengthen its position in the Pacific. In 1803, A.J. van Krusenstern set out from Krondstadt on Russia's first circumnavigation of the globe. The purpose of this voyage was to see if Russian Pacific interests could be more easily supplied by water from Europe. In the course of the voyage, extensive mapping of still-secluded Japan was accomplished.[14] Russia sent expeditions to Polynesia in 1804 and Hawaii in 1809, and even claims to have discovered Antarctica before the United States in 1820.[15] President Thomas Jefferson of the new United States declared in 1807 that Russia was his country's firmest friend because of their common struggle against British and Spanish colonialism. In 1809 the United States and Russia established diplomatic relations.

However, Russia was looking after its own interests and found its biggest opportunity in the collapse of Spanish power during the 1820s. California thus appeared to be open to Russian influence, but the Russians were distracted by events in Europe and lacked the fleet to support its pretensions or to provision its settlers.[16] It also had to compete with United States and British interests on the American Pacific coast.

The United States government at the time saw Russia as a tacit ally in dislodging Britain from its dominance of trade and its spreading power across British North America. But Russia had overreached in the Pacific and by 1824 had begun to retreat across the northern Pacific. Fort Ross was abandoned in 1839, and Russia concentrated instead on China and Japan thereafter. The need for an alliance with Britain because of the wars being fought in Europe was evidence of Russia's real priorities.[17] Consequently, the United States itself had to apply pressure to limit British and Spanish, and indeed, Russian influence on the American Pacific coast.[18] As in the case of Russia, the United States was to establish itself both on land and by sea. But the land base eventually provided the firmer footing for American interests in the Pacific.[19]

The focus of the Pacific had clearly shifted north and into the hands of the two newest Pacific empires, the United States and Russia. But unlike previous white intruders, these empires were land based and there to stay. Although Russia was arguably an old empire, it was nevertheless a new Pacific power even though it retreated across the Pacific after its initial enthusiasm. The United States continued to expand its influence all the way to the coast of East Asia. The older powers of the Pacific were in a state of disarray, unable to meet these new challenges. Japan was in self-imposed isolation. Southeast Asia was fragmented and dominated by rapacious European empires. China, the saddest case of all, lost ground as the European world leapt into the industrial revolution.

The Rise of Japan

On 8 July 1853, Commodore Perry sailed his squadron of black ships into Yedo Bay to force Japan to open its doors to foreigners.[20] The United States had taken the leading role because it wanted a base for its expanding whaling interests. On 31 March 1854, in a treaty signed at Yokohama (called the Treaty of Kanagawa) Japan agreed to open its ports to the United States. Similar treaties with the envious British, Russians and Dutch followed in less than two years. The Russo-Japanese treaty of February 1855 was the first ever between the two near-neighbours.

The Japanese door had been prised open, but what emerged was a dynamic people ready to assert their place as a new force in the Pacific. The United States, Russia and indeed all the other great powers would have cause to regret that they had stirred the Japanese out of their slumber.

Just as the United States and Russia had shifted the locus of Pacific power northwards and out of the hands of the Europeans, so Japan now gave it an Asian dimension. Not surprisingly, as Japan grew strong and independent, it also emulated western ways in its foreign policy. The obvious targets for Japanese imperialism were neighbouring Korea and China, both of which were failing to meet the challenge of modernization. In 1871 Japan signed the Tientsin Treaty with China, thereby gaining commercial rights already enjoyed by Europeans in China. In 1876 a similar treaty was signed with Korea. But Japan was hardly satisfied with such gestures. It stirred up turmoil in Korea in order to break the Chinese grip there and to enhance its own international standing.

The main challenge to Japan was not from China, or even from the European empires, but rather from that hybrid power, Russia, with an old boot in Europe and a new, very restless foot in Pacific waters. In 1855, Russia and Japan had established diplomatic and trading relations but, as Japan grew stronger, Russia recognized that Japan was more likely to be a rival than an ally in the Pacific.

The retreat of Russian sea power had not been a sign that Russia was giving up on Asia. Russia was merely consolidating its position, leaving Pacific waters to the United States and, later, to Japan. What interested Russia most was the scramble for lucrative pieces of decaying China—the so-called sick man of Asia. In treaties in 1858 and 1860, Russia gained territory from China in the Amur basin that eased access to the Vladivostok region. The 1858 treaty was also notable for its banning of British, French and American ships from navigating the Amur, Sungari and Ussuri rivers. The 1860 treaty made possible the establishment of Vladivostok, the main symbol of Russian power in the Pacific.

The Russians also made fresh attempts to reinforce their base in Northeast Asia. From the 1860s, some of the newly emancipated Russian serfs drifted out to Siberia and the Pacific; Russia's territory in Asia served partly as a prison, but it also was a new frontier, offering greater freedom and opportunity.

Russia, however, remained reluctant to expand beyond the western shores of the Pacific. Unable to afford its far-flung Pacific pretensions, in 1867 it sold Alaska to the United States for $7.2 million (the United States being seen as a lesser threat than Britain).[21] It strengthened its base in Sakhalin but relinquished its claims to the central and northern Kuriles to Japan.[22]

Japan remained the main threat to Russian interests. Its claim to ancient rights led Japan in 1894 to seize Korea and to attack Chinese forces at sea and in Manchuria. By the April 1895 Treaty of Shimonoseki, Korea was declared independent but was in reality under Japanese control. The Liaodong peninsula was ceded to Japan, as were Formosa and the Pescadores. Japan also opened more treaty ports in China thereby assuming the role coveted by Russia—the leading imperial power in China.[23] Russia then joined with France and Germany to force Japan to give up the Liaodong peninsula. The balance of power in Asia and the Pacific was suddenly shifting, and the Russians clearly needed to adjust the focus of their concern to include not only China but also Japan as a Northeast Asian rival.

With the defeat of China by Japan, Russia wisely calculated that it shared a common interest with China in containing Japan. In a secret treaty in 1896, the two parties agreed to help each other against what was by then an increasingly confident Japan. Russia nevertheless took a leading role in punishing China after the Boxer rebellion in 1900, sending a large contingent of troops in an apparent effort to consolidate its hold on Manchuria as well as to continue the obvious process of Russianization in such towns as Harbin. Even though Russia perceived China as an ally against Japan, it nevertheless placed its own interests first, even at the expense of the Chinese. Such sudden shifts in the balance of power appear to be endemic to northeast Asia.

Russian policy recognized and sought to increase the strategic importance of Harbin and Manchuria. Russia built railways to the Pacific through Manchuria, seeing these as fundamental for its Pacific position.[24] With completion of the rail lines, the fastest route from Europe to East Asia became the trans-Siberian.

Japan and Russia not only competed with each other in the northwest Pacific to slice up China, but they also competed in generally expanding their empires. Japan was determined to make up for the lost time of its isolation and strengthened its position by forming an alliance with Britain in 1902. Britain was weakened by the Boer war and was concerned about Russian threats to India, and Japan wanted greater freedom in Korea and coveted Russian assets in Manchuria.[25] Japan felt itself the equal of other great empires in the Pacific. The result was the 1904–5 Russo-Japanese war.

The humiliation of the decaying tsarist regime was total. Although the war was fought at Russia's furthest reaches, the Japanese were considered inferior to Europeans and had only recently opened up to the outside world. Tsar Nicholas himself referred to the Japanese as 'little monkeys'. Therefore, defeat by the Japanese was a major blow to the Russians and lowered their prestige in the eyes of their neighbours in the Pacific.[26] Russia, thus humiliated, was forced to give up some of its territory. The psychological damage done by the Russo-Japanese war to Russia's sense of power in the Pacific continues to this day. The essential vulnerability of an overstretched empire that fails to modernize is still a powerful image for modern Soviet foreign policy in the Pacific.

Under the 1905 Treaty of Portsmouth, arranged under United States mediation, Russia lost Liaodong, Port Arthur and the southern railways in China and south Sakhalin. Russia and China were plainly aware that emergent Japan was being used against them both by the fading European powers and the rising United States. In fact, the very boldness of the American calculation of the balance of power led Japan and Russia to develop an appreciation of each others' natural interests in Manchuria. Japan was a rival of Russia, yet one with whom it was still possible to do business.[27] Nevertheless, the Russians hesitated to become directly involved in Korea, where Japan was clearly the leading force.[28] The lessons for Russia were to appreciate the weakness of its position in East Asia and also to recognize that Russian influence could be enhanced by manipulation of the complex regional balance of power. As for Japan, thanks to the shortsightedness of the

Europeans and the preoccupations of the United States, its power in the Pacific went virtually unchallenged for the next 30 years.

By the turn of the century, the battering of China forced it to give up its struggle against modernization. The main push for revolution came as a result of domestic decay, but the incessant hammering on China's doors by Japan, Russia, the United States and European powers helped topple the old Chinese order. Yet even though the republican revolution of 1911 soon faltered as well because it did not provide a coherent alternative, China had nevertheless taken the first step on what was to be a very long road back to great power status in the Pacific.

Meanwhile, Japan lay in wait, anxious to pounce on the spoils of revolution. Its opportunity came with the outbreak of World War I, when the attention of its rivals was diverted to Europe. No other power was anxious for Japan to join the war against Germany. Japan knew it could seize German concessions in China and deal with China without too great a risk. It swiftly seized the German holdings in Shandong, disregarding China's neutrality in the war, and in 1915 presented China with 21 demands that, had they been accepted, would have reduced China to the status of a Japanese puppet. The upshot was a dominant Japan in the northwest Pacific, even though the 1919 peace conference refused to recognize all the Japanese gains.

Japan had led the attack on Russia in 1918 following that other great revolution of the decade, the Bolshevik uprising. It also sent the largest contingent of troops to defeat the Bolsheviks but was forced to give up its expansionist desires when the allied mission collapsed in disagreement over objectives. Japan was the last power to withdraw its troops because it stood to gain the most from carving up Russia. Japan finally withdrew completely from Russia in 1922.

From the point of view of the new Soviet state, the Japanese-led campaign not only marked Japan as a rapacious neighbour but also underlined the vulnerability of its position in the Pacific. The Soviet Union had established a Far Eastern Republic (FER) in its far eastern territories in the hopes of exploiting anti-Japanese sentiment and playing down the communist component of the new regime in European Russia, but disbanded the FER when Japan retreated in 1922.

Communist politics came to the Soviet Pacific much more slowly than to any other border region. Between 1922 and 1938, the territory across Siberia to the Pacific was given special status. Its politics remained consistently less revolutionary than those of European Russia, while repeated promises of massive investment regularly went unfulfilled. Although the main colonization drive that had brought the Russian population to the region occurred after the war with Japan and the construction of the rail link, the new generation in the Soviet Far East was still too young to be either trusted or subjected to radical campaigns.[29] Vladivostok remained a remarkably cosmopolitan outpost, to some extent like Shanghai, for a long time after the revolution. The perception of the Soviet Far East as a frontier also meant it was an insecure region from the Soviet point of view.

Despite its forced retreat from China and Russia, Japan remained the most vital force in the Pacific. The European powers were exhausted by the war, and China and Russia were recovering from revolutions. The Soviet Union's pressing foreign policy concerns were in Europe rather than in East Asia. Only the United States was in a position to offer resistance to Japan, but its preoccupations were at home, to some extent in Europe, and on the coast of Asia rather than in Pacific waters.

This was above all a period of flux in the Pacific. Some powers, such as Spain and the smaller European nations, had faded, and new states, such as Australia and Canada, were emerging as important actors alongside the United States and Japan. Yet there was no system of international order, whether in military, economic or cultural terms. Not surprisingly, the next 25 years were to be some of the most bloody in Pacific history.

1925–1945

After World War I, the European powers were at least temporarily chastened by their recent experience.[30] In the Pacific, the conflagration was still to come, as rival empires sought to shape a new order. At the start of the period, dynamic Japan looked for a new position that granted it greater recognition. When it encountered the incoherent policies of the Americans and other great powers, Japan took the opportunities for expansion that came its way.[31] Russia, which had previously been the most dynamic of the new Pacific powers, spent most of this period engrossed in domestic and European affairs. The United States, the region's leading power, remained in self-imposed isolation. China, the sick man of Asia, was recuperating from abortive revolutions and was a ripe target for Japanese imperialism.

So long as Japan had a weak China to pick on, Japanese imperial instincts were largely satisfied. But by the second half of the 1920s, China was progressively united by Chiang Kai-shek and Beijing fell to his Guomindang in 1927. China then set about undoing the damage of the unequal treaties with various imperial powers, Japan included.[32]

Japan's other rival, the Soviet Union, remained unsettled in the 1920s. In 1925 Japan recognized the Soviet Union and received coal and oil concessions in exchange for northern Sakhalin. Japan was much less fearful of communist ideology than were many western powers.[33] What concerned Japan more in the late 1920s was Soviet pressure on China and the fear that a resurgent Russia would reassert its rights in Manchuria. Japan was already eyeing this territory north of the Great Wall, seeing it as a bulwark against Russia and a source of raw materials and living space for a tiny island people. With Europe distracted by the rise of Germany and Manchuria in turmoil as warlords fought off the centralizing pressures of Beijing, Japanese militarists saw and took their chance in the so-called Manchuria Incident of September 1931.

The pusillanimous response of other powers to Japan's attack on China is largely explained by the particularly complex limits on their foreign policies.[34] The failure of international diplomacy, treaty obligations or the League of Nations to prevent the dismemberment of China was further evidence of the absence of international order in the Pacific. With Japan, the United States and the Soviet Union outside the League of Nations (until 1934), this already marginal body became a total irrelevance for Pacific politics. As Japan stormed out of the League, Hitler assumed control in Germany and riveted international attention on Europe. The Pacific world, in disarray, was powerless in the face of Japanese imperialism, which thus set the agenda for the region.[35] Russia, like the other Europeans, attended to the more pressing problems of European insecurity.

The precise causes of the first genuine 'war of the Pacific' cannot be clearly identified. The Soviet Union was not a major actor at the time, although it too played a part in allowing Japan to increase its power in the region. The Soviet Union was consolidating its control of Mongolia and was increasingly concerned with Japan's alliance (in November 1936) with anti-Soviet Germany. Sporadic border clashes with Japan continued from 1935. Russia then consolidated its relations with China, taking advantage of the new ostensibly official unity between the communists and Chiang Kai-shek.

Tension in East Asia was, at least until the outbreak of war in Europe, a separate conflict, although there were some inter-connections. For example, Japan's enmity with Russia was linked to the Russo–German tension. However, the causes of the Pacific war were to be found primarily in the long-standing rivalries of Pacific powers, the decay of European colonialism and the varied domestic politics of local states. The expansion of Japan's war effort in the Pacific would probably have come, even if there had been no war in Europe. But with the Europeans and the North Americans distracted by that war, it is not surprising that Japan accelerated its invasion plans.

The two great imponderables for Japan were the reactions of the Soviet Union and the United States. By securing a nonaggression treaty with Russia in April 1941, Japan felt free to move south. From the Soviet point of view, and despite the rhetoric of collective security, the calculation was simple enough. The main threat was in Europe, and the Soviet Far East was unlikely to be an early target for Japanese aggression. The Soviet Union needed a breathing space, and its Pacific territory had the most space to breathe.

Until Pearl Harbor, the Pacific war was really an East Asian war. Although Europeans were involved in the first phase by virtue of the threats to their colonies, the wider war reached Australia and even Hawaii. The conflict itself was determined primarily by the ability of the United States economy to support a protracted naval strategy at long distances.[36] This conflict was the first war to be fought across the expanse of the Pacific, a bloody struggle for scattered islands on the way to Japan. The United States was finally to live up to Henry Luce's description of the twentieth century as 'The American Century'.[37] The Soviet Union, by contrast, stayed out of all but the final hours of the conflict and therefore developed no sense of the breadth of the Pacific in military terms. Thus, whereas the Soviet Union fought its way into positions of influence in the postwar settlement in Europe, it barely expanded at all in the Pacific.

The conduct of the anti-Japanese war was overwhelmingly directed by the United States. In March 1942, Churchill and Roosevelt agreed that the United States should wage the Pacific war while the British directed combat in the Indian ocean as far as Singapore. The Soviet Union was rarely consulted until the end of the war. China was placed in the United States sphere, and Southeast Asia (as it became known at the time) was a no man's land.[38] The United States came to scorn Britain's Asian efforts and, as it pushed towards Japan from the sea, it paid decreasing attention to British and Chinese efforts to attack Japan from Eurasia. The only significant contribution of the land war came from the Soviet Union in 1945, but by then the war in the Pacific was all but over.[39]

Until 1945, the only significant cooperation between the United States and the Soviet Union was the provision of Lend Lease aid to Russia via the Pacific. Convoys to Vladivostok began in 1942 and carried 75 percent of the tonnage of United States aid. In order to avoid the problem of the Soviet-Japanese neutrality treaty, United States-built ships, under Soviet registry and with Soviet crews, were used. Nearly 15,000 Russian sailors were trained in Alaska, and American airmen made discreet emergency landings in Russian territory after raids on Japan.[40] The 1,600-mile highway linking Alaska and Canada, completed in 1943, allowed the easier flow of aid and the closer integration of the north Pacific.[41]

Clearly, by mid-1942, the United States was replacing Japan as the leading power in the Pacific and the Europeans were soon to leave the area. But the roles of Asia's two other great empires, China and Russia, were less certain. By virtue of its European contribution and its Pacific territory, the Soviet Union earned a place in the consideration of how to defeat Japan. The United States had become the arbiter of the China theatre, but Russia would benefit by the post-1945 rise of the Soviet-supported Chinese Communist Party. Another uncertainty was what Russia would do in the Pacific after Hitler was defeated in Europe.

The United States realized that the Soviet Union could take what it wanted in mainland Northeast Asia and thus eventually involved Moscow in the wartime planning. Furthermore, the United States also feared a bloody fight for every inch of Japan's home islands and so wanted Soviet help in the Pacific war.[42] At Yalta, in February 1945, it was agreed that Russia would join the war and in return get southern Sakhalin, the Kuriles, the lease of Port Arthur and its rail interests in Manchuria. The United States was clearly reluctant to protect Chinese interests and was prepared to tolerate a variation of European-type spheres of influence.[43] US policy favored a balance of Russian and Chinese power that would allow the United States to dominate the Pacific. The feared loss of China to Russia would ruin that neat model. At Potsdam, in August 1945, Russia also agreed to enter Korea.

The dropping of the atom bomb and the sudden ending of the war only partly invalidated US concern about getting Russia into the war. The Soviet invasion of Manchuria would probably have taken place in any case.[44] By the end of the war, the United States was certainly confident that it held a dominant position in the Pacific. Thus, the war had revolutionized the basic pattern of politics in the Pacific. At the cost of very few lives, the Soviet Union gained some territory. Above all, it gained by virtue of the decline of other powers (such as Japan and the Europeans) and by the expanding opportunities that came with decolonization. It also was soon to gain an important ally in China.

The most obvious change in international terms was the emergence of the two superpowers and the cold war. Although most of the rhetoric of the iron curtain was Euro-centric and inapplicable to the Pacific, the superpower confrontation was at least more simple than the interwar diplomacy of confusion, even if it was less applicable to the Pacific than to Europe. From the Soviet point of view, their obvious gains were counterbalanced by the even greater gains made by their main rival, the United States. On any Pacific-wide survey, the United States clearly predominated in terms of territorial control, economic clout and political influence. As an American official stated to a visitor from London, 'It is now our turn to bat in Asia.'[45] The Soviet Union would find this political reality uncomfortable.

4
Ideology and Culture

The Soviet Union's role as the home of a Marxist-Leninist ideology has been a key factor in any analysis of Soviet power and influence. Of course, that ideology is of global importance, even though it has its roots in Europe. When turning to the Pacific, however, one finds that conditions are very different. Although there were seven communist states in the Pacific basin (compared with nine in Europe before January 1990), with a much larger population and land area than in Europe, the divisions among the communist states were more profound in the Pacific.[1]

The region itself is also much less coherent than Europe. Therefore, the divisions within the communist world in the Pacific are perhaps less important because the non-communist world is also divided along often deep and intersecting fault lines. A major cause of the cleavages in both communist and non-communist parts of the Pacific relates to the diversity of cultures and political traditions around the Pacific rim.

Thus, in order to assess accurately the options for the Soviet Union in the Pacific, certain questions must be answered. To what extent does the Soviet Union have cultural and ideological ties that bind it to the region and help shape alliances and enmities? Implicit in this question are the more complex considerations of how Soviet ideology has changed since 1945 and the extent to which the Soviet Union dominates ideological matters. At a time of major revisions in the ideology of the Soviet Union, this final question, the extent to which the role of Soviet ideology has changed, becomes a question of primary importance.

CULTURE

The Pacific has few clear patterns of culture. From the perspective of the Soviet Union, which can claim to have solid ethnic and cultural links to Europe, the Pacific is seen as a much more diverse place. But even considering the diversity of the Pacific, it is striking just how unconnected the Soviet Union is to the Pacific in cultural terms. A brief survey of the political culture of the Pacific can identify the very limited cultural world in which the Soviet Union fits.[2]

Language

Measured by asolute numbers of speakers, the primary language of the Pacific is Chinese. Approximately 55 percent of the population of the Pacific basin are native speakers of Chinese, although only 75 percent of this group speak the main dialect of Mandarin.[3] However, Chinese is of little use outside China and the few other countries in which a significant Chinese minority lives. There are approximately 15 million people of Chinese origin in Southeast Asia and in other smaller communities dotted around the Pacific rim. The Soviet Union has no significant Chinese community and thus little ethnic link with China. At the frontier between the two countries there are a number of peoples of mixed origin, few of which are predominantly Chinese. To the extent that there are common Sino-Soviet ethnic concerns, these relate to the Muslim minorities that straddle Chinese and Soviet central Asia.

The speakers of Malay, the second largest language group in the Pacific, constitute 9.5 percent of the people of the Pacific. Malay is spoken only in Malaysia and Indonesia. The third largest language group, Spanish, is spoken by 9 percent of Pacific people, most of whom are concentrated in Latin America. Spanish is rapidly losing its foothold in the Philippines.

Of the other languages spoken in the Pacific, only Japanese (6 percent) and Korean (3 percent) are significant. The Soviet Union has no Japanese minority population. Those Japanese who were captured at the end of the war in 1945 were not allowed to settle on Soviet territory. By contrast, a significant number of ethnic Koreans used to live on Soviet territory, but even they were relocated and dispersed on the orders of Stalin.

The most peculiar case of all the Pacific languages is English, spoken by 9 percent of the population. Like all other major languages in the region, it is the mother tongue of people in a concentrated area (Canada, the United States, Australia, New Zealand). In contrast to the other languages, however, it has a wider international reach, including Singapore (where it is an official language) and the Philippines. In fact, if calculated on the basis of use of the language, rather than its identification as a mother tongue, English has the only claim to be a Pacific-wide language.

Even the Soviet Union tends to communicate in the Pacific in English. As a superpower with a difficult language not much used outside its territory, the Soviet Union has had to take the study of foreign languages seriously. Apart from some communication with close allies in Russian, most communication is either in the language of the specific state or in English. It is notable that when the Soviet Union held its first major international conference on Pacific cooperation, in October 1988, the official languages were English and Russian. In fact, Soviet diplomats around the region speak English as much as the local languages.

The strength of English, according to some people, is that it is easily spoken badly.[4] Other observers note that its widespread use obviously relates to the British colonial legacy as well as to the modern influence of the United States and to the status of English as the unofficial language of international commerce. Japanese has more than 20,000 English words in its vocabulary, and many more are used in the gibberish of international advertising patter.

By stark contrast, the language of nearly all of the 17 million citizens of the Soviet Pacific is virtually useless outside Soviet territory. Although Russian is used extensively in Eastern Europe, in the wider Pacific region it is spoken only in Mongolia by a significant percentage of the elite. The large number of Chinese who were taught Russian during the 1950s have now either died or lost their expertise. In the spirit of Sino-Soviet detente of the 1980s, Russian language study has been revived among the Chinese, but the numbers pale in comparison with the numbers learning English. (Yet in 1989, China's foreign minister, defence minister and even prime minister and party general secretary all spoke Russian.) Similarly, in North Korea and the Indochinese states, only a small section of the elite speaks Russian.

The cultural isolation that naturally follows from linguistic isolation might have been a greater problem for the Soviet Union if the other cultures in the Pacific were not also relatively isolated from each other. Thus, most international communications in the Pacific are conducted in either a foreign tongue (usually English) or through translation. At least the Soviet Union can claim to be as much a part of the cultural patchwork as the Koreans or the Thais.

Religion

Language is considered a reliable guide to culture, but religion, in contrast, is a less useful guide. Everyone need not be a believer, and modernization has tended to undermine religion. In the Pacific, there are few international religious connections and religion thus plays an even less important role than in Europe in shaping the pattern of international contacts. The Soviet Union, as an officially atheistic state, contributes little to the international religious connection. Adherents to Russian Orthodox Christianity, counted among the Christians, who constitute the largest group of active believers in the Pacific (330 million people, mostly in the Americas), have little in common with the believers across the water. In fact, Russian Orthodoxy barely extends beyond the Soviet Union's frontiers— only a handful of believers live in northeast China.

The small Siberian population of Islamic origin has somewhat more international significance. Both China and Mongolia have similar minorities. All three countries have an official policy of not encouraging religious identification. The fear that such cross-border allegiances will be formed tends to unite the three communist regimes. In 1989, when China and the Soviet Union were both troubled by unrest in the further reaches of their territories, it was notable that both countries supported each other's attempts to exercise firm control of Islamic minorities.[5]

Islamic unity, however, has not been a particular problem for Pacific states despite the presence of more than 170 million Muslims in the region. Most Muslims are concentrated in the world's largest Islamic state, Indonesia. Certainly the Islamic factor has not had the effect of linking Indonesia and the Soviet Union. Indeed, given the tendency in non-communist states such as Indonesia to pay greater attention to Islamic issues, and the simultaneous worry about the spread of such noxious ideas as Islamic unity in the communist world, the Islamic issue has, if anything, posed a persistent problem for the Soviet Union.

The third most significant religion in the Pacific, Buddhism, is based mainly in Southeast Asia, and like Confucianism (if that can be counted as a religion) in much of the rest of East Asia, has little influence within the Soviet Union. Thus, the Soviet Union remains isolated from most religious dimensions of international relations in the Pacific. In a region in which religion is already so deeply fragmented or of declining importance, this is hardly a handicap.

Migration

It is remarkable how little the huge flow of people around the world in recent centuries has involved citizens of Russia. In the nineteenth century, it is true, many people left Russia—some moved to North America, but most of them migrated to neighbouring territory that was then absorbed back into Russia and eventually the Soviet Union. To an even greater extent than China, Russia tended not to export people. The upshot of this almost natural tendency of a great continental power is that few significant Russian expatriate communities exist, and Russians have little tradition of travel. Not surprisingly, the demographic connections in the Pacific have almost no Russian threads. Other European colonial powers not only implanted their own people around the rim (for example, in Australia or the Americas), but they also moved millions of others (such as Chinese) from one part of their Pacific empires to another. Russia, unlike Britain, cannot be blamed for the sort of ethnic divisions that were created in Fiji or Malaysia, but neither does the Soviet Union have many culturally affiliated people anywhere in the Pacific.

The few communities of Russian origin in the Pacific region are mainly in North America, with small clusters in Australia. Yet, if one thinks in terms of Russian territory in the Pacific as neo-European, then it is little different from Australia or Canada. The major difference, of course, is that the European-Russian presence is not now in a separate, sovereign state, even though in the seventeenth-nineteenth centuries there may have been little to differentiate Russian and British settlements. Whereas Canada, the United States, Australia and New Zealand have advantages when establishing Pacific-wide links because of the further spread of British imperialism, Russia remains locked in its northern bastion.

Moreover, little has happened since 1945 to alter the Soviet Union's relatively isolated state. The Soviet Union still sets firm limits on both emigration and immigration. Minority populations in the Soviet Union, such as the Japanese inhabitants of the northern islands taken after World War II, were quickly returned to their homelands by the Soviet authorities. The territory was thereby mostly made clean and the isolation of the Soviet Union preserved. Of the remaining minorities on Soviet territory, few are present in sufficient numbers to cause any particular problems.

Among the exceptions are the Koreans living in Sakhalin. As part of the generally more liberal approach towards emigration under Gorbachev, the Korean minority is apparently being allowed to leave. In April 1989, the Soviets granted permission for the first time to a Soviet citizen to travel to South Korea—but only after representation from the governments of Japan and South Korea.[6] Another possibly important exception are the Aleuts in Kamchatka who, like their North American cousins, inhabit sparsely populated areas that some people consider to be strategically important.[7] But, unlike the Koreans, they have no ethnic ties to another country that will support their cause.

Human rights cases concerning movements of people rarely occur. Japan does broach the matter with Soviet officials occasionally, but human rights are seldom problematic.[8] When Japan and South Korea raise such issues, they are more interested in visits to reunite families or pay respects at a grave site. Although the increase in Soviet contacts in the region will lead to the raising of some uncomfortable issues such as these, by and large, the Soviet Union does not share the ethnic origins in the Pacific as it does in Europe, and which provided such prominence for human rights issues.

Remarkably few foreigners have been allowed into Soviet Pacific territories. Considering the labour shortages in the Soviet territory, the occasional Vietnamese or North Korean labour brigade remains a curious exception to the Soviet policy of isolation. Besides the flow of Soviet advisers back and forth to China (in the 1950s), to Mongolia and, to a lesser extent, Vietnam and North Korea, Soviet citizens have not travelled on a regular basis in the Pacific. Indeed, few Soviets have travelled as tourists to any country except to the East European states and India.[9] The very caution on the part of the Soviet Union in allowing foreigners in, or their own citizens out, ensures the continued isolation from the people-to-people politics of the Pacific.

China is now the only exception, receiving significant numbers of Soviet visitors each year. After the souring of relations in the 1960s, the numbers of Russian visitors had dwindled until by 1982, only 5,400 Russians were visiting China each year. But then numbers rose sharply as political relations improved so that by 1987, the USSR and Eastern Europe accounted for 35,000 of the visitors to China, 2 percent of the total (or about 10 percent of the total of American visitors to China). Approximately 5,000 Russians visit Australia each year and in 1983 8,600 visited Japan. New Zealand saw just over 1,000 Russians in the same year and the Philippines received similar numbers. No other countries in the non-communist Pacific received as many. The occasional and often quaint contacts between inhabitants of Siberia and Alaska suggest just how limited the potential for people-to-people contacts is.[10]

Tourists to the Soviet Union are, in some cases, more common, but still rare. By far the largest number come from Japan, which sends 50,000 in a year. China is rapidly gaining on the Japanese figure, and because of the sharp increase in cross-border contacts, apparently more visitors go to the Soviet Far East from China than from anywhere else. The new ease with which it is possible to cross the frontier also means that counting visitors is more difficult. But apart from these two East Asian giants, no Pacific country sends a significant number of tourists to the Soviet Far East.

Clearly, potential for increased people-to-people exchange exists, but of course there must be more progress in local reforms within the Soviet Union, not to mention the creation of a more sophisticated tourist infrastructure. Vladivostok, the largest city in the Soviet Pacific region, remains closed to foreigners, although promises have been made to open it to the outside world. Much work must be done to make tourists welcome—hotels are now of the standard familiar to rugged visitors to provincial China—but as China has shown, the Soviets can also make rapid progress in developing a service sector amenable to Western, cash-carrying tourists, as long as they seek new ideas and foreign advice.

Since the Gorbachev reforms, there has been increased speculation that the Soviet Union will begin to undo the damage of its isolationist policy. China, another communist state, acutely concerned about the spread of bourgeois influences, realized at an early stage in its reforms that it needed to open up to the outside world in order to borrow the best of foreign ideas and expertise. The creation of special economic zones and a booming tourist industry were parts of the so-called open door policy. The balance of costs and benefits for China was obviously sufficiently favourable for the policy to be maintained. Despite the initial fear that China would close the door following the events of May and June 1989, it seems that the door was merely swung a bit less open than it had been. Thus, as Soviet reformers look for other socialist models, the Chinese experience is an obvious one to study.

It is still too early to tell how serious the Soviet Union is about its own type of special economic zones or, indeed, about being open to more joint ventures and international tourism. The Chinese lesson suggests cautious optimism about the pace of such reforms. The risks of reform are at least as great for the Soviet Union as they were for China. China could open several doors to the outside world and still be sure that, because of its large population, foreign influence would remain diluted. In addition, China was not dealing with a remote part of its territory far from central control and with a tradition of independent policies. In all these respects, the Soviet Union has greater cause for caution. Vladivostok, like Shanghai, had a tradition of cosmopolitanism before World War II. Vladivostok today remains a vulnerable outpost in a region in which most neighbours have large populations and very different cultural backgrounds.

Although a sense of insecurity is likely to keep Soviet reforms under strict control, a more adventurous Soviet Union may yet take a more positive view of increased contacts with the people of the Pacific. The priority for the Soviet Union must be China, but then the risks of opening its doors to China must also be greatest. The Russian fear of being swamped by the Chinese masses seeking living space remains very real. Yet in 1988, the Soviets lifted visa restrictions on travel between China and the Soviet Union, thus permitting 10,000 Chinese workers in to staff Soviet factories and farms.[11] Tens of thousands of Chinese tourists are also crossing the frontier, as are a somewhat smaller number from the Soviet Union.[12]

From the Soviet Union's perspective, it can also be argued that it is perhaps easier to contemplate opening up the Far East to foreign contacts, at least in comparison with the Baltic republics in the West. With its smaller population and fewer contacts with groups beyond Soviet frontiers, the prosperity of the Soviet Far East clearly depends on contacts with the outside world. These contacts are no more likely to create a threat to Soviet national security and identity than are

Australian or Canadian contacts with states in the Pacific. Cultural factors create a challenge and an opportunity for Soviet policy in the Pacific.

Communication

The building of Pacific consciousness has depended to a great extent on the ability to create channels of communication across the vast spaces of the region. Fibre-optic cables make possible the 24-hour trading system for world stockmarkets. The more developed states of the Pacific have placed special emphasis on ensuring rapid communication. Some of the region's poorer states have skipped stages of development, but there remain significant differences between states in terms of their capacities to use the new technologies.

The use of technology and the resulting patterns of communication are also affected by political issues. The Soviet Union, like North Korea, Mongolia and the states of Indochina, remains cut off from the new patterns of communication—more by choice on the part of its government than by any limitation of economic development. One-party states, acutely sensitive to the need to control communication within their borders as a means of maintaining power, find it equally necessary to control communication with the outside world. Consequently, the socialist states of the Pacific are even more isolated from their region than the states of Eastern Europe were from their neighbours in the West. Telephones, facsimile machines, photocopiers, not to mention personal computers, are in short supply and under strict control in the socialist states, while in most of the non-socialist world, access to this technology facilitates international contacts.

Perhaps the most obvious example of the Soviet's lack of effective communication with the Pacific is in the area of civil airline connections. Even though the Soviet Union likes to point out that its territory provides the fastest route from Europe to East Asia, it has so far failed to exploit such geographic realities. Until recently, the only air link between the Soviet Far East and its Pacific neighbours was a twice-weekly flight to northern Japan. As part of new, more open relations with China, a flight to China's northeast has been added. But the changes need to be more extensive. It was a great embarrassment to the Soviet organizers of the Vladivostok conference on Pacific cooperation in October 1988 that nearly all delegates from the Pacific had to travel to Vladivostok via Moscow. It was actually quicker for the Chinese to trek to Moscow than to take any local service. Even Soviet observers note the absurdity of requiring members of the Far Eastern branch of the Soviet Academy of Sciences to travel to Moscow before they can get a visa to visit Japan.[13] Considering the booming air traffic across and around the Pacific, the absence of Soviet links with the region is particularly glaring. Even scientific and academic meetings around the rim rarely include Russians.[14]

Television and radio in the Pacific are a complex mix of the broadcasting of mass culture from North America and Western Europe and the narrowcasting of local stations using new, inexpensive technology. The more developed societies of the Pacific are already well integrated into the global market of news and entertainment, and indeed many countries, particularly Australia and Canada, actively contribute to the media melange themselves. Other developed states such as Japan, or developing ones such as Taiwan or South Korea, have made fewer contributions but can be expected to produce more of their own material in the future.

There is little that can be called Pacific-wide broadcasting. The Asian-Pacific Broadcasting Union is broader than the Pacific and does not include most communist states of the region. Although the communist states do it more comprehensively, all states maintain strict control over their broadcasters, striving to preserve sovereign control over their broadcasting. The relatively less expensive new technologies of satellite broadcasting and video technology allow even poor states to produce local narrowcasts and home-grown artistic material.

New technologies can also bridge gaps in international communication. Videos provide an easy way to watch unofficial material. Satellites can beam broadcasts across state borders with only the absence of a receiver preventing the breaking of the state broadcasting monopoly. The broadcasting of the unrest in China in May and June 1989, largely made possible by the presence of the international press corps for the Sino-Soviet summit, indicated the growing problems for communist countries wishing to keep their worlds closed.

The more developed states find it increasingly difficult to keep the receiving technology out of the hands of their people. But the less developed states, and especially the communist states, which have more rigid control over their people, can still restrict access to foreign broadcasting. North Korean radios reportedly have no tuning dial, and even if they could tune into non-North Korean broadcasting, the evidence from East Germany suggests that the system is not immediately subverted as a consequence. Yet Chinese authorities certainly made great efforts to rewrite the history of 1989 by using modern technologies to communicate their own version of events.

For all their strict control over what their own people can hear, these communist states also make a great effort to reach other peoples beyond their borders. The Soviet Union still runs the most extensive international broadcasting network in the world, and China and North Korea retain formidable capability.[15] Yet no reliable information suggests that this massive broadcasting output has the slightest impact on the Pacific world outside the communist states. The Soviet Union provides much of the satellite technology to its friends in the Pacific, but unlike the situation in much of the non-communist Pacific, the new technology has not been used to increase the diversity of programming or sources of information.[16]

Thus the Soviet Union on the one hand remains locked behind a relatively soundproof wall in the Pacific and on the other hand is equally unable to reach the hearts and minds of people outside its own gates. This isolation has proved to be a major problem for the Soviet Union in Europe, where its attempts to establish informal communications with the people of Western Europe have been mostly unsuccessful. In the Pacific, however, the Soviet Union's failure is similar to the experience of most states in the region. Unlike Europe, the Pacific remains fragmented, and, in an age of increasingly sophisticated narrowcasting, the trends do not suggest that the Soviet Union will be under increased pressure to open its ears to other cultures.

China, which has opened itself somewhat to the pressures of international capitalist advertising and the broadcasting media, also recognized the problems of spiritual pollution at an early stage. Chinese citizens in contact with foreign tourists, business people or more open societies such as Hong Kong, have caused particular problems. The unrest in Beijing in May and June 1989 was vivid evidence of the difficulties in controlling the foreign ideas. Yet as the ensuing crackdown has shown, at least in the short term, a huge continental power such as China is has a sufficient buffer against outside influences, even in the age of a shrinking globe.

Arguably, China's relative invulnerability, as is that of Japan and to some extent South Korea, is in part due to the distinctiveness of its culture. The global culture of modern Western mass media is more obviously different to the eyes of these inheritors of the Confucian tradition than it might be to the transposed Slavic culture of East Europeans now living in the Soviet Far East. Thus, the Soviet Union might well run greater risks in opening its doors to those aspects of the global culture that ricochet around the Pacific. The probable gains from becoming open to the outside world are few (from the government's point of view at least); thus, the Soviets have little incentive to change their present isolated position.

Cultural contacts

In fact, the isolation of the Soviet Union is apparent across a range of cultural dimensions. In the arts, sports and even food of the Pacific, Russia remains an isolated culture. In Europe, Russian music, art, literature and films are regularly appreciated in both East and West. By contrast in the Pacific, the Russian cultural tradition is seen as yet another dimension of European culture. Of course, in East Asia the different cultural threads rarely mingle anyway.

This type of continuing narrowcasting in culture means that the Soviet Union's culture is perceived as a different tradition along with that of the United States and Australia. To be sure, at certain levels of so-called high culture, the wealthier people in the Pacific can tap into global culture. Haute couture, artistic films or even trendy eating habits reveal an increasingly complex mix in a global melange of wealthy world culture. This process is more global than Pacific-wide. Where the Russian contribution is apparent, it is made via its ties to broader European culture.

From the Soviet Union's point of view, there are benefits to this pattern of cultural individuality in the Pacific. Unlike in Europe, where human rights issues figured—often embarrassingly for the Soviet Union—in such international agreements as the 1975 Helsinki pact, human rights issues are not a major concern in the Pacific. Given the wide cultural diversity, and the collectivist tradition of human rights in the so-called Westernized states (such as Japan or South Korea), these issues are not placed on the international agenda.[17]

At times in the postwar period, the Soviet Union has been remarkably successful in transferring some aspects of its cultural tradition. The transfer of socialist realism to China and other communist states took advantage of already existing predispositions to monumentalism and cults of personalities in these countries, and the style in the art, architecture and even music borrowed heavily from Soviet models. Of course, China has now moved beyond this stage of learning from the Soviet model and has returned to its own cultural roots. However, as part of its open-door policy and the more recent phase of detente with the Soviet Union, Russian cultural influence is increasing again in China.

The normalization of cultural relations between the two countries began in 1985, and a two-year cultural plan was signed on 4 May 1988, providing for an extensive exchange of major artistic companies and tours.[18] In 1989, the Bolshoi returned to China for the first time since 1959, and in 1990, circus companies will be exchanged. As China opens several doors to foreign contacts, it easily assimilates Russian culture as part of the European tradition. Because of the Soviet and Chinese concern with their shared ethnic populations, some of the cultural exchanges also include exchanges of minority art—for example, the Soviet exhibition of the decorative arts of Kazakhstan shown in Nanchang, Fuzhou and Beijing.

As both countries are state socialist, the organization of much of this cultural cooperation takes place on the basis of coordinated plans. This process highlights the extent to which the two states still share some aspects of ideology and social system: both are concerned that the arts and the media should serve the broader political cause.[19] Direct contacts between the creative unions of both states build a level of interstate contacts unavailable in relations with the non-communist world. Other communist states also receive the same treatment from the Soviet cultural authorities, but none are as attractive to the population of the Soviet Union as is the culture of China.

Vietnam has had a full slate of official cultural links, beginning with the 1957 agreement on cultural cooperation. A Vietnamese film won the gold medal at the Moscow film festival in 1959, and between 1946 and 1965 more than 50 books by Vietnamese authors were issued in more than two and a half million copies in Russian. Some contacts strike the outsider as bizzare; for example, a Siberian folk dance company gave 36 concerts in tropical Vietnam in the 1960s. On a more practical level, 500 Vietnamese studied music, art and entertainment at Soviet educational establishments over a period of 15 years, and more than 100 Vietnamese became candidates of science. As part of the Soviet attempt to build Vietnamese socialism, they trained much of the leading cadre of official Vietnamese cultural leaders. Although there is reportedly a limited market for Vietnamese culture in the Soviet Union, Soviet publishers are still producing a special book series called 'The Library of Vietnamese Literature'.

On a much smaller scale, thousands of students from Laos and Cambodia have come to study in the Soviet Union since 1975. The Khmer national ballet has appeared on Soviet television and Soviet publishers have recently begun to issue books by Cambodian authors. Soviet officials claim their books and films are 'very popular' in Laos and Cambodia, but there is little evidence from the Indochinese states that this is the case.

Similar patterns are evident in cultural relations with longer-standing allies in Mongolia and North Korea. A treaty in 1961 with North Korea laid the basis for cultural contacts as did a treaty in 1956 between Mongolia and the Soviet Union. Almost 800 Soviet artistic companies have toured Mongolia since then, and Soviet and Mongolian books are regularly translated into each other's language. These cultural contacts are primarily seen as part of the process of transferring socialist values. However, at a time when the definition of these socialist values are under review in the Soviet Union, it seems inevitable that the basis of Soviet cultural contacts with the Pacific will also be reassessed. To be sure, certain aspects of Soviet culture are attractive to some states in the region, but in comparison with Western influences, the Soviet Union really appeals only to the high-brow audience.

The high-brow strategy is certainly evident in Soviet contacts with the so-called neo-Europes of Canada, Australia and New Zealand. Not surprisingly the exchanges make much of the common European heritage. Contacts with Canada are primarily in the Atlantic region, including the shared obsession with the less-than-high-brow ice hockey. Similarly, most contacts with the United States are part of the European and Atlantic worlds. The curious exceptions, such as the Soviet-US expedition of cross-country skiers crossing the Bering strait is the exception that proves the rule.[20] In April 1989, the governments of Alaska and Magadan signed an agreement calling on their respective governments to allow Eskimos unrestricted travel in the area. But the signing ceremony itself demonstrated why the

Soviet Union might hesitate to take such a sensible step: two Russians—reportedly students from far-away Moscow—took the opportunity to defect in mid-ceremony. A Russian oil-skimming ship was also sent in 1989 to help clean a major oil spill, but in the best spirit of *perestroika*, the Russians charged $15,000 a day.[21]

Bilateral governmental agreements regulate much of the more conventional cultural contacts in the Pacific region, as was evident in the special agreement with Australia for the bicentennial celebrations in 1988. In 1987, 400,000 Australians applauded Soviet performers, including the Bolshoi Ballet. Many Soviet groups then moved on to New Zealand, where 70,000 saw the Bolshoi perform. The number of Australian groups visiting the Soviet Union is smaller but the audiences that greet them are much larger.

The country that has led the field in cultural contacts with the Soviet Union in the non-communist Pacific is Japan. Soviet officials proudly describe the cultural cooperation as 'stable and versatile', even at a time of political coolness. During the past few years, more than 10 million Japanese have watched Soviet performers, including the Bolshoi, the Gorky Drama Theatre of Leningrad and the Moscow Chamber Choir. Russian drama is of particular interest in Japan as are the Soviet Union's collections of European art. Japan has reciprocated by sending its own collections of European art for exhibition.

In turn, the Soviet Union has long been fascinated with Japanese culture.[22] The Kabuki theatre has visited the Soviet Union three times. The Soviet Union's respect for Japanese culture even extends to the realm of sports. The Soviets, ever desirous of excelling at sports, have even attempted to learn about baseball from Japan. Baseball will become an official sport at the Barcelona Olympiad in 1992, and the Soviet Union is eager to learn all it can. The Japanese city of Maizuru is twinned with Nakhodka, and the Japanese have provided 100 copies of a baseball rulebook translated into Russian.[23]

Although Japan and China certainly have the best and most far-reaching cultural contacts with the Soviet Union, other smaller Pacific states have made contacts as well. Curiously, the Philippines has the best cultural relations among ASEAN (Association of South East Asian Nations) states. A 1978 intergovernmental agreement set the stage for broader contacts, including a visit by the ubiquitous Bolshoi in 1980. The demise of the Marcos regime led to a hiatus in cultural contacts, but the exchange of delegations resumed in 1987. During the observance of the millenium of Christianity in Russia, the

Russian Orthodox Church sent icons to a church being opened in Manila.

Cultural contacts with Thailand have been avowedly unstable. In the absence of a common European heritage or a Russian fascination with the great traditions of Asia, Thailand and the Soviet Union have little to offer each other. The ballet company of the Tajik Opera visited Thailand in 1979 as part of a regular exchange of provincial touring groups. However, only a handful of Thai artists and writers have visited the Soviet Union. Similarly, Malaysians remain indifferent despite regular Soviet efforts to interest them in Soviet cultural diplomacy. More surprising, given the political warmth of the relationship, even Indonesia has had only poor cultural contacts with the Soviet Union.

Singapore, with its more cosmopolitan population, has had more regular contacts with the Soviet Union since 1966. A cultural agreement was signed in 1974, but the Soviet Union is still disappointed with the level of contact. As is the case with most ASEAN states, the Soviet Union sends many more groups on visits to the local states than are sent in return. In 1980 a new form of cultural cooperation was established when Moscow began providing a regular flow of soloists to perform with the Singapore National Symphony. Yet before 1986, only two major cultural events were organized in the Soviet Union by Singapore.

Thus, the pattern of Soviet cultural influence is restricted but not atypical in a region whose cultural interrelations are complex and usually incomplete. The communist states of the region share to some extent a common communist culture. There can be a mutual fascination, as between the Soviet Union and Japan. But these contacts are limited and far outweighed by traditional political cultures that create the great diversity in the Pacific.

In a time of reform in the Soviet Union and, indeed, of rapid change in the Pacific, change in these patterns of cultural disunity is possible. The Soviet Union may, like China, open itself to the influences of the region. Certainly, if it fails to open its doors, the Soviet Union runs the risk of missing the opportunities for taking part in the process of building a Pacific consciousness.

Attempts to build a Pacific-wide pattern of political culture will more likely come to nothing, however. The trends in the region suggest a complex mix of, on the one hand, regional subdivisions and national styles and, on the other hand, increasing globalization of culture for the rich and the elite. The Soviet Union has so far contributed little to the globalization of mass culture, even via its European doorway. The key to Soviet integration into these international patterns lies in its opening of various doors to the outside world, although there is unlikely to be any kind of coherent pattern of Pacific culture into which the Soviet Union might fit.

The inclination to open such doors has been rare in Russian history. Yet there have been times of such openness, and the most illustrious period, under Peter the Great, was also a time of great exploration in the Pacific. There is little inherent in the communist system that prevents such connections with the outside world, as the examples of Hungary or especially China suggest. As the Chinese experience shows, such involvement in the international system can help reshape that system. The Chinese experience also shows what risks there are in any such open-door strategy. At a time of major debate in the Soviet Union about the direction and pace of reform, the Chinese experience may be used by both conservatives and reformers. Nevertheless, the Soviet Union does have opportunities in the Pacific. Whether they are seized depends on the extent to which the old thinking is reformed in a way that makes new Pacific connections possible.

IDEOLOGY

The pattern of ideologies in the Pacific is nearly as complex as the pattern of cultures. Unlike the European and North Atlantic world, where relative stability in ideology had been evident between 1945 and 1989, the Pacific has witnessed major changes.[24] The process of decolonization created new states, and five countries in the Pacific region have joined the communist world since 1945. Indeed, the coming of communism to the wider Pacific inevitably offered the greatest opportunities for the Soviet Union. As in Europe, possibilities were opened for a coalition of like-minded states and an extension of Soviet influence. However, the coalition was never built and Soviet influence remained restricted, causing the Soviet Union to miss an historic opportunity. In an age of major reform in communist ideology and the collapse of communism in Eastern Europe in 1989, most observers would agree that the opportunity for building a new form of communist solidarity is even more remote than ever. Nevertheless, to the extent that some aspects of the ruling ideology of communist states was reformed in tandem, important lines of communication and cooperation did develop in Asia. By 1990, the entire question of communist party rule in the Soviet Union was in doubt, thereby making it more than likely that the role of ideology would change yet again.

China: Moscow misrules

It can be argued that the greatest success communism had in the post–World War II world was the Chinese revolution of 1949. Certainly the Chinese Communist Party (CCP) has almost as many members as all other communist parties put together. But it would be far from accurate to attribute this success to Soviet foreign policy.

In its origins, communism is a European ideology. The original idea of democratic centralism came from Karl Marx and the system of party and government control was translated by V. I. Lenin. Before World War II, communism was confined to two states—the Soviet Union and Mongolia—and both pursued policies more or less determined in Moscow. China has had a communist party since 1927, and one that often ruled large swathes of territory, even if it rarely controlled the same areas for very long. The early history of the Chinese Communist Party is punctuated by periods of direct Soviet control followed by periods in which Moscow was too distracted to interfere with the Chinese revolution. The earliest lesson learned by Chinese communists was that the Soviet Union's so-called leading role in the international communist movement was both variable and inconsistent.

Yet despite the Soviets' intermittent interest in China, major political factors nevertheless bound the two parties together. The essential characteristics of Chinese and Soviet communism were the same, including a one-party state governed by the communist party operating according to Lenin's principle of democratic centralism. The state controlled the commanding heights of the economy and indeed society at large, leaving little room for individual rights or anything but a socialist definition of the rule of law and the structure of society. The common ideology also included support for socialist internationalism and the inevitable triumph of the revolutionary cause around the world.

Although the degree of unity was broad, important differences still existed in the ways the two parties had evolved. Given the great political and cultural traditions of China, such differences were only to be expected. Given traditional Russian authoritarianism and Chinese pride, not to mention the supposed scientific character of communism, these Sino-Soviet differences were bound to make relations touchy. Thus, Chinese communism stressed the rural roots of the revolution and relied more on the peasantry than on the urban proletariat as the shock troops of the cause.

The triumph of Chinese communism was a long time in coming. In the process, the Chinese comrades learned to be independent of Moscow. Despite some aid at various stages, the Chinese revolution was basically homemade and distinctive. Stalin had underestimated the basis of CCP support and was prepared to deal with Chiang Kai-shek's regime as the legitimate government of China. Although Moscow obviously welcomed the triumph of communism in China when it came, the Soviet Union could claim little credit and had exerted little control over the process.

Yet Russian hubris, enhanced by its victory at the end of World War II and its roaring return to East Asian politics in its sweep through the collapsed Japanese army in Manchuria, led the Soviet Union to believe it could now take control of Chinese communism. Mao, for his part, realized that China had little option but to turn to the Soviet Union for support. Both communist nations shared a perception of Japan and the United States as enemies. The result was a honeymoon in Sino-Soviet relations, a formal treaty of alliance and close cooperation at various levels of society, government and ruling party.

The Sino-Soviet honeymoon was based on more than just a coincidence of interests. China implemented the so-called Soviet model, with its stress on heavy industry, its styles of management, influence in culture and education, and even its system of running the armed forces. In foreign policy, the Chinese line throughout most of the 1950s was, superficially at least, virtually indistinguishable from that of the Soviet Union. Soviet advisers came to China by the thousands, and China's main allies in the world were in Eastern Europe.

With hindsight, it is clear that China's leaning to the Soviet side, which characterized the early period of the cold war, could not last long. By the mid-1950s, China began to feel confident enough to seek its own routes to economic prosperity and social revolution. The results were the Great Leap Forward and a growing rift with Moscow. It is also possible to argue that even though China would ultimately have to reject the Soviet model, it still ought to have avoided the lunatic policies it chose to follow instead. The death of some 25 million Chinese as a result of failed economic policies and related natural disasters in the early 1960s was only the most obvious evidence of the Chinese ideological bankruptcy.

The Soviets watched with horror as China drifted away. By the time of the open split in the early 1960s, Moscow saw a virtually irreconcilable ideological rift. Although Chinese leaders recognized they had failed to find a viable alternative to the Soviet Union's view of communism in government, Beijing knew it could not return to the Moscow-run ideological fold. The result was yet another great heave in Chinese political thinking, namely, the great proletarian cultural revolution.

Among its other peculiarities, the cultural revolution was aimed at discrediting what the Chinese called revisionism—Soviet-style stagnation and abandonment of revolutionary idealism. If the Russians had been under any illusion that the ideological breach with China could be quickly healed, the cultural revolution cured them of such dreams. In 1969, the two communist states even came to blows along the frontier, and the Sino-Soviet split reached its most acrimonious stage. Both communist states were locked in a vicious struggle for control of the international communist movement, with China claiming to lead its most radical and revolutionary branch.

By the mid-1970s, the Soviet Union could be pleased that it had won the international struggle with China, but it was still concerned that communist movements around the globe were split and that China had become its main adversary in the Asia-Pacific region. The setback to Soviet foreign policy that the rift with China caused was the worst since World War II. China was clearly the key to Soviet policy in the Pacific, and yet relations with China could hardly have been worse.

From this low point, the Soviet Union moved again towards improved relations with China and a firmer position in the Pacific. The process initially had little to do with changes in Soviet policy and more to do with changes in China. The post-Mao reforms led to a desire for a peaceful international environment and hence a reassessment of the threats facing China. Beijing decided that the Soviet

Union was not as dangerous as was once thought, and by 1982, Sino-Soviet detente slowly moved forward.[25]

The key to the detente was the mutual recognition by the Chinese and Soviets that they were both still socialist states. Chinese reforms had clearly brought the CCP back from the wilderness of radical ideology. The gap between Soviet and Chinese socialism had become narrower than at any time since the 1950s. As one astute observer noted, both countries were now 'mirrors' for each other's socialism.[26]

In the broader sweep of Sino-Soviet detente, relations were restored at various levels of society and government. The pace of this return to normality was dictated to a large degree by the pace of domestic reforms in both communist states. While Chinese reforms shuffled forward, the Soviet Union floundered around waiting for a leader who had both longevity and new ideas. The coming to power of Mikhail Gorbachev in 1985 marked a new stage in Sino-Soviet detente.

By May 1989, Sino-Soviet relations were normalized.[27] The final seal on that process was the restoration of party-to-party ties at the Sino-Soviet summit, 23 years after they were broken off in March 1966. As one of its concessions to the Chinese in 1986, the Soviet Union allowed its East European allies to resume normal inter-party relations with China even before the Soviet Union could do the same. Yet China still held the Soviet Union at bay, demanding concessions on other political issues, most notably an end to Soviet support for the Vietnamese occupation of Cambodia.

A key factor facilitating Sino-Soviet ideological detente was the evidence that the Soviet Union was no longer determined to lead a uniformly obedient communist movement. Gorbachev had sufficient humility to recognize that the Soviet Union did not know best, at least at a time of major reforms in the Soviet Union's own ideology. Inasmuch as these Soviet reforms involved learning from the experience of others, including China, other communist states could be pleased that Soviet policy was genuinely changing.

The road to treating fellow communist states as equals in the late 1980s was long and hard. In fact, only China could plausibly claim real equality with the Soviet Union. As China became more stable, successful and sensible (at least until May 1989), and the Soviet economy staggered into decline, it was easier for all concerned to accept a relationship of greater equality. Without the recognition of such equality with China, the Soviet Union could never hope to regain a significant, dominating ideological position in the Pacific.

When China started to take the Soviet reforms seriously, Moscow's position in the region improved. By 1988, with reform on the Soviet agenda, and China as a living example of its benefits, Sino-Soviet ideological cooperation became a useful tool in Soviet attempts to urge its East Asian allies to adopt reforms of their own. At no time since the 1950s was there such solid foundation for Sino-Soviet ideological cooperation. In the 1950s the cooperation was based on Soviet guidance, but in the 1980s the cooperation was more firmly based on a mutual perception of the value of each other's experience. Although Chinese reform led the way in economic terms, the Soviet Union seemed more advanced in some aspects of political reform. Whatever the case, with both countries openly experimenting, neither was likely to demand ideological orthodoxy or adherence to a specific line.

The reversal in the Soviet ideological position by the late 1980s was impressive and important. Just as the original split with China had done more damage to the Soviet position in the Pacific than any other single process, so the healing of that breach was the single most important success for Soviet foreign policy to date. But the success did not mean a return to the position of the 1950s. Sino-Soviet detente of the 1980s was completely different. In fact, it looked to be longer lasting because it was based on genuine equality, as well as a genuine spirit of ideological inquiry and reform in both states. As Sino-Soviet relations were normalized in May 1989, Soviet and Chinese officials began calling each other comrade, a term both sides vested with some meaning and one that could not be used in relations with non-communist officials.[28]

Party-to-party relations were restored at the summit in Beijing in May 1989.[29] China was impressed that the Soviet Union was actually willing to grant independence to fellow members of the international communist movement. With the Soviet Union admitting there was no single road to socialist construction, China in turn was willing to restore party ties on the understanding that they could all learn from each others' reforms.[30] In an age of reform, communism could include a wide range of ideas. Thus, Soviet economic reformers could often point to China for example of more daring ideas, just as marching Chinese students could look to Mikhail Gorbachev for inspiration for political reform.

Indeed, it was ironic that the peak of the Sino-Soviet summit was so obscured by the gathering student unrest in China. Even before

Mikhail Gorbachev had left Beijing, the attention of the world had shifted to the crisis in China. By 3–4 June, when Chinese troops massacred hundreds on the streets of Beijing, it had become clear that China had lost its status as the capitalist world's favourite communist regime. With so much simultaneous Western interest in the Soviet reforms, the immediate winner was the Soviet Union.

As the West threatened to close China's open door from the outside in the aftermath of the massacre, some might have thought that Sino-Soviet relations would grow much closer. But the view from Moscow was far less favourable. In the first place, Mikhail Gorbachev was personally displeased that his success at the summit was ruined. He was also repeatedly embarrassed by his subsequent inability to openly condemn Chinese brutality. As a result, critics of reform both within and outside the Soviet Union even more insistently questioned the Gorbachev experiment. Those critics urging a more cautious approach to reform inside the Soviet Union could point to the Chinese experience as a reason to go slow on reform. Critics outside the Soviet Union, who claimed Gorbachev was bound to fail, could make equally powerful use of the so-called Chinese lesson. Just as Chinese success had been a cause of debate in the Soviet Union, so Chinese failure was also a major feature of Soviet debates from mid-1989.[31]

On the brighter side, Moscow formally managed to stay out of Chinese politics and, as a result, could not be accused of playing the elder-brother role that had so harmed earlier Sino-Soviet relations. Assuming that there was no radical reversal of verdicts in Beijing, the Soviet Union was unlikely to be criticized by China for how it handled the events surrounding the Beijing massacre. The Soviet Union was certainly less likely to allow recent events to harm what it still judged to be two of the most important improvements in its position in the Pacific—Sino-Soviet detente and the restoration of party-to-party ties.

Of course, party-to-party ties in 1989 meant less than ever before, especially as the East European comrades slipped towards pluralist government. For Soviet leaders increasingly moving away from communist party rule, it was necessary resolutely to argue that the so-called Sinatra Doctrine ('you do it your way', as the Soviet Foreign Ministry spokesman noted) applied to all cases. But as the paths of China and the East Europeans diverged, unofficial Soviet criticism of China's hard line on political reform was stated plainly.[32] The Tiananmen model played the role of 'negative example' as East

Europe abandoned communism. By early 1990, most people in Moscow would claim that ideological discussions with China had become far more complex after normalized relations than they were before. Indeed, it is probably true that the Soviet Union was more upset by the events in China in June than was any other foreign country. Equally, China and other East Asian communists were more upset with Gorbachev as the architect of the collapse of communism in Europe.

The troublesome Koreans

Besides China and Mongolia, North Korea is the only other Pacific state to share a land border with the Soviet Union. Because of the closeness and because the Soviet Union occupied North Korea and was present at the creation of its modern communist state, North Korea has a special relationship with the Soviet Union. However, because of the Koreans' proud character and history of struggling against arrogant, great-power neighbours, North Korea has also been more than just a mirror for Soviet policy or even for Sino-Soviet relations. As in the case of China, the situation in North Korea has no parallels in pre-1989 Eastern Europe. The Soviet Union was forced to learn how to cope with yet another distinctive communist state.

Like the Chinese Communist Party, the communist party in Korea was founded in the 1920s and immediately disintegrated into factions. Unlike China, however, the Korean communists never seized a base area or actually governed their country until Soviet troops entered Korea in 1945 as part of the great power division of East Asia. Then, as it did in Poland, the Soviet Union set about consolidating communist rule and clearing up factionalism and resistance. A unique factor in the process was the presence of Koreans who had spent a great deal of time in China with the CCP. Particularly given China's continued interest in its eastern neighbour, the Korean communists clearly had more than one political heritage to draw upon.[33]

The Soviet Union finally organized a coalition between the Chinese faction and the communist party to form the North Korean Workers' Party in 1946.[34] Considering the state of relations between Chinese and Soviet communists at the time, the merger was somewhat premature. By 1948, when the Democratic People's Republic of

Korea was established, relations among all of Northeast Asia's communists were growing warmer. The Korean Workers' Party (KWP) was created in June 1949, three months after an aid treaty was signed between North Korea and the Soviet Union. North Korean trade was reoriented so that by the late 1940s some three-quarters of North Korean trade was with the Soviet Union.[35]

As in Eastern Europe, Soviet advisers were soon operating at all levels of North Korean society. Whether or not the Soviet Union was actually involved in planning the North Korean attack on South Korea in June 1950, the attack certainly could not have been launched without Soviet assistance.[36] China likewise hardly opposed the war. Both China and North Korea were still struggling with US-supported rivals for control of their countries.[37] Yet although China probably saw its interests in Korea as very different from those of the Soviet Union, given its internal distractions, China was content to let Moscow bear the burden of control and support in Pyongyang.

The course of the war led to a consolidation of Kim Il Sung's rule, although factional disputes still continued within the KWP. However, the decision to end the war lay ultimately with the Soviet Union and China, both of whom provided the vital material and men with which to wage the war. As independent as Kim might have felt, there were limits to his power in time of war and need. As a result of the Korean war, Chinese influence in North Korea increased, although Beijing remained locked in a struggle with Moscow for relative influence.

In 1956, Kim, like leaders in most other communist states, formally embraced the cause of de-Stalinization. North Korea—and China as well—had resented how major shifts of policy were summarily imposed from Moscow. Kim resisted efforts from both communist patrons to dictate policy and by 1958 he was steering a course midway between Moscow and Beijing—the much vaunted claim of self-reliance. North Korean independence was only possible because of the increasing rivalry between its communist friends. Unlike the East European communist parties, the East Asian communists had the opportunity to find greater independence in the crevices of the Sino-Soviet conflict.

Because the Soviet Union was the leader of the international communist cause, North Korea always officially accorded the Soviet Union formal primacy. Certainly, throughout the 1950s the Soviet model served as a guide for North Korean development. The trick in the 1960s was to avoid antagonizing either ally while convincing them both that North Korea should be wooed.

North Korea emulated some of China's domestic experiments that played such a vital part in the Sino-Soviet rift. Given that conditions in North Korea were closer to those in China than in the Soviet Union, such experimentation was not entirely unexpected. The Great Leap Forward had its parallels in the Flying Horse Movement, but Korean communes remained smaller than their equivalents in vast China. On foreign policy, North Korea stuck with Moscow in shifting towards peaceful coexistence.[38] Considering that the North Korean desire to reunify with South Korea would be delayed by East-West detente, this accommodation of the Soviet foreign policy line on East-West detente was a significant Korean compromise because of the need to balance between communist allies.

Sino-Soviet competition for Pyongyang's favours settled into a pattern of cautious balancing. The Soviet Union and North Korea signed a friendship treaty on 6 July 1961, and five days later, North Korea and China signed a similar pact, only without the heavy economic aid promised in the Soviet version. By the time the Sino-Soviet rift became fully public in 1963, North Korea was siding more openly with China on the major issues in dispute. For a time, North Korea was China's most vociferous supporter in the East Asian communist world, although North Korean support was not on a par with Albania's rabid support.

By 1964, North Korea had leaned too far to the Chinese side, thus losing its sense of independence. China was unable to provide the levels of support needed to replace the Soviet Union's. China's economy was having its own problems and Soviet military aid had been especially vital to North Korean foreign policy. The purge of Khrushchev in October 1964 gave North Korea an opportunity to drift back towards the Soviet Union without jeopardizing its agreement with China about the degree of threat coming from the United States and about the perils of detente. By that time, the Soviet Union had learned to be more sympathetic to North Korean concerns about independence, much as Moscow had learned to tolerate some East European diversity. The prize was North Korean support for so-called united action against the United States in Vietnam, a policy opposed by an increasingly radical China. North Korea's concern was the practical struggle with the United States and its allies rather than China's more theoretical belief in revolutionary purity.

In fact, the more radical the Chinese line became during the cultural revolution, the more the Soviet Union was perceived by other communist states as a sensible ally. When China set out to split revolutionary movements around the globe, the North Korean communists, who had depended on such movements for support, gravitated to the Soviet side of the Sino–Soviet dispute—a realistic position for them to take in a time of polarization in the communist movement.

The return to sanity in Beijing in the early 1970s allowed North Korea to drift back to the centre ground of communist politics. In fact, Pyongyang was well on its way to evolving a distinctive version of communism, notable for its absurdly developed cult of the personality of Kim Il Sung. Although Lenin might have recognized some aspects of this system, Marx would have found it more difficult to understand.[39] From the Soviet point of view, North Korea was still a communist state, albeit one of the most peculiar national varieties.

The Soviet Union could claim little credit for the shifts in North Korean policies—to say that the Soviet Union controlled North Korea is to stretch the meaning of the word. Moscow did try to restrain North Korea during a series of incidents with US armed forces in 1969 and the 1970s, which upset Pyongyang. But China's detente with the United States in the same period was even more upsetting because the Chinese had reversed their policy so completely. In fact, North Korea was shocked to discover that, as both communist allies simultaneously improved relations with the United States, there was much less freedom to manoeuvre for smaller, independent-minded communist states.

The dilemma for North Korea was clear. In times of East–West detente, Pyongyang either had to pursue its own detente policy also, or else find some other ally. When all its allies were pursuing the great-power detente game, North Korea was not strong enough to pursue its own policy of independence. Independence was viable only when the allies upon whom it depended were falling out.

North Korea tried the road to detente with South Korea only as long as necessary. Of course, neither Korea liked being pushed into detente by their great power patrons and so were, at some level at least, happy to explore the possibility of the relative independence that might come from inter-Korean detente. But with the old communist leadership still in power in North Korea, the weight of conservative tradition and suspicion of new ideas was heavy. The pressure of stagnation might have become unbearable if it had not been for the downturn in East-West detente in the late 1970s. As superpower relations cooled, Soviet pressure for North-South Korean detente waned. North Korea also drifted towards closer relations with the Soviet Union because Chinese domestic reforms were reshaping Chinese foreign policy in ways that worried Pyongyang.

China now had less tolerance for Kim Il Sung's Stalinist and isolated ways of development. As China opened its doors to Western aid and trade, it also offered less aid to North Korea. Furthermore, China opened trade relations with South Korea, which, by the late 1980s, was worth several times the value of trade with North Korea. To survive such pressure from China, North Korea moved closer to the Soviet Union.

By the late 1980s, the pressure was back on Pyongyang. Mikhail Gorbachev, like Deng Xiaoping before him, saw the need to open doors to the capitalist Pacific, including South Korea. Soviet domestic reform was rapidly affecting Soviet foreign policy. The fact of North Korea's real dependence, despite the slogans of independence, was driven home. Both Moscow and Beijing tacitly cooperated in controlling Kim Il Sung's wilder ambitions and both urged domestic reforms on this, one of the most Stalinist governments in the communist world.

The most painful pressure of all on North Korea came from a Soviet-supported change of policy by East European states towards open contacts with South Korea. Hungary even went so far as to establish official diplomatic relations with South Korea in 1989, much to the anger of its North Korean comrades. By 1990, when communism had collapsed in Eastern Europe, nearly all of Moscow's former clients in Europe had recognized two Korean states. Between 1988 and 1989 many East Europeans were eager to show North Korea, and indeed the world at large, that they could have their own foreign policy options.[40] The ideology of reform, together with the growing diversity in the communist world, divided the communists of East Asia, even as it also improved the position of the Soviet Union in the Pacific.

Yet the Soviet Union itself was still dragging its feet in establishing formal diplomatic relations with South Korea. Although it encouraged the East Europeans to be more bold, Moscow was anxious to stay closer to Pyongyang, at least until the successor to Kim Il Sung was known. But as we will see in the later sections on Soviet trade policy, there was a clear connection between the reform of Soviet ideology at home and its determination to avoid ideological limitations on relations with South Korea.[41]

The lessons for Soviet foreign policy were clear. North Korea, like most allies, was happiest in an environment in which relative diversity was tolerated. But diversity could get out of hand. In Eastern Europe it erupted in Hungary in 1956 and Czechoslovakia in 1968. In East Asia, diversity got the Soviet Union into minicrises with the United States in Northeast Asia and bargaining with North Korea over balancing Chinese favours. The Soviet position was much more difficult in many senses in East Asia because it was not the clear and undisputed hegemonic power in that part of the communist world.

When Sino-Soviet relations improved, however, or at least when the two tacitly followed similar lines, life was easier for the Soviet Union. North Korea, unlike even East Germany, had nowhere to turn for friends and could be pressed to change or at least have its demands controlled. At the end of the 1980s, the latest phase of tacit Sino-Soviet cooperation had just begun. With a change in leadership imminent in North Korea, all parties were proceeding especially cautiously. But as long as Sino-Soviet detente and reforms held, North Korea would soon be forced to toe the line.

By late 1989 and because of the rapid moves towards German reunification, the Soviet Union also grew more ready to contemplate Korean reunification. Indeed it could be argued that Soviet contact with South Korea was part of this new policy. In the end, avoiding new conflict and a more peaceful Northeast Asia will please both Moscow and Beijing. The Soviet Union has an intrinsic interest in Korea because of the economic benefits that can be gained from cooperation with South Korea. Only a reformed North Korea could argue that cooperation between Moscow and Pyongyang could serve the interests of greater Soviet integration into the Pacific region.

A watchful eye on Mongolia

The Mongolian People's Republic is, of course, the Soviet Union's oldest ally and the first East Asian state to become communist. Surrounded as it is by the Soviet Union and China, and fearful of

Chinese irredentism, Mongolia has always sought Soviet friendship as a guarantee of independence. But independence and equality of sovereign states have always been difficult concepts for the Soviet Union, especially with neighbours and ideologically like-minded regimes. The result has been a dominating Soviet influence in Mongolia more akin to old-style Soviet-East German relations than to Soviet-North Korean relations.

With a population of no more than 2 million, Mongolia is the smallest outpost of the communist movement. With more than a billion people in neighbouring China, and Beijing's long-standing desire to control all of Mongolia, it is not surprising that the 1921 revolution in Mongolia was opposed by Chinese forces. Moscow immediately signed a treaty of friendship with the new Mongolian revolutionaries and has since been the only outside power to provide significant amounts of aid.[42]

In fact, in the 28 years after 1921, the only other country with which Mongolia signed a treaty of friendship and established diplomatic relations was Tannu Tuva, which was later absorbed into the Soviet Union in 1944. Diplomatic relations with China under the Guomindang were established in 1946 and with communist North Korea in 1948. Other Eastern bloc states followed soon thereafter and Mongolia was admitted to the United Nations in 1961.

Despite the apparent lifting of its isolation, however, Mongolia was nevertheless one of the most secluded states.[43] At the time of close Sino-Soviet relations, Mongolia was supported by both states but always suspected that China had ulterior motives. When the Sino-Soviet split occurred in the 1960s, Mongolia became more dependent on the Soviets. The temporary stationing of Soviet troops in Mongolia as Sino-Soviet border tension increased was as much to defend Mongolia from China as to provide a forward base for Soviet defence. Unlike most East Europeans who are pleased to see the withdrawal of Soviet troops, Mongolia and the Soviet Union had common interests. During the radical phases of the Chinese cultural revolution, anxiety about China was most acute.

During the 1970s, when both Mongolia and the Soviet Union had aging and conservative leaders, the basis of Soviet-Mongolian relations remained stable. But as with so much else in communist East Asia, the situation changed with the shift to more reformist policies in the Soviet Union and the onset of Sino-Soviet detente. The deployment of Soviet troops in Mongolia was one major obstacle to

Sino-Soviet detente—Soviet troop concentrations along the frontier. Soviet-Mongolian relations were also part of a broader, but unstated obstacle—the Soviet policy of firm control of a relatively monolithic bloc governed from Moscow.

From the mid-1980s, both aspects of Sino-Soviet relations changed, with major consequences for Mongolia. The Soviet Union increased pressure on Mongolia to improve relations with China, and Moscow began discussing so-called third-party issues, including Mongolia, in talks with China.[44]

Above all, the reform of Soviet communism was felt in Mongolia. The Mongolian leader, Tsedenbal, was replaced by Batmonh in 1984. Mongolia soon took up the Gorbachev battle cry of reform, albeit with some reluctance and with more emphasis on the economic than the political dimensions. Continuing Soviet pressure, including the withdrawal of most Soviet troops by the late 1980s, did not encourage a sense of confidence in Mongolia. But as a state so clearly dependent on the Soviet Union, Mongolia could do little. After all, fear of China in the first place had driven Mongolia into the alliance with the Soviet Union. By early 1990, with reform in the Soviet Union moving faster and Chinese reform on hold, Mongolia fell into line and agreed to a sweeping political reform in Moscow's mould. Just as Mongolia followed a conservative Soviet line in previous decades, so it adopted reform when the Soviet Union pushed hard enough.

Of course, Mongolia is not entirely without options or self-esteem. Soviet support has allowed the creation of a relatively independent Mongol state that compares favourably in how Mongol minorities are treated in either the Soviet Union or China. Although Mongol culture has been scarred by its contact with communism, the country does retain a distinctive character. The traditional way of life has been transformed by communism, yet Mongolia still remains a distinctive Asian society.[45] Despite the influence of Soviet-bloc culture in the form of films and even architecture, the country remains more obviously different from the Soviet model than any pre-1989 East European state. But unlike the North Koreans, the Mongols have had to make more compromises with Soviet demands, if only because of the obvious lack of alternatives. In an age of reform in the Soviet Union, Mongolia, like other allies, has been encouraged to experiment with national characteristics of politics.[46] But Mongolia, perhaps more than any other state has nowhere else to go for friends.

From the Soviet point of view, Mongolia is first and foremost useful as a military buffer. With communism a fading force in Soviet foreign policy, the ideological peculiarities are less important and less bothersome to the Soviet Union. The exception is when Mongolia stands in the way of Soviet foreign policy priorities. Like North Korea, Mongolia is an issue in Sino–Soviet relations. But even less so than North Korea, the Mongols have little chance to resist Soviet pressure for change. Once again, the Soviet Union finds that most ideological issues in its East Asian foreign policy return to the centrality of China. If relations with China are good, then the rest of Soviet East Asian policy seems to sort itself out.

Influence in Indochina

Unlike the three other northern Pacific communist states, the three communist states in Indochina do not share a frontier with the Soviet Union. Soviet influence is therefore more akin to that in Cuba—moderate and rarely a high priority. Yet, Indochina has been at war for most of the post-1945 period, often drawing a number of great powers into conflict and tension. Furthermore, Vietnam is the world's third most populous communist state and a rival to China. Arguably, from the Soviet perspective, Vietnam is the next most important East Asian communist state after China, but given the distance from Soviet power, Vietnam has had more room for manoeuvre than any Soviet ally in the Pacific.

The Vietnamese Communist Party was formally established on 3 February 1930, and like the CCP, it experienced both Soviet support and cavalier disregard of local conditions in its early years.[47] With the coming of the Japanese and the decay of French power, Ho Chi Minh took his forces into the countryside and, in Chinese style, governed some rural areas. Vietnam's route to independence helped reduce Soviet influence.[48]

In fact, when Japan was defeated, Ho's forces marched into Hanoi and proclaimed a provisional government in 1945. The eventual return of French power led to the first Indochinese war in which Chinese communists were clearly the main supporters of their Vietnamese comrades. But there was also a traditional Vietnamese suspicion of Chinese hegemonic aspirations in Indochina that, despite Vietnamese needs for support against the French, led them to be wary of Chinese intentions. The success of Chinese and Korean communism was important evidence to the Vietnamese of the need to be both independent and yet make use of comradely support.

During the Sino-Soviet alliance, the Soviet Union was clearly prepared to allow China to make the most of helping the revolutionary cause in Vietnam. At the 1954 Geneva conference, both communist allies urged a partition of the country, which fell well short of Ho's desires. China took the lead at the conference and therefore incurred most of the Vietnamese suspicions.[49] The war continued towards what is now known as the second Indochinese conflict, this time drawing in American military power more directly. Thus, Vietnam had to rely on its communist supporters, while swallowing some of its pride. From 1954 the Vietnamese communists had a state of their own to govern, yet this state-building process provided more opportunity for more direct Soviet influence.

The Vietnamese Communist Party's policies originated in a distinctive interpretation of Marxism-Leninism. To the extent that there was a model for development, it was more Chinese communism than the Soviet variety. By the time of the triumph of communism in Vietnam in 1975, the Vietnamese communists already had plenty of experience and required no ideological leadership. The split with China that followed had its roots in interstate rivalry and had very little to do with a clash of domestic policies.

Soviet influence in Vietnam increased from 1965. With the political demise of Khrushchev and the increasing tempo of the American war effort, Soviet leaders reassessed their Indochina policy. As China slid into the chaos of the cultural revolution, Vietnam obviously needed to improve relations with the Soviet Union. Yet despite the vastly increased levels of Soviet aid, the Soviets exerted remarkably little influence in Vietnamese ideology or domestic politics. Vietnam might as well have been a non-communist regime, despite the rhetoric of revolutionary solidarity. Vietnamese communism was as different from the Soviet variety as that of China—in fact, any peasant-based revolution would likely differ from the Soviet model.

Even during the late 1970s, a period of loud Sino-Soviet polemics, Vietnam supported the Soviet side in foreign policy while ignoring the Soviet practice of building communism domestically. In the early 1980s, just as China was experimenting with the agricultural reform, Vietnam adopted its own form of contract system in the countryside. Although the Vietnamese were much less adventurous and successful than the Chinese, they certainly paid little attention to the Soviet experience.[50] Even though Vietnam joined the Council of Mutual Economic Assistance (COMECON) in 1978, it saw the organization as providing further aid and a wider range of markets.[51]

The stagnation of the Vietnamese economy was primarily due to the burden of its relatively rigid, wartime economic policies and to the cost of its occupation of Cambodia (from 1979). The Soviet Union was unwilling to intervene on either of these two issues so long as Sino-Soviet relations were cool and the Soviet Union itself was avoiding its own pressing need for reform.

As we have already seen elsewhere in the communist Pacific, the mid-1980s saw Sino-Soviet detente and Soviet domestic reforms sweep the communist world. Although Vietnam could help ensure the Soviets' good behaviour by threatening to withdraw access to Vietnamese bases, the Soviet Union held the more useful instrument of economic and military aid. When Moscow realized that Sino-Soviet detente also meant that they would have to pressure Vietnam to withdraw from Cambodia, the Soviet Union did so. Hanoi baulked for a time, for, like Mongolia, it feared selfish Soviet policies.

With the rapidly sinking Vietnamese economy in the last half of the 1980s apparent to all but the most diehard conservatives, the Vietnamese changed their leadership at the end of 1986 and began the painful process of reform in earnest. The new leadership was much more amenable to the reforms being urged by the Soviet Union, if only to make better use of Soviet aid. When all but the most old-fashioned communists were exploring the possibilities for reform, the Vietnamese found it fruitless to hold out. Certainly, the Chinese example showed that quick gains could be made by rural reform in peasant societies.

Thus, the model for reform was neither Soviet nor Chinese, but rather a distinctive Vietnamese alternative. Yet the Soviet Union could claim some of the credit for engineering the change. The more successful the communist regimes in the Pacific, the less isolated and pessimistic the Soviet Union would feel. Although the price of Vietnamese success might mean less Soviet control, Moscow had already learned that it exercised little real influence in Vietnam anyway. If there was another successful East Asian socialist regime in a poor peasant country besides China, the Soviet Union could claim some of the credit.

The Soviet Union might also hope that a reformed Vietnam might exercise less control over its allied Indochinese states, Cambodia and Laos. The resulting increase in regional diversity might allow more room for Soviet influence, not to mention fewer economic and political burdens in the region. But the Soviet Union was unlikely to have any illusions that Cambodia and Laos might be especially friendly to them, for Soviet influence in Indochina has rarely extended beyond Vietnam.

Neither the Cambodian or Laotian communist movements were allowed close relations with the Soviet Union. Both China, and especially Vietnam, guarded their influence. In any case, the Soviet Union had little to offer as a model for development, or in large-scale aid.[52] The struggles within both movements had more to do with national rivalries and/or groups with links to the Chinese or Vietnamese.

In its Cambodian policy, the Soviet Union was poorly advised, for it maintained relations with the Khmer Republic until the bitter end in 1975. The reasons for the error in Soviet policy are difficult to fathom. Moscow might have been distracted by its backing of other Marxist tendencies in Cambodia, or perhaps it simply disapproved of the direction of the specific variant of communists that came to power. Like China and Vietnam, the Soviet Union had seen Vietnam as the main theatre of operations and both Laos and Cambodia as a sideshow. After 1975, when communism came to power in all three Indochinese states, Moscow was especially unprepared for the new world of an expanded communist Pacific.

But it would be unfair to suggest that Pol Pot was emulating Chinese practice when he implemented the most radical revolution ever seen in the communist world. The brutality and consequences of the Khmer Rouge's policies might have tarnished the name of communism in general if it had not so clearly been a product of national chauvinism and revolutionary extremism. As the Khmer Rouge fell further into conflict with Vietnam, the Soviet Union could wholeheartedly support Vietnam.

In fact, there is little evidence that the Soviet Union opposed the Vietnamese invasion of Cambodia in 1978. After Sino-Soviet border clashes, the world had already become accustomed to communist killing communist, and the Pol Pot phenomenon was already doing serious damage to the image of communist ideology. From the Soviet perspective, a defeat of Chinese-supported communists at a time of Sino-Soviet conflict was not an unattractive prospect.

But, if the Soviet Union had any expectation of influence in Phnom Penh after the defeat of Pol Pot, it had misjudged Indochinese communism yet again. Vietnam was sufficiently suspicious of Soviet motives to keep the levers of control firmly in its own hands, despite drawing Soviet aid for their Cambodian allies. But once Soviet pressure began to work for a Vietnamese withdrawal from Cambodia, the Soviets had a chance to improve their position in Indochina.

Cambodian and Laotian nationalism had been suppressed by Vietnamese control. In an age when the communist world outside of Asia was shrinking, the rival ideologies of Vietnam, China and the Soviet Union offered different ways of organizing the socialist Pacific. In the more than 40 years since World War II, the Soviet Union clearly lost control of its ideology in the Pacific. The resulting diversity, however, has taught the Soviet Union important lessons about how to deal with other, proud states. By the late 1980s, it could be argued that Soviet ideology was less relevant and less of a problem than at any previous point. Whether that ideology still had any long-term appeal would depend on the success of domestic Soviet reforms.

Nonruling communist parties

The total number of communist party members in East Asia outside the seven ruling parties in the Pacific is less than 600,000—about the size of the French Communist Party. The Japanese communists account for 80 percent of the total membership in non-communist East Asia, but not even in the Japanese case does this membership constitute even half of 1 percent of the local population.

The appeal of communism to the people of the Pacific is limited and has faded as time has passed. The Sino-Soviet split tore most of those movements apart in the 1960s, and the various unsuccessful wars in the region led to most of the parties being banned and isolated. In any case, most of these revolutionary movements were more pro-Chinese than pro-Soviet. The states in the non-communist Pacific can be divided into four groups: (1) pluralist democracies with tiny communist parties (Japan, Australia, New Zealand), (2) states that have successfully contained once-significant communist movements (Indonesia, Malaysia and Thailand), (3) states still struggling against a significant communist force, and (4) states that successfully ban the existence of a communist party (Singapore, Taiwan, South Korea).

In no case does any movement draw significant inspiration from Moscow.

The pluralist democracies with communist parties bear a strong resemblance to their European counterparts. In Japan, the Japanese Communist Party (JCP) won 45 seats in the House of Representatives (9.6 percent of the vote) in 1949, but when it moved to harder anti-American policies in the early 1950s, it lost all its seats in 1952. By 1961 the JCP had shifted back to support for parliamentary procedures, but in 1963 it sided with China in the Sino-Soviet split. The pro-Soviet section of its leadership was expelled in 1965, but by 1967 the party had drifted back to a more independent position between the two communist giants. It has since condemned the Chinese attack on Vietnam in 1979 and in 1989 was the first of Japan's major parties to denounce the Beijing massacre. The JCP also took a firm line against the Soviet invasion of Afghanistan, Soviet policies in Poland and even the occupation of the Kurile islands. The JCP's vote still hovers at about 9 percent, and in the mid-1980s the party had a membership of just under 500,000.[53]

The Australian Communist Party (CPA) was founded in 1920. It was banned at various times, but an act banning the CPA in 1950 was ruled unconstitutional. The Sino-Soviet conflict led to a drawn-out debate in the movement, resulting in a split and the triumph of the pro-Soviet faction. The CPA then moved towards Eurocommunist-like policies, including criticism of the Soviet invasion of Czecho-slovakia. A pro-Soviet splinter group broke away in 1971. However, its membership of under 2,000 makes it irrelevant in Australian politics.

The New Zealand Communist Party (CPNZ) became pro-Chinese during the Sino-Soviet split, leading to a splintering of the party. But the original CPNZ broke with Chinese revisionists in 1978 and declared Albania to be its socialist fatherland. With 50 members, it is half the size of the pro-Soviet Socialist Unity Party (SUP). The Soviet Ambassador to New Zealand was expelled in 1980 for passing money to the SUP, but Moscow still sends fraternal greetings, if not more, to the party.[54]

In comparison to these curiosities of democratic politics, there have been more important communist movements in the Pacific, only one of which was of any significance in the late 1980s. The party that made its presence felt first was the Communist Party of Malaya (CPM). It won its stripes by fighting the Japanese in the 1940s. The party was banned by the British in 1948 when it started a bloody guerrilla campaign. Peace talks in 1955 failed and the revolt was essentially crushed by 1960, at which time the state of emergency was lifted. The leadership of the CPM decamped to Beijing and small bands carried on isolated activity in the bush area near the Thai frontier. In 1980, the then chairman of the CPM returned to Malaysia and surrendered to the authorities. The defeat and virtual elimination of this movement were evidence that not all states in Southeast Asia need go communist and emphasized that Chinese rather than Soviet communism was the threat.

Another important communist party was formed in neighbouring Indonesia. The Partai Komunis Indonesia (PKI) assumed its present name in 1924 but had its roots in the earliest communist party in Asia, the Communist Party of the Indies. After fighting the Japanese and then the nationalist government, it adopted more nationalist positions after 1951. Its membership grew and in the election of 1955 it gained 16.4 percent of the vote, making it the fourth largest party. Some members joined the government and in 1965 the party claimed 3 million members, making it the third largest communist party in the world. The PKI was a strong supporter of China in the Sino-Soviet split.

In October 1965, a group of communist officers, believing a right-wing coup was imminent, carried out a coup of their own. The PKI-supported revolt was crushed almost immediately, and 500,000 people were killed in the ensuing massacre. The PKI was banned in 1966 and since then there have been periodic arrests and executions of members. The tiny factions remaining are still mostly pro-Chinese, and the Indonesian government remains more anti-Chinese than anti-Soviet as a result of having had to wage internal war on Chinese communism.

Pro-Chinese communists in Thailand followed a less violent path. The Communist Party of Thailand (CPT) was founded in 1942 by ethnic Chinese, and although it had representation in parliament in 1946–7, it was banned in 1952. As part of the pro-Chinese tilt in the Sino-Soviet split, the CPT concentrated its effort on guerrilla war in the countryside. Most operations took place along the Laotian and Malaysian frontiers, and active support was given by China and North Vietnam. The triumph of communism in neighbouring Laos and Cambodia put acute pressure on the Thai government.

The split between China and Vietnam tore apart the CPT. At first, the party took a pro-Chinese line and offered support to the government in the struggle against Vietnamese forces along the frontier. But fighting soon broke out between pro-Vietnamese and pro-Chinese factions. To make matters worse for the CPT, both Vietnam and China were anxious to improve relations with Thailand, and so both cut back aid to the local communists. Thousands of CPT members then defected, taking advantage of the amnesty declared by the government. Despite occasional reports of rebel activity, for all intents and purposes the CPT had ceased to operate as a force in Thai politics in the 1980s.

The last significant nonruling communist party in East Asia is also in Southeast Asia—in the Philippines. The Partido Komunista ng Pilipinas was founded in 1930, banned in 1932 but legalized again in 1938. It was banned again in 1948 and then broke up in 1968 with a splinter group following the Chinese line. The pro-Chinese faction now claims 30,000 members and has successfully pursued a form of guerrilla warfare in the countryside. Its New People's Army controlled vast portions of rural Mindanao and tied down 60,000 government troops. According to some analysts, there is a real chance that unless far-reaching reforms are undertaken in the Philippines, the Maoist strategy of a peasant revolution beginning in the countryside and moving into urban areas may be successful.

But like every other case of a nonruling communist party in East Asia, the Chinese rather than the Soviets won control of the majority of the movement. When the Chinese shifted to more pragmatic reforms in the late 1970s, further splits took place, and the remaining Maoist movements became increasingly indigenous and less guided by Chinese policy. Like nearly all of the ruling communist parties in East Asia, local characteristics also came to dominate party authority and ideology. Even though communist ideology continues to be important for many of these states and movements, it is unrecognizable as a Soviet or even Chinese ideology.

Soviet ideology in the Pacific

Clearly, the Soviet Union is less closely tied by culture or ideology to the Pacific than it is to Europe. European culture and ideology have been much more coherent than Pacific culture. Although it is true that the Soviet Union is not a natural power in East Asia, it is just as natural in cultural and ideological terms in the Pacific as the other neo-Europes in the Americas or the South Pacific. When thinking Pacific, the Soviet Union has real potential as an effective, local power.

Yet it has taken the Soviet Union a long time to feel at home in the Pacific's political diversity. In the early postwar years its attempts to impose its own ways on its allies failed with all but Mongolia. The results were a split with China, trouble with North Korea, and the loss of most communist movements in the Pacific. The road to establishing a strong Soviet position in the Pacific has been long and arduous.

The recent reforms in the Soviet role have been marked by several important developments. First, the shock to the Soviet system from the so-called loss of China eventually led to a reassessment of how to treat allies. The related problems of how to cope with diversity in international communism in Europe in the ensuing decades also helped move the Soviet Union away from the idea that it must maintain rigid control of a relatively unified bloc. Second, the Soviet relationship with other developing states, most notably India, reinforced the lesson that friends had to be treated with greater respect and care, rather than as puppets.

Third, the Soviet Union found it easier to tolerate diversity when it saw that other communist powers, most notably China, were also suffering from similar effects of ideological hubris. These Chinese reforms were accompanied by acknowledgments of past failures in trying to spread and dominate international communism. Fourth, the failures of others also led some nations, such as Vietnam or even North Korea, to seek greater friendship with the Soviet Union.

Fifth, and perhaps most important, in the mid-1980s the Soviet Union began to rethink its own grand strategies in the developing world in general, and in the Pacific in particular. In fact, the changes in the Pacific may be a major motivation for Soviet foreign policy reform. A whole range of new ideas began to be discussed and developed in the Soviet Union. Not only had the Chinese shown that major reforms in a large communist power could bear remarkably swift and sweet fruit, but the apparent failures in the Soviet Union's own system also made it imperative to begin reforms of its own. Furthermore, the booming Pacific produced a diversity of ideologies, not all of which could be rejected out of hand. The experience of the so-called Confucian states in particular provided alternative models, some of which were less incompatible than European capitalism.

The state-dominated economies of Japan and the NICs helped push the Soviet Union to rethink their own approach to competing ideas for economic development.

Whatever the specific causes of the new thinking in Soviet ideology, by the mid-1980s Moscow was acting less like a bully in the region. The new spirit was crucial in easing the fears of communists and non-communists alike that the Soviet Union was still pursuing a hegemonic policy. The result for the Soviets has been mostly improved relations with both communist and non-communist states in the region.

Sino-Soviet detente has had far-reaching implications for Soviet ideology in the Pacific. The mutual processes of reform helped improve relations with the largest communist party—in China—and it also helped place greater pressure on other nations in East Asia to pursue reform. At the price of minimizing its role as an ideological leader, the Soviet Union was able to raise its standing in the region to the highest levels since the end of World War II.

By early 1990, it was next to impossible to be certain about any ideological component of Soviet policy. The era of communism in Europe and the radical reform in the Soviet Union made Soviet ideas about communism hard to pin down. At a time when nearly all communist party states were in East Asia, the Soviet Union seemed to be giving up on the ideology it once claimed as its own. If the Soviet Union was to be a power in East Asia, it would probably be as a non-communist power.

5
Military Issues

The Soviet Union has been described as an 'incomplete superpower' because of its undue reliance on military power and its weakness in economic and general political power. This judgment applies in differing degrees to the various areas in which Soviet foreign policy operates. In Europe, Soviet power is more complete, while in the Pacific, an area of rapid economic and political change, the Soviet Union's incompleteness and its past reliance on military power alone, has seemed more glaring.

In the late 1980s, as Soviet military power in the Pacific relatively declined, the Soviets reassessed the usefulness of military force as an instrument of policy. Clearly, armed force has been less important for the Soviet Union in the Pacific than many observers had previously thought. The Soviet Union itself recognizes these changes, and it needs to find other less threatening means of bolstering its power and influence in the Pacific region.[1] To be sure, there has been an obvious buildup of Soviet forces at various times, but it is much less clear that these forces have done much more than defend established Soviet positions or safeguard the newer gains that had fallen into the Soviet Union's lap. It is certainly very difficult to find anything that might be graced with the term 'strategy' when describing the way Soviet military power has been used in the Pacific.

Gorbachev's reforms have made possible a new agenda in Soviet policy in the Pacific. The so-called Gorbachev doctrine gives priority to defending the home territory. The Soviet Union has let its allies know that they have to fend for themselves much more. The Soviet Union has been retreating from past foreign military engagements and is newly determined to project a less threatening image by emphasizing arms control and confidence-building in its regional policy.

However, the new Gorbachev diplomacy is risky. Since the Soviet Union has few instruments of policy in the Pacific, apart from its military power, a minimizing of that military power makes it harder to take the Soviet Union seriously in the Pacific. Unlike the United States, which managed to minimize the damage done by its military retreat because of its economic power in the Pacific, the Soviet Union has little else on which to build its presence in the region. Nevertheless, the Gorbachev gamble is based on the longer-term view that unless there is less reliance on military power, and more serious attention to other aspects of Soviet power, the Soviet Union stands no chance of being taken seriously in the Pacific century.

Superpower conflict

The conflict between the superpowers is often described as an East-West conflict, deriving its geographic images from the European and the Atlantic theatre where the Soviet Union and its allies are to the east while the United States and its West European allies are to the west of the ideological dividing line in Europe. Of course, in the Pacific, the Soviet East lies to the west, and the American-led West is to the east. This is only one of the more trivial, but symbolically important differences between the superpower balances in the Pacific and Atlantic theatres.[2]

More important, since 1945, the superpowers have come close to war more often in the Pacific than in the Atlantic. The conflicts in Korea and Vietnam are only the most notable cases in which the superpowers supported opposing sides in a hot war. Soviet citizens were killed by US attacks in both wars, and tens of thousands of US citizens were killed by Soviet-made weaponry. However, the superpowers never found themselves as close to *direct* conflict as they were during the Cuban missile crisis or the various turret-to-turret confrontations in Berlin. Even the Middle East war of 1973 brought the two superpowers to a higher state of military alert than any conflict in the Pacific.

Nevertheless, the Korean and Vietnam wars were probably more damaging to superpower relations than any other major postwar conflict in the developing world. Only after the end of the Korean war was it possible to begin superpower discussions on disarmament. The Vietnam war stifled superpower detente and complicated the early arms control agreements of the 1970s. The Soviet-supported Vietnamese invasion of Cambodia in 1978 was seen in Washington as yet another sign of Soviet perfidy and helped destroy the SALT II agreement.

Yet crises in Korea after 1953 were increasingly well managed by the superpowers and not allowed to harm grander Soviet-US strategies of detente.[3] China's involvement in the offshore islands crises with Taiwan in the 1950s was controlled by the United States and the Soviet Union.[4] Even during the Vietnam war, the super-powers were finally able to conclude the first SALT agreement, and as US involvement in the war decreased, the superpowers were also able to clink glasses at the high point of detente in the early 1970s.[5] Although these wars complicated superpower relations, they were eventually kept from contaminating the atmosphere when the superpowers both saw strong reasons for strategic detente. Such insulation of their relations from regional confrontations was more possible in the Pacific than in Europe because, with the exception of Japan, the Pacific allies were seen as less important.

Another major difference between the superpower confrontation in the Atlantic and Pacific is the absence of clear lines of demarcation in the Pacific. Even though the superpowers actually do share frontiers in the Pacific (in the Bering strait), these northern wastes are not of primary strategic concern because they are sparsely populated and the physical geography is forbidding. Only in Korea does the United States station troops to defend a US ally that directly confronts a Soviet ally bordering on the Soviet Union. Yet the Soviet-Korean frontier is only 12 miles long and North Korea hardly serves as a strategic glacis as did the East European states to the Soviet Union's west.

US forces were deployed in strength in South Vietnam in the 1960s, but most of them had been withdrawn by 1973 and all US personnel left the country in 1975. In mainland Southeast Asia, only Thailand still receives large-scale US support, but this entire area is as far from the Soviet frontier as Morocco. Vietnam and Moscow's other Indochinese allies are more akin to Cuba and North Yemen than to Eastern Europe in the Soviet strategic calculation.

Thus, it is difficult to know where the lines of containment and conflict in the Pacific cold war should be drawn. Although it took some time (as well as the 1948–9 and 1961 Berlin crises and the 1956 Hungarian and 1962 Cuban crises) to etch the dividing lines so deeply in Europe and the Atlantic, uncertainty about the political geography in Europe was never as great as it was in the Pacific. Most observers would now agree that one main cause of the Korean war was the Soviets' lack of understanding that the United States was committed to defend South Korea. The Vietnam war in the 1960s had a great deal to do with US attempts to prop up what it perceived to be toppling dominoes in East Asia and to halt the communist advance there.

The crucial difference between the balance of power in the Pacific compared to the Atlantic is the presence of China. Until the 1960s, the United States perceived China as part of a solid Sino-Soviet alliance. Despite the Sino-Soviet split, the United States still perceived China as merely the more radical exponent of communism, but essentially a supporter of Soviet interests.[6] Joint Sino-Soviet support for Vietnam in the 1960s was seen as a case in point. Not until Sino-Soviet border clashes in 1969, and the Kissinger-Nixon reassessment of US foreign policy, was China's potential as a genuinely independent power recognized. Some observers even thought China might be helpful in the confrontation with the Soviet Union. Chinese communism was then re-interpreted in a more moderate light and was found to have its own national drives and interests—a trend that in practice did not show itself fully until the Deng Xiaoping reforms of the 1980s.

The transformation of China from being an ally of the Soviet Union to being an enemy was the single greatest strategic loss suffered by the Soviet Union after 1945. It was not the result of anything orchestrated by the United States. Clearly, however, the Soviet need to redirect spending to the Pacific theatre to meet the Chinese threat was of huge benefit to the United States. As the old and nearly universal adage has it, 'The enemy of my enemy is my friend'. Equally, and nearly opposite, the slow but steady improvement in Sino-Soviet relations in the 1980s has reduced Soviet anxiety and represents the single most important gain in the Soviet strategic position in the Pacific in 40 years. Once again, the United States was not responsible for this shift, although its relative position in the Pacific has not apparently suffered to any great extent.

In military terms, there is no strictly bipolar confrontation in the Pacific. China has certainly turned the old two-power balance into a triangle since the 1960s. The growth of Vietnamese power in the 1970s made it even more difficult to calculate a Southeast Asian balance of power. Japan used to be a military power in the Pacific, but after 1945 has eschewed a military role outside of its own immediate security zone. Although its booming economy is able to support the world's third largest defence budget, Japan, unlike China, has not used its force in anger against any other state. Japanese forces remain configured for defence, and the state is highly vulnerable to blockade and nuclear threat. Thus, the Pacific theatre is more complicated than the Atlantic one, but not as complicated as it was before 1945.

Another major difference between the Atlantic and Pacific arenas is the relatively more diffuse nature of the superpower tension. In Europe, the lines of confrontation were immortalized by Winston Churchill as an 'iron curtain' hanging across the heart of Europe. There was never similar drapery in the Pacific, except for the heavily fortified Korean frontier that bore some resemblance to the pre-1989 inner-German frontier. Of course, by early 1990 and with the collapse of communism in Europe, it could be said that the European balance of power was rapidly reaching the level of multipolarity long in evidence in East Asia. The most heavily fortified frontiers in the Pacific are between communist states, rather than between communist and capitalist ones. The real dividing line of superpower influence, especially since the triumph of communism in Indochina in 1975, basically runs through the waters dividing eastern Eurasia from its offshore islands. Japan, Taiwan and the Philippines are the US-oriented states closest to the mainland.[7] In contrast, the Atlantic system had its dividing line on land.

This mostly offshore US influence in the Pacific has led to an emphasis on naval power. In Europe, the sign of US commitment to its allies was more visible—troops in barracks and tanks rumbling across fields. The almost total absence of US land forces in East Asia makes it more difficult to provide symbols of deterrence and friendship.

Furthermore, the traditional strength of Soviet military power has been its land-based forces. Thus in the Pacific, the Soviet Union is less of a threat to the United States and also less able to engage the United States so as to maximize Soviet strengths. In order to confront US power, the Soviet Union must go to sea—precisely the arena of US strength. In any case, most Soviet ground forces are deployed against China. Therefore, any assessment of a superpower balance in the Pacific must be primarily in naval and nuclear terms.

Probably neither superpower has a usable military advantage in the

Pacific.[8] As in Europe, a rough balance of deterrence has existed for decades, although any calculation of such balance must be imprecise at best.[9] The essential basis of this deterrence is the global nuclear balance of terror. Most Soviet ICBMSs are based east of the Urals but are targeted on the United States.[10] By the early 1980s the Soviet Pacific fleet had become Moscow's largest, and nearly 40 percent of its SLBMs were based at Pacific ports. These SLBMs were part of Soviet forces in the Pacific but their task was global.[11] Similarly, the United States deployed most of its intercontinental nuclear weapons at sea and the majority were based in, or regularly traversed, Pacific waters. These forces were only properly considered part of the Pacific balance of power in the sense that the global balance determined the Pacific balance. As Mikhail Gorbachev noted while in Beijing on 17 May 1989, 'The Pacific ocean does not, in our days, divide Asia from America like a barrier. On the contrary, it acts as a kind of connecting link. Because of this, the problems of Asian security, too, are an integral part of general, global security'.[12]

Because of this problem in distinguishing between global and regional missions, it is impossible to identify the numbers of troops that the Soviet Union and the United States deploy against each other in the Pacific. From the Soviet perspective, the most salient fact is that the main theatre of confrontation is in the northwestern Pacific, where it confronts an essentially Japanese-US alliance.[13] Moreover, the Soviet Union is defending home territory and a 27,000-kilometer-long maritime frontier in East Asia, whereas the United States has nothing but allies and trust territories in the region.[14] The Soviet Union is an East Asian power by fact of geography, whereas the United States is an East Asian power by invitation of its allies. The Soviet Union is also deeply aware that it has few people in the Pacific and has trouble keeping them there. Soviet officials openly admit that the resulting paranoia has fed an excessive concern with national security, which in turn has kept ports such as Vladivostok closed to outsiders. Vladimir Ivanov has called it 'the psychology of temporary arrangements',[15] which is also a psychology of fear that does serious harm to the (nonmilitary) Soviet desire to open the region to economic contacts.

Yet the armed forces have begun to break out of this psychology of fear. Vladivostok will be opened to foreigners in the near future, much as it was opened to citizens of the Soviet Union in September 1988. A new generation of military leaders in Moscow has made its reputation in the Far Eastern Theatre,[16] and recognizes that the success of the region requires opening up to the outside world.

In terms of troops deployed in the region, there have been major cuts in the Soviet forces while those of the United States have remained steady for more than a decade. Even the number of Soviet troops outside Soviet territory in the Pacific region has been declining. At its peak in the late 1980s, the Soviet Union had 60,000 troops in Mongolia, but after 1990, when the reductions announced by Gorbachev at the United Nations in 1988 will have been completed, there will be fewer than 10,000. There are fewer than 8,000 troops in all of the rest of the region. A relatively unseen but nevertheless important Soviet presence beyond its own waters is represented by its SSN torpedo-attack submarines, which have nearly doubled in number in the decade since 1977.[17]

By comparison, the United States deploys 140,000 of its 520,000 troops abroad in the Pacific and East Asia, 33,000 of them afloat. However, at least one estimate suggests that only 14 percent of the United States defence budget in 1987 was earmarked for the defence of the Pacific.[18] The total US force in the Pacific in 1989 was less than half the number deployed in Europe, although the naval contingent represented more than half the total number of US servicemen afloat. The US forces in the areas of the Third and Seventh fleets added together, including those on US soil, are more than 50 percent greater than US forces deployed in Europe. But taking the smaller, and more comparable figures, there are 32,000 with the army in Korea and Japan, 42,000 with the Seventh fleet, there are 38,000 marines and 37,000 in the air force.[19] Japan plays host to about 2,400 US army personnel, 8,100 from the navy, 38,000 marines and 16,200 airmen. Korea is host to 29,000 army and 11,000 air-force personnel, while the Philippines plays host to 5,900 navy, 1,200 marines and 9,300 air force. The US navy also deploys 4,900 of its personnel in Guam and the air force deploys 4,200 others. Approximately 250 other air-force personnel are based in Australia, with 29,926 stationed along the Pacific coast of the United States and a further 10,800 in Alaska.

A comparison of naval forces also reveals some US advantages, but none that confer any decisive ability to defeat the Soviet Union. As the US Pacific Command stated, in the early 1980s the US position in the Pacific was better than it was in the NATO theatre.[20] At least according to the International Institute for Strategic Studies (IISS) in London, the balance in Europe provides neither side with a usable military advantage.[21] The two US fleets in the Pacific regularly deploy seven aircraft carriers as compared to the two, much less impressive, Soviet carriers.[22] The Soviet Union has a greater total number of surface ships as a result of a major naval buildup in the 1970s. However, since 1980, its Pacific fleet declined as a proportion of the total Soviet navy while nonetheless undergoing modernization.[23]

By the late 1980s, Soviet naval strategy emphasized deployment closer to home. There were 30 percent fewer operations out of the home areas by the Soviet Pacific fleet—part of a general reduction in Soviet naval operations in the Third World.[24] The Australian foreign minister even said in April 1988 that the Soviet Pacific fleet was at sea up to 50 percent fewer days as compared to the late 1970s.[25] Admiral Sidorov, the deputy commander of the Soviet navy, said on 4 February 1988 that there had been a reduction in the number of days spent by Soviet ships at Cam Ranh bay.[26] Major-General Batenin, and Vice-Admiral A. Kuzmin said a year later that the pattern of Soviet naval exercises had been changed in order to concentrate on operations closer to home in the northwest Pacific.[27] Vice-Admiral Kuzmin claimed that the number of warships in the Soviet Pacific fleet had reduced by 57 ships during the four years before 1989 and there was *de facto* corroboration in the figures produced by the IISS in London. In 1988 the number of Soviet strategic submarines was at 75 percent of its 1986 peak, the number of nonstrategic submarines was at 80 percent of its 1984 peak, the number of primary ships was at 82 percent of its 1983 peak and naval combat aircraft were at 87 percent of their 1986 peak.[28] After the Sino-Soviet summit in May 1989, Soviet officials said a further 16 warships would be retired from the Soviet Pacific fleet, making the total 73.[29]

Other Soviet analysts noted that like the Japanese, and unlike the United States, Soviet forces lacked the kind of offensive forces—such as attack aircraft carriers and large numbers of marines—that give a country an offensive military potential.[30] Nevertheless, despite major cuts in the ground forces facing China in the Pacific and cuts in naval forces, the Soviet Union was making most of its reductions in forces along the Chinese frontier. As Defence Minister Yazov noted on 28 May 1989, the grouping of Soviet forces in the Far East deployed against the United States and its allies comprised 326,000 men, 870 aircraft, 4,500 tanks and 55 major surface ships.[31] It seemed that even with the clear reduction in the number of ships in the Soviet Pacific fleet, only 30,000 soldiers would be removed from this group by 1 January 1991. Nevertheless, the Soviet Union still apparently sees less use for its armed forces in the Pacific than at any time since the buildup began in the Brezhnev years.

As was the case in Europe, cuts in the size of the Soviet Union's armed forces challenged the notion of a Soviet threat and helped set a new agenda for the international relations of the region. Soviet officials were increasingly able to make a credible case that they, and not the United States, were genuinely reducing tension in the Pacific. Soviet officials were quick to remark that even though both superpowers were genuinely discussing mutual force reductions in Europe, the United States did not seem interested in making such cuts in the Pacific where the US advantage was more evident.[32]

In the Pacific, the United States, Japan and some smaller allies began urgent consultations in early 1989 to formulate a strategy to meet the new reality.[33] In Europe, divisions in the Western alliance emerged, but in the Western Pacific, where no multilateral alliances existed to bind allies together, the divisions were even deeper. Although the Soviet Union was not losing its status as the Pacific's second greatest military power, its cuts in military strength were reshaping the regions' balances of power. Moreover, under the Reagan administration, US naval power had increased just as the Soviets retreated.[34] US officials increasingly saw their country as the 'traditional guarantor of regional security', which was even more necessary at a time of great change in the strategic balance.[35] Needless to say, the Soviet Union saw the US role in a less benign light. But at least by early 1990 the Soviet Union was somewhat more sympathetic to the American argument, especially as Defence Secretary Cheney made it clear that the US would also now be reducing its forces in East Asia. Indeed, as the level of uncertainty in Europe grew so quickly in the lead-up to German reunification, the Soviet Union suggested, informally at least, that stability in East Asian security would be greatly appreciated.

Of course from the narrow perspective of the Soviet armed forces, these changes only added to their sense of military weakness. The Soviet Union always had been less able to deploy military power at sea. Although combat close to Soviet shore-based facilities would minimize the US carrier advantage, the United States has a string of bases and allies all along the Eurasian coast, stretching 10,000 miles from the Aleutians to Australia.

The only significant Soviet bases in the Pacific are facilities in

Vietnam and Cambodia obtained after the defeat of the United States. However, Soviet facilities are not permanent and are no match even for US facilities in the Philippines. The Australian defence minister pointed out in 1987 that these Soviet bases would not survive one day of war and are more important as a political symbol.[36] As Soviet naval operations decrease in the Indian ocean, the need for Cam Ranh bay also diminishes. Indeed, in his speech at Krasnoyarsk in September 1988, Mikhail Gorbachev offered to relinquish Soviet access to the Vietnamese bases if the United States would give up its bases in the Philippines. The offer was clearly disingenuous, but it did highlight the fact that the United States has much more important facilities in the region. The Soviet offer also made it more difficult for the United States to continue complaining about the Soviet presence in Vietnam. Soviet Foreign Minister Shevardnadze said in Manila in October 1988 that the Soviet Union might even unilaterally leave its bases.[37] By 1990, when the worldwide retreat of Soviet power was accepted as real, the Soviet suggestion that it might quit East Asian bases was more credible than ever.

The Soviet Union once had access to bases in northeast China but surrendered them in 1954. The primary missions of Soviet naval forces now seem to be to protect its Northern Territories from US attack and, most of all, to guard its sea bastions in the sea of Okhotsk for the safe launch of SLBMs. Perhaps the greatest weakness of Soviet naval forces in the Pacific is the difficulty of getting the navy out of this sea bastion without being tracked by the enemy. The narrow choke-points make it highly likely that the Soviet fleet in the sea of Japan will remain bottled up during a war.[38]

The idea of threatening sea routes farther south in Southeast Asia is unlikely to be a Soviet priority.[39] In economic terms, these sea lanes, especially those through the straits of Malacca, are vital for Japanese import of oil and other natural resources, not to mention the trade on which the prosperity of many states is built. Yet in wartime, the free passage of ships is also vital to the Soviet Union for reinforcing its Pacific flank.[40] Some estimates indicate that up to 80 percent of Soviet supplies for its Pacific coast come by sea, and the difficulties in developing the trans-Siberian rail links suggest the Soviet problem is a long-term one.[41]

Although it made use of the Malacca straits during the Bangladesh war, the United States is particularly interested in a less observable route from Guam to the Indian ocean and Diego Garcia. The Malacca straits are too shallow for secret passage of submarines but the Ombei-Wetar and Lombok-Makassar straits in Indonesia (as well as the Timor sea) do allow such secret passage. New Trident submarines reduce the need for such channels and therefore make the task of Soviet trackers even more difficult.[42]

The United States relies heavily on its bases at Clark Field and Subic bay in the Philippines to keep open these sea lanes. As many as 70 ships a month refuel and resupply at Subic bay. Clark is the base for the Thirteenth air force, which is responsible for the western Pacific and Indian oceans. Fifty percent of shipped world oil traverses these waters as does 80 percent of Asia's trade with the United States and Japan.[43] However, the two bases are only rented from the Philippine government and the existence and terms of the lease are regularly debated. Perennial unrest in the Philippines makes these US bases unreliable in the long term.

Yet during any superpower cold war—a war in which no shots are fired—these bases would retain a more political than military role.[44] The United States understood this point much earlier than the Soviet Union, and thus established its string of bases down the coast of East Asia by the early 1950s.[45] Although the improvements in modern technology make such bases less vital, the growing US presence, and the war in Vietnam, underline the importance of forward bases. The changing US definition of the adversary, as a result of detente with China and the retreat from Vietnam, led to a debate in Washington about keeping Pacific bases. The triumph of Vietnamese communism and the Soviet use of Indochinese bases, however, underlined the continuing need for US bases in the western Pacific. Not surprisingly, the decision by President Carter to remove troops from South Korea was quickly revoked.

Despite the growth in Soviet and US naval power in the Pacific, the Pacific is not more liable to have superpower conflict as compared with the immediate postwar period. By the late 1980s, there had been no major wars in the regions where the superpowers were actively involved in supporting opposing forces. The United States had virtually no troops on the East Asian mainland, and the role of a more independent China ensured that both superpowers were uneasy about calculating a possible winning coalition for war. By the 1980s, even the Soviet Union was talking of a Helsinki-like arms control measure for the Pacific, while the United States and its friends were more concerned with ensuring a peaceful atmosphere for economic development.

Yet despite all these positive trends, there were some distressing signs of possible conflict. As part of a more forward naval strategy, US naval exercises in the Pacific, such as Fleet Ex–85, operated carrier battle groups close to Soviet waters. The Soviets protested but also carried out their own exercises by flying simulated bombing missions against US carrier groups.[46]

Of course, similar manoeuvres also take place regularly in the Atlantic. All the same, there were still no clear signs that the Soviet Union was prepared to challenge US dominance of the Pacific as it sometimes did in the Atlantic. In the mid-1980s there appeared to be new Soviet interest in the Pacific islands, but it was difficult to point to any obvious Soviet gains.[47] Disputes between the United States and some Pacific islands originated in the United Nations Law of the Sea conference that created exclusive economic zones 200 miles around even the tiniest coral atoll. The refusal of the United States to pay more for fishing rights in island waters led to bad feeling that was further aggravated when the Soviet Union signed a fishing accord with Kiribati in 1985 on terms favourable to the islanders. A Soviet deal giving landing rights to Aeroflot in Vanuatu soon followed.[48] The military coup in Fiji in 1987 removed a government interested in similar accords with the Soviet Union.[49]

For all the flurry of activity in south Pacific waters, most of the events there involved US refusal to provide the miniscule amounts of extra money needed to keep the islands happy. The risk of an island going communist could not be discounted entirely, but the real threat in individual islands was more from domestic unrest, resulting from local inequalities, rather than from trouble fomented by the Soviet Union.[50]

One of the most peculiar conflicts in the Pacific is a minor dispute between the two superpowers over their mutual boundary. The frontier at the Bering strait was not set clearly in the 1867 agreement by which the United States purchased Alaska from Russia. The two superpowers began negotiations in 1981 to resolve the problem. Talks were inconclusive and ended in 1983, only to be resumed again in 1984. The dispute mainly concerns the possible exploitation of mineral resources (no population is involved), but it has also been distorted by the overarching concerns of superpower relations.[51]

In sum, the superpowers are clearly the most important military powers in the Pacific, but a real superpower balance does not exist there because their zones of influence are not as clearly identifiable as in the pre-1989 Atlantic. In any case, any such balance is best described as 'western Pacific', because despite the Soviet submarine threat, the reach of Soviet power barely extends beyond that of shore-based aviation. In comparison to Europe, Soviet military power is much more circumscribed. By early 1990, when European security became more multipolar, it gradually became much more akin to the long-standing multipolarity of East Asia.

If there is any element of a balance in the Pacific, it is derived from the global superpower balance of terror. This is not to suggest that the superpowers are irrelevant in military terms in the Pacific (or, indeed, that the Pacific is irrelevant to the two superpowers), but rather that their roles must be understood in specific conflicts in which more complex local balances of power can be identified. Certainly Soviet analysts are clear that the main focus of conflict is in the so-called *T* of East Asia—the region running across the Sino-Soviet frontier and out to Japan and south from Kamchatka to the South China sea.[52] The cross of the *T* is in Northeast Asia, and the Soviet Union thus sees the United States as the main supporter of Japan and South Korea and as part of the complex regional balance of power. As the Soviet Union knows only too well, its strategic military power, as impressive as it might be, has rarely been especially useful. In fact, the limits on Soviet power are most clearly apparent when contemplating the number of Northeast Asian adversaries.

The Sino-Soviet conflict

The Soviet-US rivalry in the Pacific is mostly at sea or linked to a global balance of terror. However, the more immediate dangerous conflict in the postwar period has been the Soviet Union's rivalry with China. The contest between the Soviet Union and its southern neighbour is one of the oldest in the Pacific, although the protagonists have changed shape and ideology over the centuries. Since 1945 when the Soviet Union, the largest Eurasian power, pushed the Japanese forces off the Eurasian land mass, China has faced only one major land-based challenger. In 1949, when the communists came to power in China, they hoped for genuine independence if not for the return to the grandeur of the pre-Western imperialist age. But while sea-based Western imperialism and even offshore Japanese power could be controlled, the Soviet Union was established in the northern reaches of the Pacific basin and was poised for action on the roof of China.

The Soviet Union had felt that its rightful position in the Pacific in the twentieth century had been steadily eroded after the rise of Japanese power and the reunification of China. When Japan was defeated, the Soviet Union had expected to return to Pacific waters as a superpower and claim a major part in shaping the postwar order.[53] Soviet expectations in the Pacific were not quite as high as in Europe, but then the situation in the Pacific also appeared to be more disorderly and therefore to offer more opportunities for new initiatives.

A return to the earlier balance of power was impossible because the ideological inclinations of the Chinese and Russians had changed. Both were now nominally united in their communism and opposed to the United States, Japan, and its other allies in Europe and the Pacific. Thus the fundamental tensions that have beset the great power politics in the postwar Pacific were established. China was an ally of the Soviet Union, but also potentially a rival. China was at first dependent on Soviet assistance, for example, in the Korean war and in facing nuclear threats from the United States. But China also hoped it could eventually free itself of its alliances with the Soviet Union, which it still saw as a European power.

On 14 February 1950, Stalin and Mao Zedong signed a treaty of friendship, alliance and mutual assistance in Moscow that included a Soviet pledge to surrender rights to the Manchurian railway and to hand over the Port Arthur naval base to China. There was no explicit entangling military alliance, but Soviet aid to China during the Korean war was that of a close comrade-in-arms.

The reasons for the falling out of the two communist giants were primarily related to the changing Chinese approach to revolution at home and Moscow's difficulty at the time in accepting that any communist state could pursue an independent path of development.[54] Military matters were not a primary cause of the dispute, although the two sides did differ on such issues as the Sino–Indian war of 1962, the Cuban missile crisis of the same year, and the Soviet Union's cautious line on supporting world revolution and using its nuclear weapons when challenging the United States in crises. In 1963, when the Soviet Union signed the Partial Test Ban Treaty with the United States and Britain, the Sino–Soviet split was publicly acknowledged. This period, as indeed much of Soviet history, is now being scrutinized in light of Gorbachev's reformist ideas. Some of the most notable reformers and new thinkers in foreign policy agree that the basic cause of the original split is to be found in Chinese policy, although undoubtedly tensions were aggravated by Khrushchev's insensitivities.[55]

The ensuing contest for leadership of the international communist movement was clearly won by the Soviet Union. China was frustrated that its more radical policies were less appealing to fellow developing states than the rival, materially more useful aid the Soviets offered them to keep them out of the Chinese camp. Even in the neighbouring Vietnam war, to which China committed some of its anti-aircraft troops, Beijing was unable to supplant Soviet influence. The one exception to this pattern was quirky, lonely European Albania.[56]

The militarization of the Sino-Soviet conflict actually began in 1964–5 after the failure of efforts to arrive at a new detente following the purge of Nikita Khrushchev. For all his undoubted widening of the Sino-Soviet split, Khrushchev had been responsible for some of the most serious cuts in Soviet deployments on the frontier with China.[57] Of course, the roots of the dispute along the frontier between the two countries extend back to the seventeenth century and the imposition by Russia of the so-called unequal treaties on a fading Chinese empire. In reality, however, the modern frontier dispute was about China's pride and determination to be treated as an equal by the Soviet Union. The Soviet Union, for reasons of both ideology and nationalism, had enormous problems in accepting the independent Chinese road to socialism. As the Sino-Soviet dispute, involving a range of domestic and foreign policy issues, became more serious, both sides looked at their long, open frontier and realized the extent of their vulnerability. China first raised the boundary question in 1963, and negotiations began in Beijing in February 1964. The increasing radicalism and anti-Sovietism of China during the cultural revolution led many Soviet officials to believe that China was unstable and liable to rash actions. A buildup in Soviet forces began in the mid-1960s and was soon more than matched in men (but not material) by China.[58]

The Soviet invasion of Czechoslovakia and the restatement of the credo that the Soviet Union reserved the right to intervene in a socialist state to safeguard the revolution (the so-called Brezhnev doctrine) were perceived as a threat by China. In the paranoid mood of the cultural revolution, China decided to teach the Soviet Union that China was not Czechoslovakia and could not be pushed around.[59] On 2 March 1969 Chinese troops apparently ambushed a Soviet patrol on Chenbao (Damansky) island, killing tens of Russians. On 15 March the Soviet Union responded with a stunning demonstration of military superiority, killing hundreds of Chinese soldiers. This was the largest-scale combat involving Soviet troops at or beyond Soviet frontiers since 1945 and remained the largest until the Soviet invasion of Afghanistan in 1979.

These were the biggest border clashes, although others had taken place before and others were to follow.[60] Apart from the loss of life, this conflict is important because it was the first between two nuclear powers and took place along a wide-open frontier whose spaces were increasingly being filled with both soldiers and equipment. From the Soviet point of view, the danger was of an uncontrolled China adding a second front to the main Soviet concern in Europe. Given the sparse Soviet population and the vastness of both the frontier and the Chinese population across it, the Soviet Union felt especially vulnerable. The great frontiers of the Soviet Pacific were now seen as a source of threat. From the Chinese point of view, the main problem was how to convince the Soviet Union that China could credibly defend itself and its idiosyncratic revolution.

The Soviet Union tried to persuade China to negotiate about the border, thereby limiting the risks of escalation and the need for further Soviet commitment. However, China refused to negotiate, despite Soviet-orchestrated border incidents in the summer of 1969.[61] The Soviet Union then increased the pressure by letting it be known around the world—especially in the United States—that it was contemplating a so-called surgical strike against Chinese nuclear weapons sites. These threats constituted the Pacific's version of the Cuban missile crisis, and by October, China was scared enough to sit down and talk about the frontier.

Although the events of 1969 resulted in little loss of life in comparison to the contemporaneous war in Vietnam, they carried the very real risk of provoking war between two nuclear powers. As such, this Sino-Soviet border conflict must rank as the most dangerous Pacific crisis since 1945 and confirmed the deep fears of Soviet strategic planners.

In 1969, the United States discovered that it also had a role in this major new conflict in the Pacific. The belated discovery of the diplomatic possibilities of the great power triangle, and the open discussion of its implications by Henry Kissinger and President Nixon, added a global dimension to what had been at first a regional, Pacific problem.[62] The growing 'strategic cooperation' between the United States, Japan and China was perceived by the Soviet Union as an even more dangerous threat. The talk of China as the sixteenth member of NATO, as well as of US arms sales to Beijing, fed the paranoia of the Soviet Union about its vulnerabilities in the Pacific. The United States may have lost the Vietnam war, but it had gained a sizeable ally of sorts in China. The Soviet Union was at its most pessimistic when contemplating its Pacific security. With deteriorating East-West relations and the cooling of Japanese ardour for contacts with the Soviet Union, Moscow felt it had few friends in the Pacific.

This mismanagement of friend and foe gave impetus to the arms race in the Pacific. The immediate Soviet reaction was to ensure its basic security first and only later to look for a political strategy that did more than simply provoke hostility from its neighbours. In the decade after 1969, the Soviet Union invested 80 percent of the increase in its military expenditure in upgrading its capabilities in the Pacific. By the end of that decade it had deployed between one-quarter and one-third of all its military power in the region, most of it aimed at China. There were more Soviet troops manning the Sino-Soviet frontier than in all of Eastern Europe. The Soviets soon had first-rank military hardware in the region and had developed their infrastructure and built extensive fortifications.[63]

By 1979, Soviet deployments had reached 52 divisions, while the Chinese deployed 78 divisions by 1980. Sporadic border incidents were reported until 1980, but with very little loss of life. The publicity given to these incidents varied according to the political winds of the day. They were political symbols in a complex Sino-Soviet detente dance.

But just as increased military tension had followed the increased tension in other dimensions of the Sino-Soviet relationship, so a real decline in military tentions awaited a broader detente.[64] The initiative for this detente did not come from the Soviet Union, although when it developed, the Soviet leadership eventually understood that its strategic position in the Pacific could be greatly enhanced. Detente developed gradually in the first half of the 1980s. Sino-Soviet trade grew much more rapidly as Soviet technicians returned to China to help in the modernization and refurbishment of old Soviet equipment and the construction of new plants. In almost every aspect of the original split, some improvement was apparent. The Soviet Union had finally broken the spell cast on its foreign policy by Sino–US cooperation in the 1970s.

Sino–US disputes over Taiwan and the generally more assertive Reagan foreign policy helped drive Sino–Soviet detente. To be sure, real disputes continued between the Soviet Union and China, most notably over the continued Soviet occupation of Afghanistan and Soviet support for the Vietnamese occupation of Cambodia. Nevertheless, military detente between the Soviet Union and China followed the generally improving atmosphere.

The scale and manner of this military detente was as complex as the original development of the arms race. Since 1982 there has been a tacit process of arms control. China pulled back many of its troops from the frontier and cut its armed forces by a million men between 1985 and 1987. Similarly the Soviet Union reduced its divisions by 80,000 men, placing the divisions on a lower level of readiness. In December 1988, Mikhail Gorbachev announced that 200,000 Soviet troops would be removed from the Far Eastern Theatre and troops in Mongolia would be reduced to less than 10,000 men. Defence Minister Yazov said in May 1989 that 271,400 troops were deployed against China, as well as 820 aircraft, 8,100 tanks and 9,400 artillery systems. Of these, 120,000 men were to be removed as part of Gorbachev's cuts. Thus, by 1 January 1991 when the Soviet cuts are complete, Soviet troop strength ranged against China may have been cut nearly in half from its late 1970s peak.[65]

Yet even Soviet sources admit they now deploy 1.7 million men in the Far Eastern Theatre. The cuts, as extensive as they undoubtedly are, do not mean that the Soviet Union will cease to be a military superpower and a threat to China. It may be of much importance that the Soviet Union is also planning to reorganize its armed forces in the Pacific into a more defensive posture. Defence Minister Yazov promised that this reorganization will involve turning some mechanized units into artillery formations and foreign observers will be allowed to verify the demobilizations.[66] Nevertheless, even after the cuts are made, the Soviet Union will remain the second largest modern military power in the Pacific, even though its offensive capability will have been severely reduced.

The normalization of Sino–Soviet relations in May 1989 owes much to the major steps taken by Mikhail Gorbachev. In July 1986, Gorbachev offered China a series of important concessions in order to improve relations. The East Europeans were allowed to resume party-to-party relations with China, and Moscow accepted the Chinese claim that the eastern border between the two countries ran through the centre of the main channel of the border rivers, not along the Chinese bank as Soviet negotiators had previously claimed. Extensive contacts along the frontier developed as both sides decentralized economic decision making as part of their economic reforms.[67] Gorbachev also decided to withdraw Soviet troops from Afghanistan, as well as to put pressure on Vietnam to reform itself and improve relations with China. In 1988, visa restrictions were lifted for travel between the Soviet Union and China; cross-border contacts increased at a rapid rate. The Soviet Union agreed to supply electric power to northeast China, and China sent workers to man Soviet farms and factories in the Far East. Both sides agreed to joint exploitation of river resources and the opening of new rail links. China and Mongolia also improved their relations and agreed to confidence-building measures along their frontier.[68] Sino-Soviet negotiators reached rapid agreement on the disputed frontier and arranged joint aerial surveys of the border region. By early 1990, China and the Soviet Union had even resumed regular exchanges of military delegations.[69]

If the Sino-Soviet split and the tensions of 1969 had been the most important shift in the Pacific military balance since 1945, then the detente of the 1980s was of nearly equal importance. To be sure, the Soviet Union still deployed more troops and nuclear weapons in the Pacific than anywhere outside Europe. Although by the mid-1980s the focus of Soviet concern in the region was US rather than Chinese power, in terms of sheer numbers and military geography, China still posed the most significant potential threat to Soviet power in the region.[70]

For its part, China still committed more troops for defence against the Soviet threat than against any other. Nevertheless, Chinese fears decreased because of (1) the challenge Reagan's administration posed to the Soviet Union, (2) China's own defence modernization and (3) the general process of detente along the Sino-Soviet frontier.[71] Chinese strategists realized that sharing socialism with the Soviet Union did not protect them from military threat.[72] Nevertheless, by 1989, following the announcement of major Soviet troop cuts and following the gradual normalization of Sino-Soviet relations, Chinese defence planners could not argue persuasively that a serious and immediate Soviet military threat still remained. The shrinking size and budget of the People's Liberation Army (PLA) testified to the crisis in Chinese strategic thinking,[73] and one Chinese official even stated that China saw 'no need to station large contingents of troops on the Sino-Soviet border'.[74]

The Sino-Soviet relationship was nearly as important for other nations in the Pacific basin. The United States has undoubtedly benefited from the divisions within communism. The drawing off of Soviet military strength to cope with the threat from China eased the burden on Europe and NATO. China's preoccupation with the Sino-Soviet dispute eased the pressure on Japan, Taiwan, and other US allies in the Pacific. The redirection of the Chinese military instrument to confront the Soviet Union accentuated the difference between warring communism and the prospering capitalism in the Pacific.

Yet the risks of uncontrolled war between Russia and China seriously concerned non-communist Pacific states. Rivalry in Korea might have led to competition to arm Pyongyang. The wars in Indochina might have spread to Thailand and ASEAN. In both cases the stability and economic prosperity of the western Pacific would be undermined, forcing the United States to resume a higher military profile. The extreme scenario of a Sino-Soviet war brought risk of United States involvement in support of China, with all the obvious dangers of a global nuclear holocaust.

The United States of course remains concerned that Sino-Soviet detente is not in Western interests. As the normalization of relations between the communist superpowers took place, and Japan's military power grew, there was an increased risk of Japan emerging as another major military power.[75] Clearly, China is increasingly worried by the trends in Japan, which may provide a basis for closer collaboration between China and the Soviet Union. After all, common fear of Japan helped create the original Sino-Soviet alliance in 1950.

The new shift in the balance of power resulting from the Sino-Soviet detente of the 1980s is not just a re-run of the 1950s. Because of trade competition, among other things, the United States now sees Japan as a growing threat. This may in turn encourage Japan to go its own way and take advantage of the shifting balance of power.[76]

At a time of Sino-Soviet rivalry, Japan was at first concerned that US renewed interest in the China factor would mean that Japan would be neglected by the United States. However, by the 1980s the possibility of Sino-US strategic cooperation had diminished. Similarly,

South Korea, Australia, New Zealand and the ASEAN states were increasingly reassured that the United States was not aligning too closely with China and ignoring its other, older allies in the region.

The smaller communist states of the Pacific at first found the Sino-Soviet split useful as a way to squeeze more aid out of their patrons. Vietnam and North Korea were past masters at this game and both suffered in the 1980s as Sino-Soviet relations improved. The Chinese and Soviet desire for detente forced these smaller communist states to compete for the favours of the communist giants instead of vice versa. As a result, North Korea felt the pressure for compromise with South Korea, and Vietnam, Cambodia, Laos and even Mongolia were under Soviet pressure to improve relations with China. The maturing of the Sino-Soviet relationship was clearly good for the stability of the Pacific region. From the point of view of Soviet strategic planners, Sino-Soviet detente was an essential prerequisite to limiting defence spending and building peaceful bridges to neighbours in the Pacific. No military issue had as much impact on the Soviet position in the Pacific as the state of Sino-Soviet relations. With the retreat of US power in the Pacific after the original Sino-Soviet split, the primacy of Sino-Soviet relations was enhanced even further. By 1989, when Sino-Soviet relations were normalized, the Soviet strategic position in the Pacific had taken its most significant turn for the better in more than 40 years.

Northeast Asian conflicts

Both Sino-Soviet relations and important aspects of superpower relations in the Pacific are played out in Northeast Asia and its adjacent waters. In fact, much of what passes for Soviet military strategy about the Pacific is really a more specific concern with Northeast Asia. The sub-region is complicated by the presence of three other states: the two Koreas and Japan. The Soviet Union has been closely involved in the security of these states and yet has been remarkably unable to control events in them satisfactorily. The conflict in Korea reveals how Soviet power is constrained in the region.

Korean conflicts

Korea has been called the Palestine of East Asia by virtue of its strategic location. Certainly Japan has considered it in its natural sphere of influence, sometimes seeing Korea as a dagger pointing at the heart of Japan. In the Soviet Union's different metaphor, Korea is a neighbour caught in the cockpit of Northeast Asia and under constant pressure from the traditional powers of East Asia. The coming of Russian power to the Pacific meant that Korea faced another possible predator when Russian was strong. But when Russia was weak, it was more willing to defend Korea from the other interested powers. A Korean proverb describes Korea as a prawn, whose back is liable to be broken by the movements of the great-power whales around it.[77] In the twentieth century, Korea has had least four whales to contend with and the prawn has literally been snapped in half. The Soviet Union has only recently become the strongest of the powers in the region.

Korea had been occupied by Japan for most of the twentieth century until Japan's defeat in World War II reopened the question of who should rule this strategic zone. Because China was split by a civil war and Japan was defeated, only two powers remained in Northeast Asian waters. The United States and the Soviet Union had not given much thought to Korea after the war, as the former was more involved in Japan and the latter more concerned about China. Thus a US proposal to divide Korea at the 38th parallel was made more out of compromise and convenience than from consideration of history or justice.[78]

Unlike divided Germany which was a vanquished nation, the Koreans were mere Asian pawns in a mainly European-focused cold war. Most of the Korean people were in the south but most of the industry was in the north. Thus, a divided Korea made no sense locally and was a recipe for war. The causes of that war have been exhaustively debated by specialists—it was the first major war after 1945 and, until the Vietnam war, the bloodiest.[79]

The formation of two Koreas was the result of global rivalries of the superpowers and was facilitated by the disarray in Korea itself. Yet neither Korea was satisfied with the division of the country, and the superpowers were less than explicit in defining the limits of tolerable change. Adjusting the borders in postwar Europe was conducted in an atmosphere of relatively careful crisis management. In contrast, poor communication and the superpowers' relative disregard for East Asia left the East Asians free to upset the less carefully managed plans of the great powers. Analysts usually blame the United States for most of the errors in policy, but the Soviet Union was as lax in its formulation of policy for the cold war in the Pacific.

To complicate matters, another great power, China, had tradition-ally (before the twentieth century) been the dominant influence in Korean affairs. The assumption of power by a communist regime determined to capture the US-supported Chinese nationalists in Taiwan parallelled the situation in Korea. As the Chinese civil war drew to a close in 1949, China again took an interest in Korean affairs, although China primarily remained focused on completing the unification of its own country.[80] The Soviet Union also wanted a communist ally in the Pacific, and it had a firmer grip on Korean rather than on Chinese communism.

The outbreak of the Korean war on 25 June 1950 seems to have been the result of North Korea's jumping the gun that was primed by Soviet aid and Chinese support. But considering the tension and confusion in the region, each state probably perceived the causes of the war differently. The North hoped for a swift victory before the United States and its allies could respond. It very nearly succeeded. The Soviet Union may not have been in complete agreement with the timing of the war, but it no doubt felt that their allies would repeat the Chinese success of the previous year in driving the non-communist forces from the country. The United States did not save Chiang Kai-shek in 1949 and, from the Soviet point of view, the risks in the Pacific were lower than in the more vital European theatre.

The Soviet miscalculation was grievous. The attack by the North reinforced the need for NATO in Europe and strengthened US commitments to its non-communist allies in the Pacific. The South Koreans were able to fight long enough for the United States to organize reinforcements and allied support under the cover of the then US-dominated United Nations. Ultimately, 15 nations gave material support to the US action in Korea.[81] The communist forces were driven back across the 38th parallel up to the Chinese frontier at the Yalu river.[82] The immediate lessons for Moscow were the impossi-bility of controlling wars in the Pacific and the need for cooperation with allies.

The Chinese, with Soviet encouragement, had warned the United States about crossing the 38th parallel. Unfortunately, the messages were not taken seriously. The forceful Chinese intervention in Korea in November pushed the United States back, and the war settled down to a slugging match around its original starting point at the 38th parallel.[83] The tiring stalemate, followed by a new Soviet foreign policy under Stalin's heirs in 1953, and a new US foreign policy under

President Eisenhower, eventually brought the war to an end with an armistice.[84]

It is difficult to decide who wins and who loses a war that ends more or less where it started. For the Koreans, the war proved that reunification could not be achieved by force. Reunification may have seemed worth the price of war in 1950 before separate traditions were established. However, in 1953 too high a price had been paid for maintaining the division for anyone realistically to suggest another conflict. The division of Korea was just as unreal as in 1950, but because so much of the population had moved during the war and because each government had gained in status simply by surviving it, the notion of division became more acceptable. Much like the effect of the Berlin crises in Europe, the Korean war stabilized the region by showing that however unnatural the status quo may be, the parties concerned and their allies were willing to fight to maintain it.

Stability in the cold war, in the Pacific, seemed to require a crisis on this scale. The United States had demonstrated its credibility as an ally. Although the United States did not fight the war primarily for reasons of Pacific security, the war did increase its military presence on the Asian mainland. The defeat of the Guomindang in the Chinese civil war had, for all intents and purposes, driven the United States off the Asian mainland in the Pacific and forced it to concentrate on Japan. The Korean war swiftly reestablished the United States in Asia, in part as a forward defence of its main interests in Japan.

The Soviet Union had stayed out of direct combat, although it reportedly provided air cover for Chinese cities and much of the equipment for the communist side of the war. Like the United States, the Soviet Union was willing to defend its regional interests, although the focus on East Asia was an unwelcome distraction from the main European theatre. The war also created closer allies out of China and North Korea, both of whom depended so heavily on Soviet support.

China was perhaps the only major great-power loser from the war. The Chinese priority had been unification of all China—including Taiwan—and peaceful reconstruction. The war allowed the United States to interpose its Seventh fleet in the Taiwan straits and cost China dearly in human and economic terms. China was left poorer, more reliant on the Soviet Union, more hostile to the United States and Japan and was still without control of Taiwan and the offshore islands.

The course of the Korean conflict since 1953 has been punctuated by periodic crises, but nothing on the scale of the 1950–53 war.[85] As these crises developed—for example over the North Korean attack on the US intelligence-gathering ship, the Pueblo, in 1968—the great-power whales of the region kept the waves to a minimum. Although local events were the main cause of such crises, the pattern of crisis management had much to do with the overarching pattern of great-power politics. The Soviet Union remained the main supporter of North Korea, although it often had to manoeuvre to keep Chinese influence under control. Until the Chinese reform of the 1980s, the two superpowers shared the greatest interest in keeping Korean crises under control. The main sources of instability in the peninsula came from local Korean politics and, to some extent, the shifting pattern of Sino-Soviet relations.

Yet in many respects the fundamental realities of the Korean conflict remain the same today as in 1950. There is a genuine cold war—a sort of no war, no peace—that generates more heat than anywhere in Europe. The two Koreas are packed into a small peninsula where modern weaponry makes both sides highly vulnerable. Most people in North Korea live within 200 miles of the inner-Korean frontier, and the capital, Pyongyang, is only 90 miles away. Seoul is a mere 30 miles south of the frontier and within artillery range of the North—or 3 minutes by air. As both societies move rapidly away from their agricultural base towards industrialization and city life, both are even more vulnerable than they were in 1950. War is not a sensible option for either side.

The balance of power has remained tense but reasonably stable. Both sides have increased defence spending as their economies have developed, but the better growth rates in the South make its defence burden progressively easier to bear.[86] Although the North has a quantitative advantage in most categories of weapons, it does not have the sort of decisive advantage that could make war seem worthwhile. The South has advantages in quality of equipment and training, as well as the presence of some 40,000 US troops and their tactical nuclear weapons.[87] Chinese forces withdrew from the North in 1958.

The Soviet Union prefers the trend towards a reduction in tension. Any war started by the North with Soviet arms would certainly destroy Moscow's chances of building bridges to other East Asian states. A war might demand new Soviet evidence of comradely loyalty to the North, which would especially upset Japan.[88] By the late 1980s, the Soviet Union was seeking new ways of making contact with South Korea: official trade relations actually began in 1989. Thus, the Soviet Union is less likely to support North Korean adventurism.

Yet Soviet military contacts with North Korea remain important to both sides. Soviet arms supplies have been maintained, and increasingly sophisticated equipment was provided to match what the United States provided to South Korea. This high-technology competition was certainly beyond China's ability or willingness to undertake. Soviet forces continued to conduct military exercises with their North Korean comrades.[89] Almost 25 percent of the North Korean navy takes part in these exercises. From the Soviet point of view, this is one of the best ways to keep in close touch with the North Korean armed forces, which are expected to play the determining role in the forthcoming succession struggle after the death of Kim Il Sung.

Despite the obvious military tension on the Korean peninsula, the chance of conflict is also reduced by the unwillingness of the superpowers to contemplate another war in Korea. In 1989, the Soviet Union even went so far as to host the South Korean opposition leader, Kim Young Sam, and the Soviets at least tacitly explored ideas about encouraging North-South dialogue.[90] The United States is primarily concerned with the peace and security of its economically prosperous allies, Japan and South Korea, and sees no advantage in coveting the territory of North Korea.[91] Much like the discussion of troop withdrawals from Europe, the problem the United States and its allies face in Korea is how to reduce the defence burden without cutting the quality of the deterrence that made economic prosperity in the South possible. As the Soviets undertake extensive troop reductions, and as South Korea increasingly calls for change in the status of US troops on its soil, it seems likely that the US presence in South Korea will be reduced in some form during the early 1990s. Moscow will undoubtedly be pleased, although it would want the reductions phased so that the risks of war would not increase.

China is belatedly but similarly interested in a peaceful Northeast Asia. In the 1970s, China's closer relations with the United States meant it had even less patience with North Korean attacks on the South. Yet China and the United States remain on opposite sides of the Korean issue, mainly because China fears losing the friendship of the Pyongyang regime in the Sino-Soviet conflict. When Sino-Soviet relations began to improve in the 1980s, China and the Soviet Union both cooperated to keep North Korea under control. The leverage that the North once had on its communist patrons, playing one off against the other to maximize their support, was declining.[92] Also, by 1989 both China and the Soviet Union were rapidly increasing their trade with the South, a further indication of their common desire for a peaceful Korea.

Clearly none of the great powers has an interest in further conflict in Korea. The risks of war must be considered minimal, although a crisis may occur because of unrest in the South or the succession to Kim Il Sung in the North. East Asian states still have enormous scope to upset the uneasy status quo beloved by the great powers.

Japan

The Soviet-Japanese relationship has changed significantly since the two states first came into contact. Earlier in the twentieth century, the confrontation had a strong military dimension as the two powers fought for the spoils in northeast China. Japan defeated Russia in 1905 and invaded deep into Soviet territory just after the revolution. Despite a wary standoff during most of World War II, the Soviet Union eventually did enter the war against Japan in 1945.

The Soviet Union's best hope was to divide Japan as it did Germany, but the war ended too swiftly for such a far-reaching advance in the Soviet position.[93] The Soviet Union did take some territory from Japan at the end of the war, the legacy of which has been a continuing Soviet-Japanese territorial dispute. Given the cold war atmosphere and US support for Japan, the Soviet-Japanese relationship developed a major role for the United States to counterbalance the preponderance of Soviet military power.

Given this obvious weakness in the Japanese military position and their growing confidence as an economic power, the Japanese have managed their territorial dispute with the Soviet Union in a most unusual manner. The Japanese may speak relatively infrequently (in comparison to the West Europeans) about a Soviet military threat, but they are seriously concerned about their military inferiority. The language of the military relationship is expressed in an idiom of 'territorial disputes' concerning the now-famous Northern Territories.

The Northern Territories are a group of islands off the northeastern tip of Hokkaido that Japan claims from the Soviet Union. Etorofu and Kunashiri are generally recognized as geographically part of the Kurile chain that currently belongs to the Soviet Union. To the south of these two islands lie the Habomai group and Shikotan. The combined land area is about 5,000 sq km. At the end of World War II, the islands had a population of about 17,000, half of whom fled Soviet occupation. The rest were interned and later forcibly repatriated to Japan between 1947 and 1949.

The history of this dispute is complex.[94] The Soviet Union's claim is based on wartime agreements, especially at Yalta, that promised control of the Kurile islands. Japan points out that the contested islands were not specified in the agreement and that in any case Japan was not party to the Yalta agreement.[95] The Soviet Union refused to sign the 1951 peace treaty at San Francisco but began talks on a separate peace, which broke down in 1956. As part of the discussions of the restoration of Soviet-Japanese relations, the Soviet Union agreed to return the Habomais and Shikotan if a peace treaty were agreed. The Soviet offer to return these smaller territories had at first been accepted by the Japanese government, but then refused because it did not include all four island groups. The complexities of domestic Japanese politics, not to mention pressure from the United States, had much to do with this change of mind.[96]

Soviet policy hardened after 1956 and Moscow then linked any deal to the withdrawal of US forces from Japan.[97] The Soviet Union opposed the 1960 Japanese-US security treaty that allowed the continued US military presence in Japan. In treaties in 1968 and 1971, Japan obtained the return of Bonin, Volcanoe and Ryukyu islands from the United States. In 1978, the Sino-Japanese friendship pact was interpreted in Moscow as an anti-Soviet gesture, and attitudes hardened even more against compromise. Fishing disputes, such as those in 1977, were resolved by accords, but fishermen operating in disputed waters were still detained. Japan then complained about the Soviet military buildup on the northern islands, including Shikotan, which had not been militarized since 1960.

Apart from the fishing rights and the complications that an accord might make for the alliance between the United States and its main Pacific ally, Japan, some of the Northern Territories are of strategic value to the Soviet Union. In the event of a war, Soviet control of the two northernmost islands might permit Soviet ships to exit from the sea of Okhotsk to the Pacific, whereas without such control the Soviets would almost certainly be contained. As Soviet policy shifted towards defending the sea bastions, the islands became important as yet another link in the chain preventing the entry of hostile enemy craft. Nowhere else does the Soviet Union face such a powerful military threat so close to such a vital base.[98]

Although a compromise along the lines of that offered in 1956 seems possible,[99] the Soviet Union will have to 'regurgitate what it has swallowed', something it has rarely done since 1945. Yet the Soviet Union needs to be convinced that a territorial compromise is worthwhile—a motive very evident in its previous concessions in Pacific territorial disputes: The Soviet Union has already returned territory to neighbouring China on more than one occasion since 1949, the latest being the promised return of islands along the river frontier. The lengthy but eventually successful process of normalizing Sino-Soviet relations despite a much more complex territorial dispute suggests that agreement with Japan is possible.

The Soviet-Japanese territorial dispute seems especially easy to resolve because of general East-West detente. Japan is the only major Western state that has not improved relations with the Soviet Union under Gorbachev, and the United States is no longer likely to impede any normalization of Soviet-Japanese relations. In the past, the prospects for a Soviet-Japanese deal have depended on the attitude of the United States and on Japanese domestic politics as much as on the more flexible policies of the Soviet Union. When Sino-Soviet relations normalized in 1989, the Soviet Union could concentrate on the last remaining foreign policy reform in the Pacific, improving relations with Japan.

The Soviet Union seems more willing to compromise, but it will want to test various offers on the territorial question first to find out which offer is mostly likely to be accepted. Since the last half of 1988, the Soviet Union has been testing the winds of compromise. The demilitarization of the islands and the eventual return of some of the Habomais (or even all of them, as well as Shikotan) seem acceptable to the Soviets. Some observers suggest that Moscow might even agree to demilitarize the two northernmost islands or arrange to transfer sovereignty to Japan while arranging a lease-back arrangement.[100] As of the visit in December 1988 of Foreign Minister Shevardnadze to Tokyo, the Soviet Union is now discussing the territorial question. Detailed negotiations are underway.[101] Soviet scholars increasingly emphasize the need to reform the Soviet position, including withdrawal of troops from the disputed areas and greater acceptance of a positive US role in the region.[102] The Soviets apparently intend to ease the fears of the Japanese, who remain concerned about a Soviet threat, without saying so explicitly.

Given the uncertain condition of Japanese domestic politics, the Soviet Union will probably not make a formal offer unless it sees a government in Tokyo strong enough to support a compromise agreement.[103] Perhaps because of this Soviet assessment of Japanese domestic politics, the Soviet Union has taken a more casual approach to Soviet-Japanese relations—the Soviets think they have plenty of time. Perhaps Moscow has also been distracted by the need to formalize detente with China. The Soviet Union has certainly argued that how Sino-Japanese territorial disputes were deferred might serve as a useful model for improving Soviet-Japanese relations.[104] However, even though the reversal in Sino-Japanese relations in the 1970s is a positive example for Soviet optimists, the careful observer of Japanese politics must nevertheless note that major foreign policy change tends to result only from 'shocks' to the Japanese system. As Karel van Wolferen has recently argued, without shock treatment, the Japanese government does not make, let alone change, policy.[105]

This Soviet-Japanese territorial dispute has a more general, symbolic quality as Japanese power increases and Soviet strength declines. Japan, at the urging of the United States, increased its defence spending so that by the late 1980s it had the world's third largest defence budget, albeit with less than 2 percent of GDP spent on defence. The Soviet Union describes Japan as 'a worthy opponent'[106] and basically classifies its power as part of an alliance with the United States. However, because Japan is on the rise and the Soviet Union was wallowing in self-doubt in the late 1980s, the Soviet Union is especially interested in the possibilities for less hostile relations with its vital Northeast Asian neighbour. The Soviet Union is fascinated by Japan and little remains in Soviet-Japanese relations of the deeper wartime hostility that still hinders US and European relations with Japan.[107] Moscow has begun to realize that it can convince Japan about its peaceful intentions by discussing such related, but still important, issues as the Korean peninsula. Japan was apparently impressed by the Soviet contacts with South Korea, its determination to attend the Seoul Olympics and the presure it applied to North Korea to keep calm.[108] Prime Minister Takeshita told *Izvestiya* on 2 March 1989 that the Soviet troop cuts, if they take place, 'can be welcomed as a manifestation of the USSR's real desire for genuine peace and stabilization.'[109]

The Soviet Union, like China, cannot be entirely sanguine about Japan as a more independent force. Will expanding Japanese military power mean a relative decline of Soviet strength? If Japan is serious about defending sea lanes to a distance of 1,000 nautical miles, then it is likely to come into conflict with Soviet and Chinese forces. Some Japanese observers argue there is no need to compromise with the Soviet Union because it is in decline and can be pushed around.[110] But the Soviet Union also knows that Japan would be fundamentally vulnerable in time of war. As a small, crowded island dependent on foreign trade, Japanese society and military power can be demolished in minutes with nuclear weapons and easily starved by mere threats of conventional blockade. Without the supporting colonies it had in the early twentieth century, Japan has no serious claim to military strength.

Unlike Britain, Japan has no multilateral alliance to support a credible defence policy and must rely on a bilateral arrangement with the United States. Only the United States protects Japanese security. When it is self-confident, the Soviet Union recognizes its essential strength when dealing with Japan. As it reforms its foreign policy and seeks to improve relations with Japan, the Soviet Union also recognizes that the key to detente with Japan depends in part on continued detente with the United States. Anomalies and ambiguities in great-power relations abound in Northeast Asia, thereby encouraging the Soviet Union to tread carefully and slowly in the vital Northeast Asian region.

Southeast Asia

The nearest part of Southeast Asia to Vladivostok is as close to Soviet territory as is Iceland or Somalia. Geography is not everything in Soviet strategy, but it does help explain the relative unimportance of Southeast Asia in Soviet strategic thinking. When calculating what is central and what is peripheral in terms of military security, the Soviets consider Southeast Asia only marginally more important than Africa. Not surprisingly, the Soviet Union has always been especially cautious in becoming heavily committed so far from home. As the number of wars have declined in the region, and Soviet out-of-area operations were scaled back in the late 1980s. The concern with military issues in Southeast Asia is less prominent than at any point since the early 1950s.

Indochina, 1955–75

The Soviet Union was slow to become involved in the conflicts of Southeast Asia, but as US involvement in the region increased, the Soviet Union gradually paid more attention. Although it was not always the main military supporter of Indochinese communists, the Soviet Union, as the communist superpower, was expected to take an increasing interest in the fate of their ideological brethren. Chinese and Soviet aid to the anti-French forces was essential, but not sufficient, to ensure North Vietnam's victory. Thus, the Indochina conflict resembled the Korean war in that the overlay of the East-West conflict helped determine who fought on which side. After 1955, the conflict moved into its next phase—local struggles for domestic power with a significant degree of external intervention. Thus, the context of East-West conflict remained the same, but the nature of the domestic conflict changed. In all three Indochinese cases— Vietnam, Laos and Cambodia—the struggle involved communist forces fighting guerrilla wars, but only in the case of Vietnam was there large-scale and direct involvement of the United States in support of its ally, the Republic of Vietnam (South Vietnam).

The 1954 Geneva conference failed to end the struggle in Laos. The Pathet Lao was a communist force created by the Vietnamese and supported by China. The fiercest fighting took place between 1960– 62 and was brought to an end by another unofficial agreement in Geneva, which had been patched together by the United States, the Soviet Union and China. The Soviet Union was barely interested in events in distant Indochina, especially when coping with minicrises in Europe while simultaneously attempting to build up its strategic arsenal.

Laos was to become neutral, but all sides seemed to recognize that the *de facto* result would be partition as long as the main conflict continued in Vietnam.[111] When China took a more active interest in the guerrilla war, the Soviet Union was happy to ignore Laos. As the tempo of the war in Vietnam increased, the Vietnamese took a more prominent role in Pathet Lao affairs in order to secure their supply routes to South Vietnam.[112] The defeat of the US-supported regime in Saigon in the spring of 1975 brought about a collapse of power in Vientiane as well.

The new communist regime in Laos owed a huge debt to Vietnam. As the split between China and Vietnam grew wider, Laos found itself surrounded by a hostile Thailand, a sullen China, a distracted Cambodia and a much-too-friendly Vietnam. By paying the price of domination by the Vietnamese, Laos retained nominal independence and peace. Laos was the only one of the three Indochinese states that was basically at peace in 1975. However, it was also isolated from the new wave of prosperity sweeping the East Asian rim of the Pacific. In the Soviet perspective, Laos remained the least interesting communist ally.

In 1953 before the Geneva conference, neighbouring Cambodia obtained independence from France. Prince Sihanouk became its leader. In contrast to their positions on Laos, the United States, China and the Soviet Union were more or less resigned to Sihanouk's neutralist and populist politics and were unwilling to make major efforts to topple him.[113] By the mid-1960s, however, as the war in Vietnam escalated, politics in Cambodia became more polarized. Left-wing pressure from local Khmer Rouge communists forced Sihanouk to break diplomatic relations with the United States in May 1965.[114]

In 1970, disputes among the conservative Khmers led to a coup by Lon Nol that brought to power a more right-wing regime, forcing Sihanouk to flee to China. These events did not create a simple process of polarization because the Sino-Soviet split meant Sihanouk was unlikely to be as favourable to the Soviet Union as he was towards China. In fact, Moscow maintained diplomatic relations with the Lon Nol regime until its end in 1975. Moreover, as Vietnam and China became estranged, the leftist cause in Indochina was further fragmented.

The main rebel movement inside Cambodia was controlled by Pol Pot. He argued for a faster revolutionary pace and rejected the more cautious approach that best served the Vietnam-first policy of the North Vietnamese. The primary explanation for Cambodian events is to be found in internal politics and the polarization encouraged by events in neighbouring Vietnam. The Soviet Union was not an important actor in the unfolding Indochinese war.[115]

The Cambodian sideshow was concluded in 1975 when Pol Pot's forces marched into Phnom Penh and declared a so-called year zero.

But unlike the situation in Laos, the radical policies of the new regime resulted in disputes with its neighbours that became new wars in the region. The new Cambodian regime was supported by different—and increasingly antagonistic—communist regimes, which aggravated the local dispute. The Soviet Union was thus an actor in the region, mostly as a supporter of Vietnam, remaining a remarkably distant superpower in Laos and Cambodia.

The Indochinese conflict clearly centred on Vietnam, the pace setter for its neighbours. The United States viewed China as the more active and dangerous part of a divided communist camp. The Soviet Union was also a threat due to its support for Hanoi, but at least it was possible to do business with Moscow.[116] The Soviet Union found that its concentration on superpower relations may have led to an improved position in most parts of the world, but its standing was damaged with movements such as those in China and North Vietnam that wanted a more revolutionary and aggressive foreign policy.

Despite the large numbers of its troops and modern technology deployed in Vietnam, the United States was unwilling, and to some extent unable, to win the war in Vietnam.[117] Opposition at home and from European allies concerned about the reduced attention to NATO hampered the US war effort. The Soviet Union perhaps encouraged this opposition to United States policy but could hardly claim credit for organizing it in the first place.

North Vietnamese resistance was fierce and well supported by its allies. Although China refused to support the Soviet idea of 'united action' against the United States, in reality it agreed with the Soviet Union in supporting North Vietnam. The shift to a more active Soviet policy in defence of North Vietnam came in 1965 when the Sino-Soviet split, the purge of Khrushchev and the increased US war effort, all combined to change Soviet policy. In fact, the period from 1965–72 was not only the peak of US involvement in the war, but also the high point of Soviet involvement. Not surprisingly, the Soviet Union conceived of its role first and foremost in terms of its relationship with the United States and only secondarily in terms of support for a specific communist regime.

In 1971, the United States faced its most difficult challenge in the postwar period as it attempted to get out of the Vietnam war without losing too much honour. The grand strategy, formulated by Henry Kissinger, was to improve relations with China and the Soviet Union, thereby encouraging both communist allies of Hanoi to force an amicable deal in Indochina. However, both China and the Soviet Union considered the US proposals solely on their own merits and declined to press Vietnam into anything that prevented it from winning the war. The Soviet Union was willing to sign a SALT agreement with the United States, but it saw no need to force Vietnam to meet US terms as part of some complex linkage of great power politics. It was already clear to the Soviet Union that their Vietnamese allies were about to win and merely needed to keep US forces at bay long enough for South Vietnam to collapse. The Soviet Union recognized the ironclad rule of conflict in the Third World—a superpower defending a winning ally is in a much stronger position than when it defends a weak friend.

The overlay of East-West relations, so crucial in previous conflicts in Indochina, had been replaced by more complex multipolar great-power relations. Now the Soviet Union became concerned with Vietnam because of both US and Chinese influence. Although the so-called great-power triangle had existed long before 1971 (in fact, ever since the Sino-Soviet split), only in the 1970s did the United States try to use the rift in the communist world as a way out of its Vietnam quagmire. That the effort failed does not obscure the fact that great-power conflict in the Pacific was no longer bipolar.

The 1973 Paris accords between the United States and North Vietnam allowed the United States to withdraw its troops from the war. Of course, the result could have been more devastating for the United States and the Pacific. War between the United States and North Vietnam's patrons in China and the Soviet Union had been avoided despite the fact that Chinese troops, and a smaller number of Soviet air defence troops, had fought in the North, and Soviet aid shipments had been destroyed in US bombing raids on northern cities and ports. The Soviet Union provided more than 80 percent of the military aid Hanoi received, and by deterring the United States from adopting more adventurous war plans, Soviet aid ensured that Vietnam could fight the war on its own terms. China was more active in the war, and for a time in 1965–6 threatened to repeat its role in the Korean conflict.[118] Also as in Korea, the Soviet Union was not the prime target of US crisis management, even though Soviet aid to Vietnam was seen as essential to the survival of the Hanoi regime.

The importance of the Vietnam war is due not only to its being the most costly war (in human and financial terms) since 1945, but also to its being the most extensive US military engagement at any time since 1945. Also, the war seriously damaged the US economy, its self-confidence and credibility, and it formalized the transition from a bipolar to a multipolar world. It transformed the map of Indochina. What were once two semineutral states and a divided Vietnam, became three communist states, with Vietnam the world's third largest and third most powerful communist state. Two of the three new states took up relatively pro-Soviet positions in the Sino-Soviet split, and the other, Cambodia, took the Chinese side. In the Pacific balance of power, 1975 is clearly the second most important time of change. The gains for communism were clear, but they were only marginally the result of a consistent Soviet policy.

Other Southeast Asian states were forced to readjust their international perspectives. The Southeast Asia Treaty Organization (SEATO) was shown to be a hollow alliance and eventually died in 1977. SEATO's failure also shattered any illusion that an alliance structure in the Pacific could be maintained along Atlantic lines. Thailand thus found itself in the forefront of the struggle against communism. Malaysia, the Philippines and Singapore stared across the South China sea at several communist regimes. Unlike the situation in Europe, the dividing line in Asia has moved since 1945, and communism was no longer monolithic.

The main loser among the great powers was clearly the United States. It had committed a large proportion of its conventional military forces to a land war in Asia and was still unable to win. The other superpower, the Soviet Union, had perhaps benefitted the most during the 20 years since 1955. Most important, it did not directly participate in the wars. Despite the complexity of local conflicts, the Soviet Union was only occasionally embarrassed (as in its continued recognition of Lon Nol in Cambodia). Military aid was not as extensive as the local communist forces wanted, but they received all they really needed. The lesson for Moscow was that military aid and superpower deterrence could work to improve the Soviet position. The Soviet Union had gained merely by keeping a low profile, while the international reputation of the United States plummeted elsewhere in the developing world as a result of its adventurism and gunboat diplomacy. Opposition to US policy also increased in the much more important (from the Soviet perspective) European theatre. The European left criticized US so-called imperialism while the right worried about the damage done to NATO and the international economy by a distracted and drained United States.

In 1975, China could also be pleased that it had helped eject the United States from Asia. Yet China worried that a defeated United States would be less useful in containing the perceived Soviet threat to China. When the Vietnam war first began, which was before the Sino-Soviet split, the United States was the common enemy. The Soviet calculation remained the same throughout the war, but China changed its mind in the early 1970s and improved relations with the United States. The defeat of the United States in Vietnam was thus a mixed blessing from the Chinese perspective.

China could also be pleased that there were now more communist regimes on its frontiers. Yet the Sino-Soviet split had taught China that not all communists were the same. If these regimes were more pro-Soviet than pro-Chinese—and Laos and Vietnam seemed to be pro-Soviet—then these communist triumphs were thus not necessarily in the Chinese interest. Certainly, a triumphant Vietnam was more powerful, confident and independent of China than in 1955 and less likely to resume the subservient relationship that China preferred in its idealized vision of traditional East Asian foreign policy.

The Vietnam war had a major impact in the entire Pacific region. The United States became less directly involved in Pacific security, if only because fewer of its men were dying in western Pacific jungles and fewer ships and aircraft had to cross the waters to supply its military forces. The retreat from the Asian land mass encouraged the United States to think about the Pacific more in naval and offshore terms.

The war also brought the Soviet Union closer to Indochina—Vietnam in particular. Before there were other communist states in the region, China had been more important and Soviet foreign policy had had fewer options. The addition of new communist regimes, especially Vietnam, which was prepared to offer the Soviet Union military facilities, gave the Soviet Union major cause to think Pacific. The expansion of Soviet military power around the globe was already underway, but the events in the Pacific presented Soviet leaders with greater success and more prospects than anywhere else in the developing world. North Vietnam's victory certainly provided the Soviet Union with much needed naval facilities in a region that had previously been stony ground for Soviet influence. To be sure, some Pacific states were scared by Soviet success. But other states, such as Indonesia, henceforth sensed a greater need to work with Moscow as a legitimate participant in the region.

New conflict in Cambodia

Various explanations have been offered for the war between Vietnam and Cambodia.[119] No single explanation is adequate, but as the Sino-Soviet conflict suggests, ideological rivalry together with underlying nationalism is a potent mix. The main destruction to the national political fabric came from disputes within Cambodia, including those between pro-Vietnamese communists and Pol Pot's Khmer Rouge.[120] For instance, Pol Pot's followers derided the pro-Vietnamese Khmer communists as 'Vietnamese in Khmer bodies'. These groups had different strategies, power bases and alliances.

After the victories of 1975, the communist powers realized that even more gains could be made. The Soviet Union believed it had earned the friendship of the local communists by virtue of its steadfast material and spiritual support. Vietnam itself realized that it was the Pacific's third largest communist power. It thus had its own aspirations for special relationships with its fellow Indochinese.[121] Potential for conflict among the communists, although not necessarily inevitable, certainly existed.

Believing that the best defence is an offence, Pol Pot's Khmer Rouge regime, already paranoid about Vietnamese intentions, insisted from the start on the withdrawal of Vietnamese troops from Cambodia. Both countries did establish border-liaison committees despite being on different sides in the still looming Sino-Soviet split.[122] By 1977, Pol Pot led Cambodia into ever more violent border clashes with Vietnam. Both sides then escalated hostilities and demands for support from their communist allies. Cambodia obtained more military aid from China even though Beijing was not pleased to see the conflict get out of hand.[123] Even so, the Pol Pot regime became increasingly radicalized as its policies at home failed. This regime, in its perverted revolutionary zeal, earned the unenviable record for slaughtering more of its citizenry than any since Hitler. By February 1978, the Vietnamese decided to invade Cambodia and install a more pliable regime.[124]

The Soviet Union was willing to support Vietnam for several reasons. Not only was Vietnam demanding little more than diplomatic and material aid—something it had done to Soviet advantage for decades—but Vietnam also offered Moscow access to military facilities in Vietnam, including the US-built naval base at Cam Ranh bay, and the prospect of improving its strategic position in the Pacific.[125] Although the Soviet Union did not gain access to Vietnamese bases until 1979, the bait was clearly dangled in front of the Soviet Union for some time before.[126] Furthermore, the growing Chinese support for Pol Pot made Moscow more anxious to balance Chinese influence and keep Beijing from dominating Indochina. Economic costs aside, the international political costs of such Soviet support were minimal because of the increasingly poor reputation of the Pol Pot regime.[127] On 25 December 1978, Vietnamese troops entered Cambodia and established a new regime in Phnom Penh under Heng Samrin by 11 January 1979. Vietnam had extended its power, and to a lesser extent so had the Soviet Union. China was the main loser.

In those days of cool Sino-Soviet relations, the Soviet Union was pleased that the war had enhanced its position. Moscow obtained access to important bases, and a former ally of China became a Soviet friend. However, the Soviet Union did not like being thought of as an imperialist out to change the nature of regimes in Southeast Asia. In contrast to the new, more Western-oriented China, the Soviet Union was getting a reputation of radicalism and adventure. The continuing Sino-Soviet split and the new Chinese opening to the West isolated the Soviet Union in Southeast Asia just when Moscow was strongest militarily. The lesson was obvious: military power often comes at the expense of political influence. In the long term, the 1979 Vietnamese triumph in Cambodia was not in the Soviet Union's best interests.

China and Vietnam

The course of the Cambodian conflict in the 1970s was very closely intertwined with Sino-Vietnamese relations.[128] Although the pace of the Cambodian events was primarily determined by the domestic policies of the Khmer Rouge, the Soviet Union and other outsiders also played an important role. The two other main participants, China and Vietnam, were reacting to Cambodian events while also pursuing their separate interests. The Soviet Union, as the main supporter of Vietnam, was called on to deter Chinese threats to Vietnam, thus demonstrating its support for an ally. The brief Sino-Vietnamese war in 1979 was a success for Soviet diplomacy if only because it projected an image of reliability without having to do anything specific.

The Sino-Vietnamese conflict can be traced back to ancient times, but the most recent disputes centred on the course of the first two phases of the Vietnam war and Hanoi's feeling that China's support was both inadequate or manipulative.[129] Had Vietnam not sided with the Soviet Union in the Sino-Soviet split, China might have been less antagonistic to Vietnamese predominance in Indochina. Had China also not been so anti-Soviet, it might have regarded Vietnam's pro-Soviet leanings as less significant. Both sides had powerful reasons for suspicion, but this suspicion also fed paranoia about each other's intentions which was soon beyond rational control.[130]

By May 1978, China had terminated its aid projects to Vietnam, and by July the two countries were fighting minor border clashes. This rapid deterioration of relations was in many respects an accelerated version of the slide towards war along the Sino-Soviet frontier in the 1960s.[131] The Soviet Union clearly concerned the Chinese, especially since Vietnam joined Comecon—the socialist bloc economic organization—in June and signed a friendship treaty with the Soviet Union on 3 November. For China, these steps provoked even deeper fears of Soviet encirclement of China. For the Soviet Union, the alliance with Vietnam was obvious, and so far, low-cost. The 1979 war would raise the price of friendship with Vietnam but not diminish Soviet satisfaction with the balance sheet.

Another interested observer, the United States, played its part in the Vietnamese tendency to align with the Soviet Union. The Carter administration was probably more to blame than Vietnam for US failure to improve relations with Hanoi, but under any circumstances the time was probably not ripe.[132] The failure to heal the US-Vietnam breach meant that Vietnam had little option but to move closer to Moscow. Against a background of escalating Vietnamese-Cambodian conflict, China accepted revised US terms for normalization of relations,[133] and the last obstacle was cleared before China could attack Vietnam.[134]

The war went badly for China, and by 16 March 1979, it was forced to withdraw without Vietnam having been taught the lesson that China intended.[135] Vietnam was not forced out of Cambodia nor was it forced to run to Moscow for assistance. China's military instrument was too blunt and rusty to force panic in Hanoi, and Beijing thus had to reassess its position. The Soviet Union had warned China not to continue its attack on Vietnam, and indeed Moscow's threat did keep China's military operations limited. China's failure to hit Vietnam hard ensured the failure of its goal to teach Vietnam a lesson. Thus, the Soviet Union could claim most of the credit for humiliating China. Equally, the image of the Soviet Union as a steadfast ally was clearly reinforced.

Towards detente in Indochina

The defeat of China at the hands of Vietnam in their short border war was the most damaging loss the PLA suffered since the 1969 engagements with the Soviet Union.[136] The first steps towards detente between China and the Soviet Union in the 1980s were taken largely because the Chinese had realized, by 1980, that its heavily anti-Soviet policy was too costly. From the Soviet point of view, the 1979 war was, like the events of 1975, a triumph. But the success of the Soviet Union was closely related to Chinese errors. When China reformed its foreign policy in the 1980s, the Soviet Union also had to reform or else see its position in Southeast Asia deteriorate rapidly.

All of Indochina, under Vietnam's sway, thus also came under Soviet power and influence. China nevertheless brought supplies to Khmer Rouge rebels and its allied opposition movements on the Thai border with Cambodia. Until 1985, China had some hope that its support for the rebels might pay off in the long run. The strategy was to bleed Vietnam sufficiently so that it would have to withdraw. But after the 1985 spring offensive by the Vietnamese, the Khmer rebels were confined to the farthest reaches of Cambodia nearest Thailand and ceased to pose a major threat to the Vietnamese occupation. Although sporadic clashes took place, the war was certainly ending. China concentrated on its domestic program of modernization, and its foreign policy priorities henceforth included improved relations with the Soviet Union.

To be sure, China continued to view the Cambodian conflict as the main obstacle to Sino-Soviet detente and maintained the linkage that had so dominated its foreign policy of the 1970s. China insisted that it would not normalize relations with the Soviet Union unless Moscow pressed Vietnam to withdraw from Cambodia. Although the Soviet Union could not do so publicly for fear of losing its bases in Indochina, it could encourage Hanoi to be more positive. The Soviets thus insisted on economic reform in Vietnam, demanded that their aid be spent more effectively and proposed to discuss the Cambodian question in the biannual Sino-Soviet talks—all of which influenced the Vietnamese.[137]

The Indochina problem not only drained the Soviet Union's budget and hindered Sino-Soviet detente, it also prevented the Soviet Union from improving relations with ASEAN states.[138] It was not even a simple Soviet calculation of whether to support socialist as opposed to non-socialist economies, for communist China made it plain that Soviet influence in the region would be limited unless it resolved the Indochina issue.

All these factors finally moved Mikhail Gorbachev to act; he pressed Vietnam to withdraw its troops from Cambodia by October 1989. The foreign ministers of China and the Soviet Union reached a joint agreement on Cambodia in Beijing in February 1989, thus clearing the way for a Sino-Soviet summit.[139] The message to Vietnam and its Cambodian allies was clear—if they did not want a virtually imposed deal, they had better reach agreement on their own. In swift succession, Vietnam satisfied Soviet (and most other people's) demands by agreeing to withdraw from Cambodia. Soon thereafter, in the spring of 1989, the Cambodian factions also quickly compromised in order to remove their country from the agenda of the Sino-Soviet summit.

Both the Soviet Union and China knew they could not actually impose a settlement in Cambodia, but they did see the resolution of the conflict as more in their hands than in those of any other great power. China explicitly told the United States not to interfere, and Soviet observers expressed clear satisfaction that China and the Soviet Union alone had made sufficient progress to resolve the matter.[140]

Although the Soviet Union seemed forced into pressing Vietnam to withdraw its troops from Cambodia, it probably did not mind applying this pressure. By appearing to have to push Vietnam into compromise, the Soviet Union could earn points both as a com-promiser and as a peacemaker in the region. Inasmuch as the Soviet Union was withdrawing from Afghanistan at the same time, it was also willing to take credit for solving the Indochinese conflict. The only way the Soviet Union might appear to be a loser was in its weakened credibility as an ally. If the regime in Cambodia is not hostile to the Soviet Union or Vietnam, however, the Soviet action will be vindicated.

The Cambodian conflict remains the last significant hot war in East Asia, but the Soviet Union refuses to be drawn into a military engagement. The failure of the Paris talks in 1989 had more to do with China's hard-line support for the Khmer Rouge and reflected well on a Soviet Union that could admit it had erred in its initial failure to criticize the genocidal policies of Pol Pot. The Soviet Union, like much of the West, waited to see the verdict of the battlefield in 1989–90. But it was a sign of the times that Soviet and West European attitudes to Cambodia were growing closer.

Even before Vietnamese troops were out of Cambodia, the Soviet Union was rapidly improving its position in Southeast Asia. Its image as a military threat was in decline. The primary targets of Soviet diplomacy were Thailand and the Philippines. The reduction of the threat along the Thai border made it easier for Thailand to improve relations with Moscow. Similarly, Indonesia looked more favourably on the Soviet Union and its various suggestions for regional arms control when the Vietnamese were in retreat.[141]

The Philippines, with its major US bases and relatively new and more moderate government, received the most Soviet attention. In 1959, Nikita Khrushchev had banged his shoe at the United Nations in protest against a Philippine speaker who compared the Soviet Union unfavourably with the United States.[142] But in 1988, the Philippines were increasingly upset with the United States, on the one hand, because of the fees for basing rights and were intrigued, on the other hand, by the peaceful initiatives coming from Moscow. Mikhail Gorbachev's offer in September 1988 to give up access to Vietnamese bases in exchange for US withdrawal from the bases in the Philippines, at least made the point that states in the region need be less concerned with the much smaller and less effective Soviet bases.

On a visit to the Philippines in December 1988, Soviet Foreign Minister Shevardnadze succeeded in showing the softer side of Soviet diplomacy. Subsequent Soviet delegations suggested the Soviet Union might unilaterally withdraw its troops from Indochina. Clearly Moscow was suggesting that it could help the ASEAN states create a more peaceful region.[143] By turning the spotlight on the United States, the Soviet Union had rapidly improved its position. Many ASEAN states then turned their attention to the next major issue that might lead to war—the South China sea. Much to the Soviet Union's relief, China, rather than the Soviet Union, was having trouble with the ASEAN states. The Soviet position in the region had never looked better.

Vietnam, China and the South China sea

The Sino-Vietnamese dispute also extends beyond the land frontiers into the much more murky political waters of the South China sea. The Soviet Union, as a superpower with a navy in transit between the Pacific and Indian oceans—not to mention its alliance with Vietnam—has taken an interest in conflict in these waters, but so far has not been directly involved in combat. As inheritors of French Indochina, Vietnam claimed the Paracel (Xisha) and Spratly (Nansha) islands in the South China sea while China claimed them as traditionally Chinese. For more than 15 years after the French withdrawal from Vietnam, South Vietnam held both groups and even removed Chinese residents from the Paracel group.[144]

In January 1974, China seized the Paracel islands while South Vietnam was too weak to act, North Vietnam and the Soviet Union were still nominally allies, and the United States was courting China.[145] It was a masterful piece of low-risk war that proved China would use force to regain what it claimed as its own.

In the 1970s, China could only grasp the Paracels, but in the 1980s, it began expanding the reach of its navy. Aircraft and ships were more frequently sent to the Spratlys.[146] In March 1988, China took advantage of its new detente with the Soviet Union to attack Vietnamese troops in the Spratlys and inflict hundreds of casualties. As in the 1974 operation, little territory was acquired, but it again displayed Chinese determination to take what it claimed as its own. The islands sit astride vital sea routes for the growing trade of the Pacific; thus, China's pursuit of its principles was seen as dangerous and perhaps even as a harbinger of a more potent Chinese military power in the years to come.

The Soviet Union, although clearly an ally of Vietnam, was of course loathe to denounce China for fear of harming the delicate Sino-Soviet detente. As in the 1962 Sino-Indian conflict, the Soviet Union was caught between conflicting interests in an Asian war. The solution was, in effect, to lean towards the new friend, China, at the expense of a more influential position in the South China sea. From the Soviet point of view, China is the most important state in Asia. It was not an easy choice for Moscow to make. When it took a nominally neutral stance in 1988, both Vietnam and China were aware of the signal that Moscow was sending. Needless to say, there was also a hidden signal that took longer to be read in Southeast Asia; the retreat of an active Soviet military power would leave others, such as China, freer to impose their will. Only in retreat did it become obvious that the Soviet Union was also a force for peace in Southeast Asia.

Conflict in the wider Pacific

Stretching beyond Indochina are the islands of the Pacific, almost none of which figure in Soviet military plans. To be sure, the Soviet Union has occasionally taken an active interest in certain events. The special case of Taiwan is an obvious exception to the general lack of Soviet interest in these more distant parts.

Taiwan

In the 1950s, the Soviet Union supported its Chinese communist ally in its determination to regain control of all its territory. Throughout the various offshore islands crises, however, the Soviet Union was somewhat less anxious than China to create a major crisis. The Soviet Union did not want to risk major tension with the United States, which supported Taiwan throughout the crises. The Soviet Union deterred US threats to China, although there is still some debate about just how firm an ally of China the Soviet Union really was.[147]

China claimed that the Soviet Union failed to offer the full fraternal support it expected in their struggle against Western imperialism. The Soviet Union argued that there were limits imposed by the need to manage crises in the nuclear age and that the United States should not be pushed to the brink of war. China no doubt was frustrated with the level of Soviet support, which reflected the different Chinese view of the world and greater willingness to take risks in the nuclear age. The Soviet Union's maturity in times of crisis was not appreciated by China's revolutionary leadership.

Following the Sino-Soviet split, the Soviet attitude towards the Taiwan problem changed. The declining necessity to support China's more radical line, and indeed China's own distraction with internal upheavals, took the Taiwan issue off the Soviet agenda. By the 1970s, when the Taiwan issue was the primary dispute preventing a normalization of Sino-US relations, Soviet ambiguity was even more evident. Although opposed to Sino-US detente, the Soviet Union could also not support anti-communist Taiwan. Thus, the Soviet Union still supported the idea of one China, but was nevertheless pleased that the issue caused problems in the relationship between its main rivals in the Pacific.

The subsequent normalization of Sino–US relations in 1979 and the compromise on Taiwan let both China and the United States concentrate on the Soviet Union as their main adversary. As Sino–Soviet detente grew stronger in the 1980s, however, the Taiwan issue resurfaced to some extent as a base for Sino–Soviet unity. The failure of the United States and China fully to resolve problems over Taiwan, including continuing US arms transfers to Taiwan and a thriving trade relationship, ensured that Taiwan remained a major obstacle in Sino–US relations. The Soviet Union could proudly point to its full acceptance of the Chinese position on Taiwan in contrast to the Sino–US disagreement.

In the 1980s, as China began to accept that Taiwan would not inevitably be reunited with the mainland, Soviet options increased somewhat. Taiwan's unnatural position—a major global trader with few diplomatic relations—ensured that any formal Soviet approaches to Taiwan would likely upset China. Yet as China itself began to develop informal relations with Taiwan, other states could more easily do so as well, so long as it was done informally. Arguably the most successful of the NICs, Taiwan was an attractive partner for many states in the global trading network. The Soviet Union, more serious about exploring the possibilities of contacts with the NICs, thus considered opening relations with Taiwan as well. In the late-1980s atmosphere of greater Chinese pragmatism, Soviet contacts with Taiwan were more possible. As Chinese military options against Taiwan became less likely, pragmatic economic calculations moved to the forefront of Soviet calculations.

The further Pacific

As the Spratly incident shows, although the Pacific has grown more pacific in recent years, several disputes may yet wreck havoc with regional stability. The least understood potential crises mainly involve maritime disputes—particularly along the coast of China. The Soviets have so far stayed out of such disputes and watched for signs of uncontrolled crisis. As in the cases of the various minicrises in Korea since the 1950s, the Soviet position has been that none of these issues are important enough to distract from the main areas of concern in Northeast Asia.

As interest increases in the new Law of the Sea and the potential exploitation of sea-bed resources, such naval disputes may figure even more strongly in the future.[148] The complex disagreements between the states of Northeast Asia are good examples of the new but, as yet, mostly low-key conflict.[149] In the more distant future are potential disputes over the mineral rights in the Antarctic.[150] However, conflict in the Antarctic—as indeed other disputes in the Pacific—involves more nations than merely the states of the Pacific, and therefore crises can be either resolved or exacerbated on a global level. The Soviet Union, as a global superpower, has an interest in controlling these conflicts. As a major maritime power with the second largest navy in the Pacific and capability in exploiting sea-bed minerals, and as a participant in governing Antarctic regime, the Soviet Union will take an active role in all these Pacific-wide issues. But the farther one gets from Soviet territory, the more difficult it is to envisage a Soviet military capability.

Thus the large but distant territories of Australia and New Zealand catch the eye of Soviet military planners, even though they offer little opportunity for Soviet action. These close allies of the United States have always been recognized as part of the US sphere of influence. Although ANZUS (Australia, New Zealand, United States) has never been a front-line alliance—it is as far from the nearest conflict with communists in Southeast Asia as Chad is from the Brandenburg gate—the allies have contributed to US-led war efforts in the Pacific since 1945. The United States regularly took a harder line on the Soviet role in the region than did its allies, but the Soviet Union has always been cautious about exploiting these differences.[151]

In the 1980s, the Soviet Union saw some of the deepest rifts open up in ANZUS, but at a time of relative retreat of Soviet naval power in the Pacific. The dispute between New Zealand and the United States over the activities of US nuclear-armed and nuclear-powered ships and aircraft led to the *de facto* suspension of New Zealand from the alliance. The Dibb report, and subsequent revision of Australian defence policy to concentrate more on defence of the homeland, added further strain to the US attempt to build alliance consciousness about a perceived Soviet threat.[152]

Yet the Soviet Union did not take advantage of these rifts in US-led alliances. A realistic Soviet assessment of its priorities puts relatively little emphasis on the south Pacific as an area of operation.[153] Despite the occasional presence of Soviet naval ships in the south Pacific, the Soviets remain overwhelmingly concerned with the north Pacific.[154] There is no regular Soviet military presence in the southwest Pacific region, although the access to bases in Vietnam in the early 1980s has brought regular Soviet operations closer to the region.

Even in the case of the most important south Pacific state, Australia, the Soviet Union remains aware of its distance and negative image. The facilities at North West Cape, Pine Gap and Nurrungar that Australia provides for the United States are recognized as vital components of the US alliance network. Although the Soviet Union has stressed that the presence of these bases makes Australia a key target in time of war, the Soviets have been unsuccessful in transforming this issue into a major problem in either Australian domestic politics or Australian–US relations. Australia's rapprochement with China after the Sino-Soviet split meant that the Soviet Union appeared even more remote and less important.[155]

Significantly, even in the 1980s, when Australia and New Zealand reassessed their defence policies, the Soviet military position in the south Pacific barely changed. A Soviet request for fishing rights within the Australian 200-mile fishing zone was deferred by Australia in November 1988.[156] New Zealand was somewhat more positive about the new Soviet foreign policy in the Pacific, for example, welcoming Soviet support for the nuclear-free zone and praising Gorbachev's initiatives at Krasnoyarsk in 1988.[157] But if only because of the sensitivity of New Zealand's neighbours about its potential for neutralism, there were strict limits on how friendly New Zealand was prepared to sound about Gorbachev's early foreign policy.

The 1980s was also a period of potential Soviet gains as the instability of decolonization beset the region. In other parts of the world, this process provided ample opportunities for improvements in the Soviet position. However, despite a number of fearful predictions of Soviet strategic gains, by the end of the decade, Soviet influence remained minimal. The Soviet Union had established diplomatic relations with Fiji in 1974, Tonga in 1975 and Papua New Guinea and Western Samoa in 1976, but in no case was a resident diplomatic mission established.[158] In 1986, newly independent Kiribati signed a fishing agreement with the Soviet Union as Moscow took advantage of the short-sighted and stingy US response to the demands of the islands for greater returns on their fishing resources. This so-called fishing in troubled water also included the establishment of diplomatic relations with Vanuatu in June 1986 and the Soviet search for greater access for its aircraft and, most important, for its global fishing fleets. Vanuatu also signed a fishing accord in January 1987 and Papua New Guinea reportedly expressed an interest in improving relations with the Soviet Union. The short-lived Fijian Labor government indicated they, too, wanted better relations with the Soviet Union, and such ideas were cited by the Fijian military leaders as one reason for their coup.[159] As one of his Pacific initiatives in 1986, Gorbachev reorganized the Soviet Foreign Ministry in order to pay more direct attention to the individual Pacific islands.

Soviet success so far has been minimal, however. Despite frequent scare stories about Soviet influence in the islands, in most cases these are merely part of what Paul Dibb has called 'playing the Soviet card'—the attempt by the islanders to obtain more Western aid by hinting they might turn to the Soviet Union.[160] In many cases, the apparent rise in Soviet influence has more to do with Western failures—for example, the French nuclear test programme, or the refusal by the United States and Japan to pay more for local fish resources. In 1982, the Solomon islands learned from the Tongan example how to play the Soviet card (1976), and in the late 1980s the newly independent islands have tried to play the game again.

It is true that the island economies are very fragile, but in most cases their political culture is fiercely anti-communist. But it is striking that the fishing agreement with Kiribati was not renewed because the Soviet Union decided it was simply suffering too much of a financial loss without any obvious gain in other spheres. By 1988, the limits of the islands' cooperation with the Soviet Union was clear. Kiribati was even refusing a joint Soviet-US scientific team the right to check ocean pollution in Kiribati waters.[161] The fishing deal with Vanuatu was only somewhat more attractive because it included arrangements for reprovisioning. Nevertheless it was not renewed.

Even though the south Pacific does not rate as an area of major Soviet interest, it is unlikely that the Soviets' less militarily threatening foreign policy will continue to be so regularly rebuffed. The positive Soviet approach to the region as a nuclear-free zone and the reduction in the perceived sense of a Soviet threat should make more Soviet progress possible. For example, a Soviet parliamentary delegation to Tonga in 1988 discussed peace initiatives because

Tonga, as the then-current chair of the South Pacific Forum, was seen as an effective avenue for an expression of the new Soviet image.[162] In 1989, Papua New Guinea announced it would allow the Soviet Union to open an embassy in Port Moresby. Furthermore, the Soviet Union probably knows more about the oceanography of the South Pacific than any other country and so has much to offer the states of the region. There is still no compelling reason for the Soviet Union to deploy submarines in the region, even though new technology does allow them to roam further than before. The testing of Soviet ICBMs has also been moved away from the south Pacific to the north Pacific. While there is some speculation that the need to control Pacific gateways as part of a Soviet SDI program will involve the Soviets again in south Pacific military concerns, such a scenario would be in the distant future.[163]

As long-range naval operations diminish and the Soviets attempt to improve their image in the Pacific and deemphasize military matters, Soviet involvement in the region enters a new era. At least in military terms, the Soviet Union is increasingly confined to being a mainly north Pacific power.

Arms control and disarmament

In the Pacific region, formal arms control has generally been unsuccessful. However, several significant tacit arms control and confidence-building measures have developed as the various conflicts in the region have been resolved. As a major military power in the Pacific, the Soviet Union has been at the forefront of implementing these special forms of arms control, and in recent years has perhaps suggested the most innovative new ideas for limiting the risks of war and reducing arms.[164]

There have been remarkably few formal arms control agreements in the Pacific since 1945—even fewer are still viable. In the two most important relationships in global terms—the superpower balance in the Pacific and Sino-Soviet relations—no significant, formal arms control agreements have been achieved. Yet, the powers in the Pacific have not entirely avoided arms control. Some agreements have been enshrined in documents, and others have emerged tacitly. The Soviet Union has been a key partner in most agreements.

The most formal arms control regime is the 1968 Non-Proliferation

Treaty (NPT). Although not strictly a Pacific treaty, it does have special implications for arms control in the region. Three states in the area have nuclear weapons—the two superpowers and China. Only two, however, have signed the NPT. China denounced the treaty as an attempt to impose superpower hegemony.

In recent years, China has become a *de facto* adherent of the NPT.[165] A notable new adherent to the NPT is North Korea. Both the Soviets and Chinese share a strong interest in controlling the Korean conflict. North Korea's signature was a precondition of the Soviet sale of a nuclear power plant to that nation. In the south Pacific, the Treaty of Raratonga for a south Pacific nuclear-free zone has also drawn the attention of the Soviet Union. The treaty would prevent the deployment of nuclear weapons on the territory of states in the area but would not ban their transit through the zone.[166] Such a partial nuclear-free zone would not make the south Pacific a nuclear-safe zone, however, as weapons can be targeted on the region from thousands of miles away.[167]

The treaty had its roots in growing concern about French nuclear testing in Tahiti and the increased risks of nuclear war affecting the one region of the world that had hoped to escape a nuclear holocaust. The disagreement in ANZUS over port visits by US nuclear-armed and nuclear-powered ships was a case in point. Not surprisingly, therefore, the United States, France and Britain refused to abide by the terms of the treaty, whereas the Soviet Union and China promised to do so.

A more successful, but not specifically nuclear, arms limitation treaty, was the Antarctic pact of 1959, which took effect when it was signed by 12 states in 1961. The 12 original signators included a wide range of states as befits the location of the Antarctic on the fringe of the Atlantic, Pacific and Indian oceans. The Antarctic treaty is a tribute to what arms control can be if it is established before a region is militarized. Admittedly, however, the treaty has also benefited from the Antarctic's remoteness and the high cost of maintaining a claim by scientific research for anyone but a wealthy nation.[168]

The superpowers have also agreed to two minor measures that can be classed as confidence-building arms control. In 1972 they agreed to reduce incidents at sea, and in 1985 they agreed with Japan to help maintain air safety after Soviet aircraft shot down a civilian Korean airliner. Both agreements remain in force and have been useful in their own minor ways. Both sides see clear limits and a useful role for measures in these essentially technical spheres. Neither superpower wants a conflict arising from uncontrolled disputes and tensions. Because the East-West division in the Pacific is less clear than the old division in Europe, it is all the more important to ensure mechanisms for limiting misunderstanding. This basic confidence-building exercise is often a first step to ensuring the stability necessary for future detente and more formal arms control.

Perhaps the most formal arms control measures in the Pacific are those agreed as part of the end of the Korean war in 1953. The armistice of 27 July 1953 created a demilitarized zone that nominally remains in force today. Four states were appointed as part of a neutral supervising commission and all were from Europe (Sweden, Switzerland, Poland and Czechoslovakia).[169] Of course, the zone has been repeatedly violated and there have been more than 30 years of very frigid cold war between North and South Korea. Arguably, arms control helped contain a conflict in the limited extent that both parties desired. But in practice, arms control has not done much to advance the cause of peace in the region.[170]

The most important detente in inter-Korean relations has occurred because of changes in the region's general balance of power, especially because of detente in great-power relations. By 1980 Kim Il Sung argued for 'One Country–Two Systems', because China had offered similar terms to Taiwan and because the Soviet Union had imposed pressure for detente. However, such pessimism about the results of formal arms control in Asia ignores the less formal achievements.

Sino–Soviet relations have benefited from tacit arms control in the form of such confidence-building measures as the thinning out of divisions along the border and withdrawals to create *de facto* demilitarized zones. The thinning out of Soviet divisions has reduced the actual number of Soviet soldiers on the frontier by about 80,000.[171] China officially cut its armed forces by one million men by 1987, roughly equalling the Soviet reduction in combat troops along the border. In December 1988, Mikhail Gorbachev announced further reductions over the next two years that would remove 200,000 troops from the Soviet Far Eastern theatre. Although 25 percent of Soviet troops are deployed in this region, the Soviet Union was making 40 percent of its announced troop reductions in this region. Moreover, China and Mongolia have agreed on confidence-building measures along their frontier, and the Soviet Union will soon withdraw all troops from Mongolia. China is reportedly planning to cut its armed forces by a further 500,000 as part of this spiral of arms control and detente. Such measures have achieved more than the long-running conventional arms reduction negotiation process in Europe, albeit without formal agreement.

Perhaps as a result of the positive example of such tacit arms control, in 1989 Japan (or at least some of its journalists) took up a Soviet offer to build confidence by attending Soviet naval exercises. Although some other invitees did not attend, the Japanese action suggested that a type of confidence-building arms control was possible.[172] The superpowers and even Britain also became involved in wider consultation that included other possible, informal measures.[173] From the Soviet point of view, the informal approach to arms reduction in the Pacific means that when the Soviet Union decides to launch an arms control initiative, it could achieve success more swiftly in the Pacific.

Problems with Pacific arms control

Most types of arms control have never been easy to achieve, even in the superpower decade of detente, the 1970s. In the more than 20 years that arms control has been a main item on the great powers' agendas (since the 1963 Partial Test Ban Treaty), a voluminous literature on the problems and prospects for arms control has emerged. Most discussion has focused on the political roots of the negotiations, the problems of what to count and the difficulty of counting anything at all. However, although these issues are important, they are not necessarily the main problems hindering arms control in the Pacific. Despite a number of general Soviet arms control proposals, even Moscow recognizes the special problems of arms control in the Pacific.[174] Five main difficulties in reaching arms control in the Pacific can be identified.

First, at least until the collapse of communism in Europe in 1989, it was clear that hot military conflict in Europe was unlikely although such wars did take place in East Asia.[175] Broadly speaking, there are two types of conflict in the Pacific—active wars and controlled conflicts.[176] The active wars are probably least susceptible to arms control because the political causes of conflict are unresolved and the combatants are still shedding each other's blood. The Southeast Asian wars seem to fall into this category. Other conflicts, however, seem to be under control and may be approaching European levels of controlled tension. These include the superpower balance in the Pacific and the Sino–Soviet conflict. The Korean conflict hovers somewhere between the two types—strong emotions are moderating as time passes. Nevertheless, conflict can easily flare up again as a result of domestic or foreign policy changes. Clearly, successful arms control in the Pacific is more likely in specific areas in which rivalries have begun to stabilize. Furthermore, the complexity of the politics of each conflict is distinctive, making a Pacific-wide approach to arms control unlikely.

Second, the Pacific does not have a simple balance of power. Thus, multilateral arms control is essential, but this is more difficult to achieve than is bilateral arms control. Soviet sources describe this condition as akin to puff pastry and recognize the difficulty in reaching any formal agreement.[177] Given the significant superpower forces in the Pacific and the substantial Chinese and Vietnamese armed forces, several balances of power exist. Needless to say, this multilateral situation is a nightmare for arms control.

Third, Pacific states are less similar. Japan is a unique case—a wealthy, developed economy with a relatively stable political system. Other countries—the Newly Industrializing Countries (NICs), for example—are booming economically but have somewhat unstable political systems. Most of the ASEAN states are less developed and many of them have serious domestic problems. The poorer Pacific states have an even wider spectrum of domestic problems that could result in international conflict as did the Vietnam war, a bloody civil war that drew in various great powers on both sides. Another serious situation concerns the radical domestic politics of the Khmer Rouge in Cambodia and Vietnam's attempt to install a more amenable regime in Phnom Penh. The Taiwan–China conflict is really an unresolved civil war. These conflicts, and indeed myriad other internal problems, originate primarily in debates about how to modernize. None of these issues are easily resolved and therefore no swift end to conflict is likely. If the conflicts remain acute, meaningful arms control will be almost impossible.

Fourth, no tradition of formal arms control exists in the Pacific, and many Pacific nations are suspicious of superpowers who try to make the messy Pacific picture fit their preconceptions.[178] The Pacific peoples instinctively reject colonial laws, legacies of imperialism and self-serving policies that often mask great-power aspirations for Pacific states. Young states with optimistic dreams often see arms control merely as a charade to restrict them and to maintain the status quo. Of course, this is not to suggest that Pacific states have pursued uncontrolled arms races and have deployed forces without concern for reducing tensions. Tacit limitations on arms transfers to various regional conflicts have been a feature of regional politics since the Korean war. But it is striking that the defence policies of Pacific states have not recognized the necessity for formal arms control. As a result of broader assessments of balances of power and the costs of unrestrained arms races, states in the Pacific have tacitly accepted restraint on weapons and tension. Thus, applying Western conceptions of arms control to the unique situation in the Pacific can easily result in distortion and misunderstanding.

Finally, for many states in the region, arms control appears inopportune at a time when leaders want to focus the public's attention on external threats and on the need to increase arms spending. For example, even though arms control could enhance security in both Korea and Japan, such an option is not encouraged by local leaders, and is only further undermined by blatantly propagandistic offers of arms control from the Soviet Union. In Japan, confidence-building measures are often seen as concessions to the Soviet Union because they might be taken as recognition of Soviet occupation of the Northern Territories. These measures might also undermine the delicate consensus on the need for increased defence expenditure.

Progress in Pacific arms control

In the past decade, there has been a flood of arms control proposals in the Pacific, but until recently few have been more than propaganda gestures. It took a long time for the Soviet Union to realize the need for more sophisticated approaches to Pacific arms control. Following the Gorbachev speech in Vladivostok in 1986, more realistic ideas finally began to emerge.

In the 1970s, the Soviet Union proposed an Asian collective security scheme—essentially an attempt to organize Asian states in a containment ring against China. Moscow found few supporters and the idea was gradually dropped. Then in a major speech at Vladivostok in July 1986, Gorbachev abandoned most of the old ideas and launched a new initiative, even offering the United States a place in a Pacific, Helsinki-like process. As Soviet officials made clear at the time, such grandiose plans were for the long-term future and took second place to more specific overtures to Japan and China.[179]

The Gorbachev initiative for an Asian Helsinki was an attempt to break up what the Soviet Union perceived as an anti-Soviet coalition in the region organized by the United States. The European Helsinki process in 1975 had caused the Soviet Union problems primarily in the sphere of human rights violations. In the Pacific this was unlikely to become an issue, for fear of harming Western relations with China as well as some of the recently favoured, but less than democratic, NICs. The advantages for the Soviet Union of an Asian Helsinki would be similar to those in Europe—recognition of existing frontiers and allied regimes. Yet the problems with such a proposal are even larger than in Europe, if only because of the lack of identifiable blocs and the lack of an agreed status quo.

In the meantime, a more fruitful strategy was to pursue bilateral, and informal arms control. The tit-for-tat arms control along the Sino-Soviet border will have cut the number of forces on the Soviet side nearly in half from its late-1970s peak. The decisions to reduce armed forces are directly related to the domestic reforms in China and the Soviet Union. The result of the reductions in arms has been the improvement of bilateral relations. The two sides are also now discussing the possibilities for formal agreements to build confidence. Soviet and Chinese foreign ministers agreed in February 1989 on the mechanism that would allow military and diplomatic experts to work on the details of such agreements.[180] The Soviet Union sees this process as including formal agreements on troop numbers on the frontier, a full settlement of border disputes and increased interaction among people along the frontier.[181] To a large extent, many of these measures have already been achieved without formal agreement.

The arms control still to come includes some of the more unorthodox measures to build confidence. Soviet officials are already talking of implementing a new strategy of 'defensive sufficiency' that includes an armed forces reformed into a 'defensive structure'. Soviet officials also speak of the need for the new negotiating teams to agree to reductions in offensive components of the armed forces, limitations on the number and scale of exercises, and establishment of means for mutual verification of military exercises and troop movements. The model, at least in the Soviet mind, is clearly the successful arms control negotiations for similar confidence-building measures in Europe.[182]

The Soviet Union also claims, perhaps more dubiously, that arms control between two socialist states is easier to achieve than between states from different social systems.[183] Progress on arms control with China has certainly been quicker and easier than in the case of Soviet-European negotiations.

The process of Sino-Soviet detente is clearly leading to a range of other possible arms control measures. For example, the Soviet Union has already arranged for Japanese observers at Soviet naval exercises in 1989, and Soviet officials have proposed that the superpowers arrange confidence-building measures in Korea.[184] The Soviets have also been active since 1987 in pressing Vietnam to withdraw from Cambodia and negotiate with China about outstanding issues. The Soviet Union is minimizing its image as a primarily military superpower by taking initiatives as a peacemaker—for example, its efforts in 1965 in South Asia, which provided enormous gains for Soviet foreign policy and helped establish a closer relationship with India. Although China and the Soviet Union are not negotiating a specific means of implementing Vietnamese withdrawal from Cambodia, both sides have discussed how the international community can best supervise the peace process.

Another serious proposal to reduce the risks of accidental war, affecting a specific zone, is the portion of the 1982 Law of the Sea treaty that ensures the free passage of ships through straits and limits the right of passage of warships into certain coastal waters. Although the treaty is not yet in operation, and many of its features merely codify sensible existing practice, it does represent a useful accord for an area such as the Pacific with so many potential naval disputes. If, as some have argued, the idea of the Exclusive Economic Zone is extended to include a ban on anti-submarine warfare (the so-called ASWEEZ),[185] then the superpowers and China will have an even greater need to ensure the smooth implementation of arms control in the Pacific. The United States has not signed the Law of the Sea treaty, but the majority of Pacific states have done so and wish to see it implemented.[186] Like the NPT, the treaty is not a specifically Pacific arms control measure. Unlike the NPT, however, it is favoured by the developing states. As a result, it may eventually be one of the best kept of any arms control agreement in the Pacific.

Finally, the superpower arms control process in Europe has influenced arms control in the Pacific. Negotiations on limiting intermediate-range nuclear forces (INF) have long been complicated by the existence of Chinese nuclear weapons and by the deployment by both superpowers of some parts of their arsenal against China. In the SALT I agreement, the Soviet Union was granted a *de facto* 'China quotient' in its long-range weaponry so as to meet a perceived Chinese threat.[187] The United States also originally conceived of its ABM shield for use against China, which led to the eventual ABM treaty as part of SALT I.[188]

In the 1970s, the Soviet Union began deploying the SS–20, an INF weapon targeted both on Western Europe and East Asia, as well as in a 'swing' mode capable of hitting both theatres. Following the deployment of NATO's INF weapons in the early 1980s, the superpowers began negotiating an agreement on limiting, and then banning, INF weapons completely.[189] The question arose whether the superpowers should retain 100 weapons in the Pacific to deal with the more complicated balance of power in that region. The Soviet Union told China that the SS–20 was targeted on Japanese and US forces, while simultaneously suggesting to the United States and Japan that the weapon was aimed at the Chinese. The Soviets offered to scrap these last 100 INF weapons if the United States would remove its weapons on ships and bases just off Eurasia.

In July 1987, Mikhail Gorbachev agreed to scrap the 100 weapons, thereby accepting an INF ban on land in Eurasia but not at sea. Thus, Europe and Asia were to be free of these weapons, but not the Atlantic or Pacific oceans. The agreement was delayed, however, because of a dispute over German INF weapons. Thus, at least on the nuclear and superpower level, regional security is clearly inseparable from global security. When finally signed in December 1988, the agreement, which had begun as European arms control, had become a major treaty affecting nuclear weapons in East Asia as well. In arms control, there was no Pacific thinking, but rather much Eurasian thinking.

As a Eurasian power, the Soviets will always have a comprehensive perspective that links its Atlantic and Pacific security. A large proportion of Soviet strategic weapons is in the Pacific region, and because these weapons can be re-targeted, they have to be considered in a number of regional and global equations of nuclear weapons. When the complicating factors of China's nuclear programme and Japanese potential are added, it is difficult to imagine the Soviet Union feeling secure about calculations of supposedly safe balances of power achieved in arms control.[190] Similarly, the Soviet Union realizes that it faces different kinds of conventional military threats in the Pacific and that any arms control zones would be different for each adversarial relationship. In order to reduce troops along the Sino-Soviet border, there would inevitably be a reduction in troops that would also face threats from Japan and the United States. As a result, it is not surprising that the Gorbachev statement of December 1988 on troop cuts involved all the major theatres of Soviet operations. The security of Asia and Europe are linked by the sprawling geography of the Soviet Union.

Clearly much more can be done in terms of Pacific arms control. The Soviet Union is still a major great-power supporter of its friends in Korea and Indochina. It is still in dispute to some extent with China, Japan and the United States in the region. The Soviet Union is still in search of a better public image in the region, and arms control would help it build a better image in the south Pacific and Southeast Asia.

However, the flood of arms control proposals pouring out of the Kremlin must be examined carefully. As has been shown, many Soviet proposals are serious, but many others have mainly propaganda purposes. The Soviet Union never actually expected the United States to trade its bases in Vietnam for the US ones in the Philippines, but Gorbachev's Krasnoyarsk initiative in 1988 nevertheless scored political points. The Soviet Union argues that talks should be held on naval arms control, particularly in Northeast Asia, yet it knows that the United States, and particularly its navy, is not inclined to reach agreement as long as it has the Soviet navy contained. Arms control proposals must be manifestly negotiable.[191]

The more specific the arms control proposal and the fewer the number of states involved, the more likely the proposal will be taken seriously. Proposals for prior notification of major manoeuvres are possible, but exchange of observers and delineation of zones of operation seem too complex to implement except on a bilateral basis.[192] Bilateral agreements, whether between China and the Soviet Union, or between the two superpowers, seem more fruitful. Crisis management in the Gulf war in 1988, and consultation between Soviet and US defence ministers, even on naval affairs, suggests that progress is possible.[193]

A major part of the problem, even in discussing narrow agreements, is the distinctive and forward deployment of the US naval presence in the Pacific. As in Europe, the United States would have to pull back farthest and would suffer particularly because of its greater reliance on naval forces. As an East Asian power, the Soviet Union is concerned with the protection of its immediate territory, while the United States is merely concerned with defending allies when it sends its ships to the western Pacific. Furthermore, the Soviet Union can urge specific types of arms control that limit so-called offensive naval systems and can complain that certain configurations of US forces appear more offensive as part of Washington's 'horizontal escalation' maritime strategy. Emphasizing naval arms control is a logical step for the Soviet Union if it is interested in removing the United States as a military factor in East Asia. Naval arms control is also a specific tactic for driving a wedge between the United States and its distant Pacific allies.

Thus, there remain important reasons why arms control will be difficult to achieve and will probably not follow the grandiose plans suggested following the Gorbachev initiatives at Vladivostok and Krasnoyarsk. A more fruitful route in the Pacific has been narrower, more pragmatic tacit arms control under circumstances in which both sides have relatively similar forces and strategic problems. Confidence-building measures have been especially useful and are likely to be a feature of further agreements, if they should be reached, with China, Japan and even Korea and Indochina.

In the final analysis, two prospects appear most promising on the Pacific arms control agenda—informal rather than formal accords, and confidence building rather than more complex and precise measures. The process of arms control is clearly useful to Pacific states as long as it is less legalistic and formal than in Europe. Arms control seems like a sensible strategy for coping with the inherent change and uncertainty in the region's conflicts. Flexible arms control based on informal self-restraint seems to be the hallmark of Pacific arms control. From the Soviet point of view, such an arms control strategy has its drawbacks. If their primary aim is to achieve symbolic agreements, they will fail because grandiose formal agreements are unlikely to be achievable or useful. Yet the recent Soviet stress on tacit, and smaller-scale agreements do suggest that new, and much more realistic, thinking on Pacific arms control is taking place.

Soviet Pacific security

The Soviet Union has been a superpower in the European and Atlantic worlds, but it looks increasingly less like one at both ends of Eurasia. The Soviet Union involved itself again in Pacific security issues after the defeat of Japan in 1945. When wars proliferated in East Asia and because Japan and China were initially weak, the Soviet Union seemed to have a secure position as an influential military superpower in the Pacific. But since the mid-1970s, and despite the growth in some of its forces, the Soviet Union has been losing its ability to use military power as an effective instrument of policy in the Pacific.

The causes of the decline of Soviet power are myriad. First, the diminishing number of conflicts in the region provided fewer opportunities for states to depend on the Soviet Union. Second, the emergence of a successful Japan and a group of NICs, all under the US security umbrella, meant the US burden of supporting allies was eased. When the Vietnam war ended in 1975, the US relative position looked much stronger. Third, and probably most important, China split with the Soviet Union and forced it to increase its forces in the region drastically. The Soviet defence burden was vast and apparently open-ended, not balanced by the emergence of Vietnam as a closer Soviet ally.

Yet the trends since the 1950s have not been all bad for the Soviet Union. First, the risks of superpower crises getting out of hand were controlled in the Pacific before they were in any other region except Europe. Second, the Soviet Union helped establish a number of like-minded communist regimes in 1975. Third, China was moving towards a more independent foreign policy by the 1980s and was thus less antagonistic to the Soviet Union. Finally, the Soviet Union grew more realistic about its effective military reach and by the late 1980s was cutting back its long-range military operations and focusing on the essentials of its Pacific security.

The Soviet security perspective remains overwhelmingly focused on the northwest Pacific. The primary interest is, of course, the defence of Soviet home territory. The two greatest threats to this security are China and Japan. Optimistic Soviet planners in the 1980s could point to detente with China and the United States, as well as to Japanese foreign policy more independent of US influence and support, as evidence of an improving Soviet security position. They could add that conflict in Korea is more under control than ever before and that nearly every other hot conflict is cooling or has ended. The Soviet fleet is now able to operate out of Vietnamese bases, and Soviet influence is spreading in the southern Pacific. Even Soviet arms control proposals are being taken more seriously than ever before and the new Gorbachev policies are projecting a new Soviet image in the Pacific.

More pessimistic Soviet planners could point to the remaining problems in relations with China and the United States and to the fear of a remilitarized Japan. They could note the decline of military influence as Soviet weapons were no longer needed in active wars. They could also indicate concern about the strength of US allies and about the poor economic condition of the Soviet Union's friends.

The arguments of both the optimists and pessimists rest on solid ground. The relative correctness of each argument depends on the new policies pursued in defence of Soviet Pacific security. There are increasing signs that the Soviet Union recognizes the need to make the best of the realities of Pacific politics. Regional diversity ensures that any calculation of security must remain uncertain, but also that a threatening coalition will probably not be created. By late 1989 even the European theatre seemed to be evolving in a similar direction of complex multipolarity. Thus, if arms control is to serve as an instrument of Soviet security policy, the emphases must be on the narrow possibilities and on the controlling of specific conflicts. A region-wide approach is less fruitful.

Yet the challenge to Soviet security—more broadly defined than just military matters—remains acute. If the Soviet Union really does feel more secure in a limited role, acting less like a military superpower, then can it ever regain full superpower status in the Pacific? What is taking place is the normalization, so to speak, of the Soviet Union in the Pacific. The decline of both superpowers in military terms means they are becoming more normal-size actors in a complex balance of power. As the balance of power is more often measured in economic terms in the Pacific, the Soviet Union must make a rapid success of its domestic reforms in order to return to the Pacific as a useful partner rather than as a threatening adversary. The transformation is difficult. However, no matter how quickly it is achieved, by the twenty-first century the Soviet Union will probably be a less important, or threatening, power in calculations of Pacific security.

6

The Economic Dimension

The Soviet Union is hardly an economic powerhouse in the Pacific. The 3.2 percent of total trade within the Pacific that it achieved in 1980 had risen to 3.8 percent in 1988—a level between that of Thailand and Canada, among the lowest ranking of the top 15 Pacific trading nations.[1] China's, and even Hong Kong's, share of Pacific trade was three times larger. France was a more important trading partner for Pacific states than the Soviet Union. On a per capita basis of the population in the Soviet Union's Pacific region, the Soviet Union moves up the list to tenth place among Pacific traders. Yet its total trade within the entire region is only slightly larger than Soviet-Czech trade.

This not insignificant, but nevertheless disappointing, Soviet standing in the Pacific economy masks more subtle features of the Soviet role in the Pacific. Soviet trade has been concentrated on a small number of partners. There have only been a few major changes in these patterns of trade, and Soviet trade with the non-communist Pacific is not much different from the low levels of Soviet trade with other non-communist states around the world. Thus, the problems with the Soviet foreign trade position in the Pacific are not necessarily unusual when viewed in the context of overall Soviet trade policy.

However, as the Soviet economy undergoes major reforms, the potential for change in the Soviet position in the Pacific is great. China, the other large socialist economy in the region, has shown that ideology need not restrict a socialist country's integration with the booming Pacific economy. As the wider Pacific economy undergoes so many major changes, the Soviet Union faces greater challenges but also greater opportunities than ever before. Whether the Soviet Union will meet the challenge depends largely on the progress of domestic reforms. The rapidly evolving Pacific and global economies themselves have played an important role in stimulating Soviet domestic reforms.

The Soviet Union and the Pacific economy

A broad survey of previous patterns of Soviet trade with the Pacific reveals a number of basic features. First, the past 25 years have shown a remarkable consistency in the percentage of Soviet trade with the states of the Pacific. Since 1968 imports and exports have each hovered in the region of 5 to 10 percent. By 1988, the Pacific was the destination for 9.1 percent of Soviet exports and the source of 7.3 percent of Soviet imports, figures that have recently climbed to their highest levels in 20 years. Yet this represents a sharp drop from the 1950s levels, when as much as a quarter of Soviet trade was done with Pacific states. More recently, less than a quarter of Soviet exports to Pacific states is actually generated in the Soviet Far East.[2]

The cause of the sharp drop in trade is obvious—the Sino-Soviet split. China formerly took more than 75 percent of Soviet Pacific trade, but after hitting a bottom of between 2 and 4 percent, China has climbed back up to between 15 and 20 percent in the late 1980s. In 1988, 16.3 percent of Soviet exports to the Pacific went to China

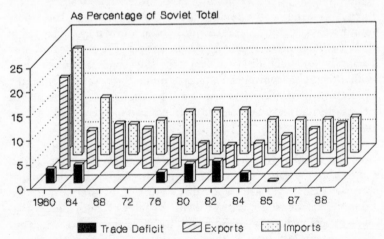

Figure 6.1   USSR Trade with the Pacific: 1960–1988
Sources: UN and IMF trade statistics.

and 17 percent of Soviet imports from the region came from China. However, except for China, Soviet Pacific trade policy has had remarkable continuity. Although a small deficit has sometimes been recorded in trade in the past 25 years, it has never surpassed 5 percent of trade.

Second, the Soviet Union has shown a distinctive pattern in the types of goods it has traded with the Pacific. As a primary producer of raw materials, it has followed the Canadian and Australian pattern. Industrial products have been imported more than they have been exported, especially after the break with China closed the one major outlet for Soviet industrial goods.

Third, Soviet trade has been dominated by a few major partners. China's leading role has already been noted. Japan accounted for nearly 50 percent of Soviet Pacific trade in the mid-1970s, but Soviet exports have fallen off since then. Vietnam has consistently provided about 5 percent of Soviet Pacific imports but taken 10 to 15 percent of exports. By the 1980s, Vietnam was taking a quarter of Soviet exports to the region, more than any other Pacific state. Mongolia provided a slightly higher percentage of Soviet Pacific imports and took about a quarter of Soviet exports during the 1980s. In 1988, Mongolia ranked fifth behind China, Japan, North Korea and Vietnam among the Soviet Union's trade partners. North Korea is

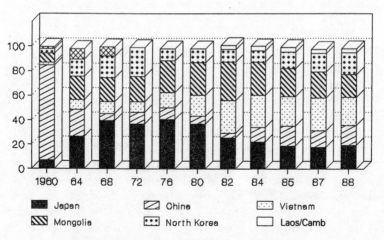

Figure 6.2 Soviet Pacific Exports: 1960–1988
Sources: UN and IMF trade statistics.

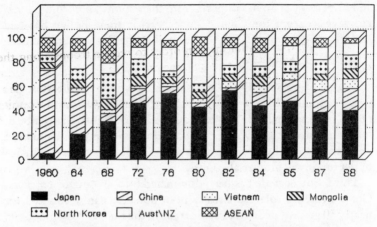

Figure 6.3   Soviet Pacific Imports: 1960–1988
Sources: UN and IMF trade statistics.

the only other significant socialist trading partner. It exported more to the Soviet Union than did any other socialist state after the Sino-Soviet split, but in the mid-1980s it surrendered top ranking once again to China. North Korean imports from the Soviet Union have mostly been around 10–15 percent of the Soviet total. The two smaller communist states of the Pacific, Laos and Cambodia, accounted for only about 1 percent of total Soviet trade in the Pacific, even in the late 1980s.

Among capitalist trading partners, few reached above 5 percent of Soviet total exports. Only Australia and Malaysia were major partners, each accounting for up to 20 percent of Soviet Pacific imports when trade relations were at their peak. By the 1980s, Australia accounted for about 10 percent of Soviet imports and Malaysia fell to below 5 percent.

Comparisons to patterns of Soviet trade in Europe are revealing. In the period of close Sino-Soviet relations, Soviet trade with the non-communist Pacific accounted for a much smaller percentage of Soviet Pacific trade than did trade with non-communist Europe did as a percentage of Soviet trade with Europe. But following the Sino-Soviet split, Soviet trade with parts of the non-communist Pacific rose in relative importance. Japan, as the largest non-communist partner, dominated Soviet trade (especially Soviet imports). Although the Soviet Union never accounted for more than 5 percent of either

Japanese or Australian exports, these figures were roughly comparable to the role played by the Soviet Union in West European trade. In Europe, trade with the Soviet Union tended to be more balanced, but still it never constituted more than 3 percent of trade for any of the big four West European economies (West Germany, France, UK, Italy). Thus, there might be some potential in terms of Soviet exports to the developed capitalist Pacific, but in general, the pattern of trade was not much different from that between the Soviet Union and capitalist Europe.

When China's trade with the Soviet Union declined, the other socialist states were unable to take up the slack. Unlike the East Europeans, the Soviet allies in the Pacific were mostly poor peasant economies. Foreign trade was less important for their economies and there was less tradition of trade with the Soviet Union. Thus, the socialist component of Soviet Pacific trade relations remained underdeveloped.

The remaining non-communist developing economies in the Pacific have always been minor partners for the Soviet Union. Malaysian exports to the Soviet Union were about the paltry level of Algerian exports to the Soviet Union, as indeed Singapore's were akin to those of Morocco. Thus, there may have been some room for improvement in Soviet trade with ASEAN and especially with the NICs, but the pattern in the Pacific was broadly in line with that of Soviet trade generally.

Compared with other states in the Pacific, the Soviet Union's trade pattern is distinctive. However, the value and direction of trade strongly resembles that of China before its domestic reforms and its opening up to the international capitalist economy. In the 1960s, the only major difference in Soviet and Chinese trade patterns was that China also traded with Hong Kong. As the Chinese reforms gathered pace in the early 1980s, however, China emerged as a more important trading partner for a number of Pacific economies.

Apart from Sino-Soviet trade, which rose in the mid-1980s, Chinese trade with all socialist economies in the Pacific declined. In contrast, Chinese trade with the capitalist Pacific moved strongly upward. By the mid-1980s, Japan was doing more than twice as much trade with China than with the Soviet Union. China also pulled ahead in trade relations with Australia, New Zealand and ASEAN. In the latter case, China was able to export to these states while the Soviet Union remained virtually unable to do so.

Nevertheless, outside of the western and southern Pacific, China remained just as insignificant a trade partner as it—and the Soviet Union—had always been. The United States and Canada did roughly the same amount of trade with both the Soviet Union and China as they had done in the past decade. China accounted for less than 1 percent of West European trade while the Soviet Union accounted for between 1 and 2 percent. In sum, China showed it was possible to improve the international trading position of a state-socialist regime in the Pacific, but it required wide-ranging economic reforms. Indeed, China also showed that when those reforms stall, the international image of a socialist state can suffer.

In sum, at least until the Gorbachev era, Soviet foreign trade in the Pacific was relatively stable, but with some important scope for change. Clearly, a more detailed assessment of bilateral relationships is required. In order of priority for the Soviet Union, the main trade partners have been China, Japan, the socialist Pacific and finally the non-socialist Pacific.

The China trade

Trade between the Soviet Union and China is unique because of the combination of three main features. First, the two countries are neighbours, and as between the United States and Canada, whose vast border has few topographical features to mark it, some trade merely ignores the unreality of the political frontier. Towns that have been traditional trade partners resent artificial frontiers. Populations accustomed to roaming across the open spaces provide some basis for natural trade.

Second, China and the Soviet Union can be seen as complementary economies. China is a poor peasant economy that specializes in the export of light industrial goods. The Soviet economy is much more industrialized, and the Soviet Far East has huge stores of raw materials for export. China also has vast reserves of some raw materials, but few are available for export because of the needs of its much larger population. The Soviet market in the Far East is one fiftieth the size of that of China, but its per capita GNP is seven times higher.

Third, China and the Soviet Union have some similarities in an ideology and system of government. In broad terms, they are both still state-socialist regimes. To be sure, real differences exist, chiefly in the peasant base of the Chinese revolution. The process of reform in each state has been different in pace and even direction. Soviet reforms have emphasized the interconnections of political and economic reforms, whereas the Chinese, most notably in June 1989, made it clear they wanted economic reform without its political equivalent. However, most Soviet reformers remain skeptical that China can ignore the need for political reform.

Both states still direct important sectors of their economy from the centre through variants of a central planning authority. Neither state has a convertible currency and therefore the planning bodies have a preference for 'planned' or barter trade. Unlike in the international capitalist economy, the two great socialist powers favour planned trade that avoids the risks of foreign indebtedness and reliance on the fluctuating fortunes of the international market economy. Even though both China and the Soviet Union have begun reforms that might close the gap between their systems and that of the international capitalist economy, the differences are still much greater than those that divide the Soviet and Chinese systems. These features of Sino-Soviet economic relations have helped shape the most distinctive and variable trade relationship in the Pacific.

Three phases can be identified in Sino-Soviet economic relations. The first is the decade from 1950, often known as the honeymoon. After the signing of the February 1950 Treaty of Friendship, Alliance and Mutual Assistance, the Soviet Union became heavily involved in assisting the new communist regime in China. The Soviet Union itself was not in a position to offer vast sums of money, given its own tasks of postwar recovery, but it did make an effort to help China. The extent of this assistance was the focus of much recrimination when Sino-Soviet relations later deteriorated.[3]

China had hoped for more aid, was disappointed with the low level of credit, and was upset that much of the aid had to be paid back when relations deteriorated.[4] However, it is also true that only the Soviet Union was willing to assist China and, given the nature of Chinese ideology and policy at the time, Beijing had cut itself off from Western assistance and trade. Western academics later regretted this isolation, but the greatest share of responsibility for the changes in policy lies with the Chinese themselves.

Sino-Soviet relations under Khrushchev initially showed improvement as compared with the Stalin period. In 1954, Khrushchev visited China, and the scale of aid and trade was sharply increased. Between 1950 and 1957 the Soviet Union provided 8.1 billion roubles of assistance for the construction of 211 projects. By 1967, the total number of projects completed was 291, worth 20 billion roubles. Khrushchev ordered Soviet advisers to return home in the summer of 1960 in an apparent attempt to show China exactly how much it needed Soviet assistance. The Soviets claim that 198 projects were completed by them, whereas some Western estimates put the number as low as 130. According to the Soviet Union, total credits to China were $2 billion, but some Western estimates put the figure at closer to $3 billion. All credit had been repaid by 1965.[5]

This period in Sino-Soviet relations has been reassessed in the Gorbachev era. Some Soviet sources suggest Khrushchev was too hasty in withdrawing Soviet advisers, not to mention too erratic in his handling of foreign policy generally, but the overall Soviet consensus is still that China is more to blame for the problems that developed.[6] Furthermore, the 1950s was a time of reconstruction in the Soviet Union, and so even the limited degree of aid that the Soviet Union granted to China was undoubtedly a sacrifice that suggested serious Soviet concern with the fate of China. It was certainly a change from the 1945–9 Soviet treatment of China, when some plants and machinery in northeast China were returned to the Soviet Union to help rebuild Soviet industry.

The period of Soviet assistance to China in the 1950s is generally known as the 'Soviet model period' and, even after reassessment by historians, it remains an accurate description. In most spheres of Chinese life, the Soviet Union provided guidance for establishing a new communist regime—from industry to education and from the arts to the armed forces. The only parallel in Pacific economic relations was the far-reaching US assistance to Japan a little earlier in the postwar period of reconstruction.

The causes of the split in Sino-Soviet relations are well known.[7] Its basic features were Chinese dissatisfaction with the Soviet model and the search for a more specifically Chinese version of communism. The Soviet emphasis on heavy industry, rather than on light industry or agriculture, was unsuited to China. The Chinese revolution had been made by proud people with a great heritage of statecraft. Unlike many of the East European regimes then being shaped by Moscow, the Chinese communists had their own revolutionary experience.

When Mao Zedong led his communist comrades towards the Great Leap Forward in the late 1950s and the abandonment of the Soviet model, Sino-Soviet relations deteriorated.[8] Sino-Soviet trade collapsed along with political relations. The absurdly optimistic policies of the Great Leap, combined with natural disasters and the withdrawal of Soviet advisers in 1960, led to the famines of 1960–61. As many as 20 to 30 million Chinese died, by far the largest single human catastrophe of the postwar world.

During the honeymoon, Sino-Soviet trade had reached remarkable levels. China accounted for three-quarters of Soviet trade with the Pacific and the Soviet bloc accounted for nearly as much of total Chinese trade. Yet in the second phase from 1960 to 1982, Sino-Soviet trade tumbled to derisible levels; in 1970 China accounted for less than 3 percent of Soviet Pacific imports or exports.

The main cause of these changes can be clearly traced to the domestic politics of China and the Soviet Union. As the Chinese drifted into the cultural revolution in 1965–9, a main target of the campaign was Soviet-style revisionism. Party-to-party ties between China and the Soviet Union were severed in March 1966, the most drastic action available to warring communist comrades.

The third phase, the recovery of Sino-Soviet economic relations in the early 1980s, was one of the earliest products of communist detente.[9] Meanwhile, in the intervening 20 years, India, and to some extent Vietnam, had taken China's place in the Soviet pattern of trade with developing states. China had also found new trade partners and most notably had opened its door to Western aid and trade. But for a

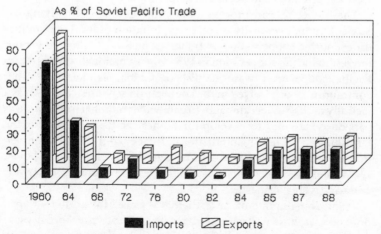

Figure 6.4   Trade with China: 1960–1988
Sources: UN and IMF trade statistics.

potent mix of political and economic reasons, both great communist powers eventually perceived a need to improve their economic relations.

From the Soviet point of view, trade with China could help provide consumer goods and food for its isolated Pacific territory. Soviet development of the region had failed to materialize to the extent planned, and even attempts to involve Japanese investment had not been successful.[10] The vast potential locked up in Soviet Asia was clear to see, but the long-term Soviet problem remained how to exploit that potential given the obviously inhospitable conditions in much of the region.[11]

As Sino-Soviet relations improved, the Soviet Union began to learn about the Chinese reforms of socialism, which included special economic zones for foreign production and the widespread use of joint ventures to acquire foreign technology and boost exports. Although the Soviet Union had been discussing the possibility of establishing some special economic zones of its own, the entire process of reform of the Soviet economy was taking longer than many officials first expected. If the idea was to stress the more independent development of the Soviet Far East, there was simply not a large amount of funds from within the Soviet Union available to develop the region. The success of plans to entice foreign investment depended on the wider reforms in the Soviet economy, few of which were expected to be in operation before the early 1990s.

The Soviet reform process looked like gradually involving the Soviet Union, eventually, in more exploitation of local possibilities for economic cooperation and trade.[12] The Soviets showed greater interest in Pacific cooperation in 1988 when a national committee on Pacific cooperation was established. China, as the only other communist state involved in the cooperation schemes, was seen as a tacit ally in the Soviet campaign to gain wider regional recognition as part of the attempt to develop the Soviet Far East. Of course, the tarnishing of China's international image after the Tiananmen massacre meant that China had become less useful for the Soviet Union and the Soviet Union's own image as a serious reformer was comparatively enhanced.

From China's point of view, there was a need for a different open door besides those ajar to Western countries. Western technology was superb but expensive and difficult to use in a developing country with insufficient infrastructure to support it. Western aid came with loans that could be difficult to finance. Western trade required foreign currency and the problem of finding suitable goods to export to highly developed Western markets. Hence, the attraction of barter and balanced trade with a neighbour that would provide somewhat less sophisticated technology. As Sino-Soviet relations were normalized in 1989, contacts between the planning authorities of the two states grew ever closer.[13]

In 1985 a major five-year trade agreement provided for the return of Soviet advisers to help refurbish 17 old Soviet plants and to build 7 new ones. Cross-border trade increased and overall trade boomed.[14] The value of Sino-Soviet trade climbed steadily in the 1980s. By 1986 it totaled $2.7 billion, constituting 4 percent of Chinese exports and 3 percent of imports. The Soviet Union was China's fifth largest trading partner and by far its largest trade partner in the communist world. Although this trade was still only about 1 percent of total Soviet foreign trade, China had become the Soviet Union's second largest trading partner in the Pacific, after Japan (if the United States and Canada are treated as Atlantic partners). China was also the Soviet Union's second largest partner in the communist developing world (after Cuba), having surpassed Vietnam in 1983. Soviet dual-use technology sales to China are increasing (free of Cocom restrictions) and include aircraft.[15]

Although trade stagnated in 1987 and China slipped back in the Soviet league table, the long-term recovery trend as seen in the 1988 trade figures still suggests that China had regained its place as the key to Soviet economic relations in the Pacific.[16] In 1988, China accounted for 16.3 percent of total Soviet exports to the Pacific and 17.6 percent of Soviet imports from the region. The trade protocol for 1989 envisages bilateral trade to rise by 17 percent. Machinery and equipment will account for 50 percent of Soviet exports to China.[17] For the first time in 30 years, the Soviet Union will provide development loans to China, most notably including a loan for $125 million to renovate the Soviet-built Baotou Iron and Steel Works.[18]

The problems in 1987 were in large measure due to the reform process in both countries. Reforms caused major disruptions, and ossified bureaucracies were slow to adapt, primarily on the Soviet side. Yet Chinese reports suggest that transport problems on their side of the frontier might have been the most pressing problem.[19] As the two great communist states struggled with the problem of how to reform massive, centrally planned socialist economies, they at least recognized the important ties that bound the two economies and societies. Chinese reforms had already been studied and, in part, incorporated into the Gorbachev reforms. Each communist state, to some extent, held up the other as a 'mirror to socialism' and both were clearly fascinated with each other's experience in reform. [20]

The struggles between rapid and slow reformers, central planners and decentralizers, were common to both states. Soviet and Chinese commentaries on each other's economies were frank but positive. They also reflected internal debates within each country on the best path to reform and further reinforced the link that politicians on both sides perceived between China and the Soviet Union. [21] When the Chinese reforms ran out of steam in the autumn of 1988 and exploded in June 1989, Soviet commentators were distressed that the cause of reform had been damaged.

At least in the early months after the Tiananmen massacre, there did not appear to be any serious change in the state of Sino–Soviet trade. One of the more distinctive, and, from the Soviet point of view, optimistic features of Sino–Soviet trade was the potential for developing closer links at the local level. By 1988, border trade had reached the value of 700 million Swiss francs (the currency in which trade was denominated), or 18 percent of total Sino–Soviet trade. The total trade between neighbouring Chinese provinces and Soviet border regions was 1,300 million Swiss francs, or about one-third of total Sino–Soviet trade. By early 1989, 14 trading posts had been opened in the Soviet Union to cope with the boom in local trade. This sharp rise from the single-digit percentages of previous years was seen as the start of a major shift to more local trade. [22]

The flood of details about local trade grows daily and includes the export of more than 10,000 Chinese workers to the Soviet Far East to staff factories and farms. Eighteen of the 25 labour contracts signed since 1986 were agreed in the second half of 1988 alone, with a total value of $100 million. Soviet and Chinese media carried a steady stream of stories explaining how the number of contracted workers was growing at a rapid rate and would continue to do so well into the 1990s. [23] Although the retrenchment in Chinese reforms in 1989 suggested such regional deals were less likely to prosper, it was certainly politically safer for the Chinese to pursue their Soviet contacts than those with the West. Indeed, it could be argued that the crackdown in China made an expansion of Sino–Soviet regional links even more likely.

The Soviet Union pays for the workers in timber, steel, fertilizer, pianos and refrigerators.[24] The Soviet Union also sells electric power as well as machinery to China. The two sides have agreed to develop their common river border jointly and to open local airline connections. The Soviet Union is helping to complete a new Chinese railway in Xinjiang to extend the range of contacts. Visa restrictions have been lifted for travel from China to the Soviet Union, and even radio broadcast agreements are being signed by local authorities. Joint ventures in the Soviet Far East include food production, the hotel business and restaurants.[25]

By the mid-1980s, Sino-Soviet economic relations had clearly become closer than at any point since the economic split in 1960.[26] China was even taking a greater interest in the soon-to-be-abandoned Comecon, and in late 1988 attended (as an observer) its first meeting since the 1960s.[27] However, the local and regional trade was probably of greater interest to both sides. China was especially interested in developing local trade in its noftheastern territory as a way of catching up with other parts of China that had greater opportunities to expand foreign trade with the West. Certainly there was growing evidence of expertise in Chinese territory bordering the Soviet Union that recognized the potential for an interlocking regional economy.[28] Heilongjiang's largest trade partner in 1985 was the Soviet Union (36.4 percent), and by 1988 the contracted trade was worth nearly $500 million and increasing. Shenyang, one of the largest cities in China's northeast, counted the Soviet Union among its top three export partners.[29]

From the Soviet point of view, the next step was to develop more complex regional links between China, Korea and even Japan. Soviet officials talk of creating a 'Far Eastern Hong Kong' in Northeast Asia as these multilateral links develop.[30] Yet before such grandiose hopes can be realized, Soviet domestic reforms must be implemented—not to mention improved trade relations with other partners in the Pacific.

The dream of Japan

Unlike the pre-1989 communist states of Europe, the two largest ones in the Pacific, China and the Soviet Union, both trade most heavily with the non-communist world. Soviet trade is heavily skewed towards Japan, which accounted for nearly twice as much Soviet trade as did China in 1988. Although this trade with Japan constitutes 40 percent of Soviet imports from the Pacific, by 1988 only 19 percent of Soviet exports to the Pacific were going to Japan. Soviet-Japanese trade had reached its height—with Japan accounting for 50 percent of Soviet Pacific imports and exports—in the 1970s, when trade with Japan was growing and trade with China was stagnant.

Soviet-Japanese trade, like Soviet-Chinese trade, also has some distinctive features. Japan is, of course, a neighbour of the Soviet Union, and the only one in the Pacific that is a developed society, hungry for resources and able to provide modern technology. This is said to provide a perfect match of economic complementarity between these two economies. Japan, however, has a large population and a dynamic economy that threaten Soviet ideology. The Japanese challenge to the Soviet Union has grown as the Soviet economy has stagnated and Japan's economy has become the world's second largest. Japan has thus challenged the Soviet claim to superpower status and thereby has encouraged the Soviet Union to rethink its economic strategy and to choose the path of reform.[31] Unlike the Chinese challenge of reform, the Japanese challenge came from the rival economic ideology of capitalism.

The 1957 Soviet-Japanese trade agreement led to a rapid increase in trade in the late 1950s and early 1960s.[32] The Japanese wanted to exploit the natural resources of Siberia in order to lessen the risks of Japanese vulnerability to blockade. Even though the Soviet Union

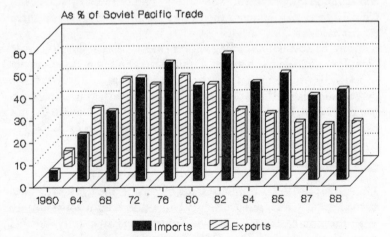

Figure 6.5   Trade with Japan: 1960–1988
Sources: UN and IMF trade statistics.

espoused a hostile ideology, Japan has always shown itself more pragmatic in its trade dealings, in keeping with its priority of an economics-led foreign policy.

The Soviet strategy, as in trade with Western Europe, was to take advantage of Western technology and to some extent to build political ties that would eventually undermine US alliances on either side of the Soviet Union. In periods of superpower detente, Soviet trade with Japan increased and the prospects for greater Japanese investment in Siberia became possible. Grandiose plans for the exploitation of Siberian resources with Japanese technology were formulated and then abandoned when the economic and political problems mounted. In history and relations with the Soviet Union, Japan was not different from other US allies in Western Europe. Japanese-Soviet trade fell off more sharply than did Soviet-West European trade when superpower relations were cool, but it is inaccurate to suggest (as Japanese officials often do) that economic problems prevent any serious levels of trade with the Soviet Union. Even in the 1980s, Japan still sent 2 percent of its exports to the Soviet Union and took 1 percent of its imports in return. These percentages are higher than those for UK-Soviet trade, but lower than that for Soviet-West German or Soviet-Italian trade. The kinds of problems in Soviet-Japanese economic relations are not much different from those in Soviet-West European relations.

Although Japan was formally bound by Cocom regulations restricting East-West trade, the Soviet Union regularly found Japan to be the best conduit for such sensitive technology as could be had. As Japan became a leader in technological innovation rather than merely a skilled copier of Western technology, the attractions of dealing with Japan naturally grew. Yet by 1977 the growth in trade had slowed sharply and stagnated until 1988.

The problems in Soviet-Japanese trade are often explained by Japanese as being basically more economic than political. An unreformed Soviet Union lacked the skills and capital to exploit its own resources. The conditions in the Soviet Far East are harsh, and Soviet ports are frozen at the peak times of Japanese demand for Soviet resources. The drop in oil prices in the 1980s reduced the attractiveness of Soviet resources and reduced the amount of hard currency the Soviet Union had for purchasing foreign goods. The absence of local initiative made it difficult to strike deals, and Japanese industry went elsewhere (especially to Australia) in search of long-term contracts for raw materials.[33]

Yet, as has been suggested, the pattern of Soviet-Japanese trade is not very different from that between the Soviet Union and the West Europeans. Japan has also been willing to become more closely involved with the Chinese and poorer ASEAN states, where the economic conditions are often considerably worse than in the Soviet Union. Japanese reluctance to deal with the Soviet Union is in part largely due to cultural antipathy and political problems related to the Northern Territories dispute.

Whatever the case, by the last part of the 1980s, the level of Soviet-Japanese trade, despite the negative publicity, was normal for that between a developed Western country and the Soviet Union. Indeed, as in most trading relations between the Soviet Union and the West, the Gorbachev initiatives in the late 1980s and the prospects for reform and development in the Soviet Far East have increased speculation that Soviet-Japanese cooperation will be expanded. Japan's need for resources in the long term is not diminished, and tensions in the Persian gulf suggest how fragile the Japanese economy might be without resources closer to home. The Soviet Union has also revised its assessment of the Japanese economy, and has begun lavishing praise on Japan's new ideas in economics and its increased international role.[34] As the Soviet Union debated the nature of a socialist economy in the new world of global economic interdependence, some Soviet officials began looking closely at the Japanese economic system. Japanese-style trading houses were attractive to some in the Soviet Union as a way of coping with the problems of 'uncontrolled decentralization' that other Soviet reformers apparently supported.[35]

The Soviet Union understood that if it was to become accepted into plans for Pacific cooperation, it would have to prove its good intentions to Japan above all. By 1988, Japan seemed to be more sympathetic to the Soviet case. Yet conditions for Soviet-Japanese cooperation have changed in important ways since the 1970s. The fall in oil prices and the rise of the yen have made the Soviet Union and Japan less attractive to each other.[36]

No doubt the Soviets desire to encourage Japanese independence from—and disagreements with—the United States, although the Soviet Union must recognize that it cannot serve as an alternative for the United States in Japanese foreign economic relations. Yet Moscow is alway aware that Japan and the United States have a highly important but unstable trade relationship of their own. As a result, the United States has been known to use Cocom regulations in order to block

Japanese firms from gaining advantages in the Soviet marketplace. The latest case, in early 1989, concerned the possible export of high-definition television technology and precision metal-forming technology in video recorders.[37] Because the trade ties to the United States are so much more important to Japan than are those with the Soviet Union, Japanese firms tend to back down when the United States particularly objects to such practices. As a result, Japanese firms are then driven to seek multilateral joint ventures with the Soviet Union in order to deflect some of the attention, while still making profits.

Serious questions remain, even for many Soviet specialists, about how much closer Soviet-Japanese economic relations are likely to get in the short term.[38] Even at the best of times in the 1970s, Soviet-Japanese trade constituted about 2 percent of Japanese trade (about 3 percent in the mid-1960s, but then overall Japanese trade totals were lower). Without major reform in the Soviet foreign trade structure, there is little reason to believe that in the medium term, Japan, like West Germany, can expand its trade with the Soviet Union much beyond 3 percent of total Japanese trade. Despite the discussion in the Soviet Union about complementarity with Japan, this is a much more limited kind of complementarity than in the case of cooperation within the European community. It should also be pointed out that many of the joint ventures between the Soviet Union and Japan concern the European part of the Soviet Union, and therefore the arguments about regional cooperation do not apply.[39]

Nevertheless, reform in communist systems can have a far-reaching impact. For example, Sino-Japanese trade soared past that of Soviet-Japanese trade in the early 1980s, when China opened up to the capitalist Pacific economy. China became Japan's third largest Pacific trade partner and Sino-Japanese trade was the fourth largest bilateral trade flow in the Pacific. Of course, there are major differences in the nature of the complementarity in Sino-Japanese and Soviet-Japanese relations, and the Chinese market is 50 times the size of that in the Soviet Far East. Nevertheless, given real reform, Soviet-Japanese economic relations, like Soviet-West European relations, can prosper.

Despite the absence of a positive political atmosphere in Soviet-Japanese relations in 1988—let alone an agreement on capital investment—Soviet-Japanese trade recovered from its early 1980s slump. In April 1989 a new think tank on trade with the Soviet Union and Eastern Europe was set up.[40] By the summer of 1989, there were clear signs that Soviet-Japanese trade was likely to develop. The long-awaited joint development project for oil and gas around Sakhalin appeared to be nearing finalization. This $4 billion project includes a small participation by Chevron Corporation of the United States, thereby helping to spread the political responsibilities, at least as perceived in Tokyo.[41]

In late November 1988 a major deal, worth up to $6 billion was signed by Mitsubishi, Mitsui and Chiyoda to work on a petro-chemical plant in Siberia.[42] There are more modest plans for developing deep-sea research and joint exploration of fishery resources. Even the waters around the disputed Northern Territories have been suggested as a possible area for cooperation in exploiting fishing resources.[43] It is a remarkable sign of the economic problems in the Soviet Union that they have been unable to earn much from the abundant fishing resources in the region. The lure of making some money may help the Soviet Union overcome its natural aversion to dealing with its great competitor in the international fishing business, Japan.

There are even more grandiose plans by Seizo Ohta, the so-called Armand Hammer of Japan, to develop a site at Kraskino, 50 km from the Chinese and Korean borders, as a site for multilateral processing of Soviet raw materials.[44] Moscow is even considering issuing its first yen bonds.[45] More imminently, Japanese firms are again negotiating with the Soviet Union about car manufacturing, although the Soviet Union wants a joint venture with Japanese finance and the Japanese want a simple technology transfer.[46]

Any such rapid expansion of trade will depend on the nature and speed of the reforms in the Soviet Union, and especially in the Soviet Far East. Joint ventures, arguments over the convertibility of the rouble and the basic bureaucratic nature of the Soviet system, are all pervasive problems limiting the scope of future cooperation.[47] Although Soviet-Japanese trade relations have made progress in 1988 despite these problems, they cannot go much further without more extensive reforms.

The Soviet Union and its socialist allies

The Soviet Union, if it is still to be seen as a socialist state, has nearly all its allies in East Asia. But the East Asians are allies of a very unique sort. The Indochinese states are poor, developing, peasant economies, and North Korea has a growing, but still young industrial base. All the socialist allies run a trade deficit with the Soviet Union, in contrast to the Soviet Union's always-balanced trade with China and Soviet trade deficits with the capitalist Pacific. Trade with socialist states is mostly planned through bilateral agreements, but most trade with the capitalist world has to be done through individual corporations. Clearly there are peculiarities about Soviet trade with the socialist world. But the most peculiar case must be that of the most complete ally of the Soviet Union, Mongolia.

Mongolia is heavily reliant on the Soviet economy and has been so ever since the communist regime came to power in 1921.[48] Mongolia, with its sparse population, remains on paper the richest Pacific socialist state, with a per capita GDP approaching half that of Taiwan's $5,000. More than half of Mongolian industry was established with Soviet aid, and Mongolia has received nearly a quarter of all Soviet aid to less developed countries in the 1955–83 period.[49] Some 80 percent of Mongolian trade is with the Soviet Union, but less than 1 percent of the total trade is strictly local trade.[50] From the Soviet point of view, Mongolia takes about 1 percent of total Soviet trade. Yet in the mid-1980s, as in past decades, that trade was overwhelmingly composed of Soviet exports. Mongolia took 18 percent of Soviet Pacific exports in 1988, ranking third among Soviet trade partners in the Pacific.

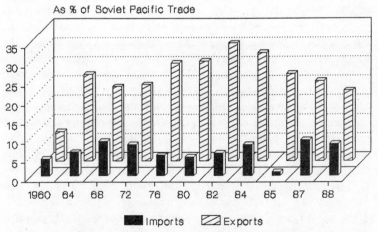

Figure 6.6   Trade with Mongolia: 1960–1988
Sources: UN and IMF trade statistics.

This enormously one-sided trade relationship makes Mongolia highly dependent on the Soviet Union to an extent unknown even in Eastern Europe. Given the small Mongolian population, the weakness of its export base and limited political options, it is unlikely that this relationship can be changed significantly. Although major reforms are now underway in the structure of Mongolian trading organizations, schemes for integration with the CMEA ultimately hinge on the question of whether anything will be salvaged of CMEA after the European revolution of 1989.[51] Mongolia might possibly allow some of its regions to establish their own contacts with parts of the Soviet Union as a means of economic reform, but this can hardly serve as a major solution to the Mongolian problem.[52]

Vietnam is the next largest recipient of Soviet assistance to Pacific states, taking nearly 10 percent of total Soviet economic aid disbursements in the 1955–83 period.[53] Unlike Mongolia, Vietnam once divided its trade more evenly between China and the Soviet Union. However, as relations with China deteriorated in the late 1970s, Vietnam also shifted to a Mongolia-type model in its foreign trade. Some trade with China continued through Hong Kong and Singapore (accounting for as much as a fifth of Vietnamese trade with these two entrepôts), but the vast majority was now with the Soviet Union and its allies in the CMEA. In 1986, 70 percent of the $800 million of Vietnamese exports were agricultural products and raw materials sent to the Soviet Union. Japan was the only significant non-communist trade partner ($280 million total trade in 1986), but under ASEAN pressure the limits to trade growth were clear.[54] Nevertheless, from the Soviet point of view, Vietnam was the largest single market for Soviet exports in the Pacific, taking nearly 27 percent in 1987 and 24 percent in 1988.

As a CMEA member since 1978, Vietnam benefited from Soviet aid, which by 1987 had reached $5 million per day. In 1987 the Soviet Union also began exerting sharper pressure on Vietnam to undertake economic reforms of its own so as to perk up the economy and lighten the burden on its allies.[55] The Soviet Union recognized that its aid to Vietnam was being wasted because of the lack of a proper economic base in Vietnam and the absence of reform.[56] Of equal importance for the Soviet Union was the fact that Vietnam stood in the way of a Sino-Soviet detente, in part because of Vietnam's occupation of Cambodia. Thus, the Soviet Union could enhance a number of its objectives at the same time by pushing Vietnam to reform its economy and to withdraw from Cambodia.

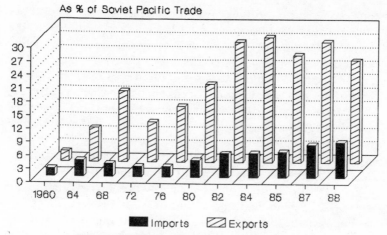

As % of Soviet Pacific Trade

■ Imports ▨ Exports

Figure 6.7 Trade with Vietnam: 1960–1988
Sources: UN and IMF trade statistics.

A special CPSU (Communist Party of the Soviet Union) Central Committee meeting was held in June 1987 to discuss the problem of economic relations with Vietnam. Although they agreed to a new plan that would increase Soviet aid, it was acknowledged that basic problems would remain for some time because of the difficulties of reform in both Vietnam and the Soviet Union. The new plan focused on greater integration and various joint ventures, but the slowness in reform was holding back the much needed wide-ranging changes.[57]

In contrast to Mongolia, however, Vietnam has a large population —it is the third most populous country in the communist world. To some extent like China, it has the potential and problems of a poor peasant economy. It can serve as a large market for Soviet exports— indeed its share of Soviet Pacific exports doubled in the 1980s to about one-quarter of the Soviet Union's Pacific total. Yet Vietnamese exports to the Soviet Union still constitute only about 8 percent of Soviet imports from the Pacific (1.3 percent of total Soviet trade) in 1988. The focus has been on the growing and processing of Vietnamese agricultural products and on the output of consumer goods.

Yet the parallels to China also suggest that the Chinese might see Vietnam as a competitor for Soviet foreign trade. For example, Soviet-Vietnamese operations to produce food for export to the Soviet Far East have experienced serious problems in handling perishable goods.[58] China's northeast is poised to help solve these food problems for the Soviet Far East and thereby cut Vietnam out of the market. Unfortunately for Vietnam, it is further from the Soviet Union, has an even less well developed export base and is politically less important than China is to the Soviet Union. As a CMEA member, Vietnam has some advantages in terms of how Soviet trade is planned and managed, but as the CMEA fades, the Vietnamese advantage may be slipping away. Thus, it is easy to see how Vietnam could import a great deal more from the Soviet Union, but it is more difficult to see why it might want to import the less advanced Soviet goods and how they could afford to do so without any huge improvement in Vietnam's export potential.

Yet there also are areas of potential growth in Soviet-Vietnamese trade. The fishing industry seems to be a primary focus for development. In 1989, in keeping with the new spirit of reform and pragmatic economic arrangements, a South Korean firm that constructs ships for the South Korean navy agreed to build ships for a joint Soviet-Vietnamese petroleum venture.[59] Soviet experience in the oil industry has already been vital for Vietnam's development of its offshore oil. The Soviet Union helped build Vietnam's first commercial oil refinery, which is already substantially cutting Vietnam's oil import bill.[60] The Soviet Union was the first to help exploit Vietnamese oil resources, and a joint venture in the White Tiger field began pumping the first oil in 1986. Oil, Vietnam's third largest export item, is being sent to Japan, France and Singapore. With Soviet encouragement, Vietnam has even opened a sea-trade link with South Korea,[61] and investment and trade may increase as the Soviet Union encourages its allies to branch out into the Pacific economy.

Vietnam has also found a ready, if sometimes uncomfortable, location for its surplus labour—it has sent thousands of workers to the Soviet Union. Some reports suggest that many Vietnamese have already been shifted to work in the Soviet Far East, processing raw materials or producing consumer goods that are of interest to Vietnam.[62] The Vietnamese, like the Chinese and Koreans, can play a crucial role in filling the shortage of labour in the Soviet Far East— one of the most basic problems limiting Soviet development of its Pacific territory.

North Korea still retains its balanced trading pattern with its communist neighbours. By the late 1980s, however, trade with the Soviet Union was worth three to four times North Korea's trade with China (the Soviet Union accounted for 40 percent of North Korea's trade turnover in 1987). In the decades before the 1970s, the trade had regularly been more balanced, but China's opening to the West meant a lower priority for North Korea. Unofficial Chinese trade with South Korea, valued by some at $3 billion in 1988, was considerably more than five times the total with the communist North.

The Soviet presence in North Korea was much less pervasive than in Mongolia, but economic ties still operated in the time-honoured fashion of coordinated central plans, project aid and close integration of specialists and technicians. The Soviet Union assisted in the construction of 70 industrial facilities that accounted for more than 25 percent of North Korean industrial output, 63 percent of generated electricity, 50 percent of its coal and petroleum products, and 33 percent of its steel production.[63]

Even the opening up of the North Korean economy to the Pacific market has been in part the result of pressure to do so from the Soviet Union at various times. For example, in the early 1970s, North Korea had been encouraged by the Soviet Union to open up to the rest of the Pacific and the world at large. But the huge problems in arranging investment, even by Japan, kept North Korea out of the Pacific pattern of trade. In the late 1980s, the Soviets have renewed pressure for reforms in North Korea.

Border trade constituted less than 1 percent of total Soviet-North Korean trade, but then the border itself is only 12 miles long. Yet North Koreans were also important to the prospects for developing the Soviet Far East because they provided up to 30,000 workers to undertake difficult tasks such as felling and processing timber.[64]

In the early 1970s, North Korea was the Soviet Union's second largest trading partner in the Pacific, providing 10 percent of Soviet Pacific imports and taking 23 percent of Soviet Pacific exports in 1972. But both figures fell by nearly half as the North Korean economy stagnated. By the mid-1980s, North Korea had slipped to fifth place among Soviet Pacific trade partners. By 1988 North Korea was back to fourth place, taking 17.2 percent of Soviet exports to the Pacific and providing 8 percent of Soviet imports from the region. However, Moscow's trade-related aid to North Korea dropped from $260 million in 1981 to $95 million in 1986.[65]

This pattern suggested that there was more potential for Soviet-North Korean trade. Yet most Soviet sources were clear about the deep-seated problems preventing a swift improvement in trade volume. A particularly outspoken Soviet analyst noted that North

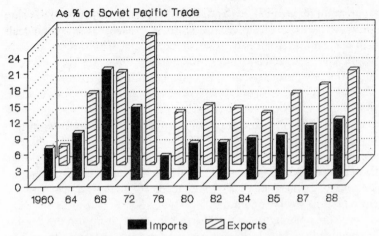

Figure 6.8   Trade with North Korea: 1960–1988
Sources: UN and IMF trade statistics.

Korea was not a suitable trade partner at a time when Soviet enterprises were moving towards more self-accounting procedures and therefore could choose their trade partners more carefully. Other problems stemmed from the failure of the North Koreans to make efficient use of Soviet products. More self-critically, Soviet analysts admitted that the kinds of cooperation were not always well suited to the North Korean economy, and many of the products supplied and produced were of yesterday's standards. Cooperation at the enterprise level had to be emphasized, as did food production and expanding the export industries.[66] In sum, there was little prospect for a rapid improvement in trade.

Yet some Soviet sources spoke of establishing joint ventures to process Soviet raw materials for export to North Korea. Even light industrial products such as furniture and clothing were seen as likely subjects for cooperation.[67] From the Soviet point of view, importing labour from its socialist allies was a quick way to solve the labour problem blocking exploitation of the Soviet Pacific territory. Yet, as with most such potential cooperation within the socialist world, improvement depended on changes in ally's domestic economic affairs.

A possible side door to economic reform in North Korea, and greater integration into the regional economy, was the possibility of multilateral economic cooperation that would include South Korea. In the spring of 1989, Soviet officials made much of the tentative agreement between North and South Korean enterprises to develop projects in the Soviet Far East and Siberia.[68] Moscow saw such deals as a way around the growing North Korean concern with its socialist allies who established economic relations with South Korea. Yet it was difficult to imagine that much would come of the multilateral cooperation involving the Soviet Union until there was a leadership change in North Korea and new thinking could be genuinely unleashed. For the time being, the only serious multilateral cooperation was likely to be between the region's socialist states; for example, the transport protocol in March 1989 that involved the four socialist states of Northeast Asia.[69]

As its two socialist neighbours reformed themselves, North Korea has also had to reform and possibly even to open up to the outside world once again. With booming growth in the South, the communist North is clearly falling behind its neighbours and the region, both materially and in terms of new ideas. North Korea remains the communist state in the Pacific most able to joint the ranks of the modernizers in the Pacific (after China and the Soviet Union), but like its communist neighbours, it can only do so when domestic reform has begun.

The two remaining states, Cambodia and Laos, are the poorest and the most isolated from the economic growth and new pattern of international relations in the Pacific. They have also been cut off from the Soviet Union, and neither accounts for more than 2 percent of Soviet exports to the Pacific. Nevertheless, there were some signs in the late 1980s of a future increase in Soviet trade with both states as the Soviet Union sought new influence in East Asia.

By 1987, Cambodia had become the Soviet Union's fifth largest trade partner in East Asia, ahead of Malaysia. The Soviet Union was by far Cambodia's main trade partner.[70] Even Laos had moved up the list of Soviet trade partners in the region, taking eighth place in 1987 and 1988, just ahead of Thailand and Singapore. Both countries receive large proportions of their foreign aid from the Soviet Union, and Moscow claims its 600 million roubles-worth in aid between 1976–88 represented more than half the Laotian total of aid received.[71]

Serious problems are bound to occur in developing trade between the Soviet Union and these two states that rank among the poorest in the world. Soviet and Laotian officials admit that Laos is unable to make the best use of Soviet aid because it simply lacks the infrastructure to support the enterprise. Soviet exports to Laos and

Cambodia are easy to envisage, but the problem has always been what the poor states can export in return. As in the case of other socialist states, there is some potential in labour exports to the Soviet Union, but such plans are much less attractive than they are for Vietnam, China or even North Korea. From the Soviet perspective, these states, despite being net importers from the Soviet Union, are more of a burden than a benefit in economic terms. Even with a future reform of their economies, it is likely they will play only a marginal role in Soviet conceptions of the Pacific economy.

ASEAN, the NICs and other capitalist economies

Besides Soviet-Japanese trade, only a small amount of Soviet foreign trade is conducted with non-socialist states of the Pacific. In this respect, the pattern of Soviet trade is radically different from that of most other states in the region. The Soviets have no official trade with two of the four NICs (Hong Kong and Taiwan) and Soviet Pacific trade with the United States is of no significance.[72] Surely there is some potential for increased trade with these key participants in the Pacific economic boom.

Yet even the more established non-communist trading partners of the Soviet Union have found it difficult to establish a new and more thriving basis for trade. There are two types of trade partners—the fully developed capitalist economies such as New Zealand and Australia, and the less developed states of ASEAN. Soviet trade with the neo-Europes of the south Pacific has been overwhelmingly unbalanced and based on commodity exports to the Soviet Union.

At times—for example, in 1980—Australia accounted for nearly 20 percent of Soviet imports from the Pacific and New Zealand provided nearly another 5 percent. But in most years, the respective percentages have been 10 percent and 2 percent (in 1988, 7.2 percent for Australia and 2 percent for New Zealand), accounting for such staple exports as grain from Australia and wool and meat from New Zealand. The problems in trade are obvious and affect Soviet-Canadian and Soviet-US trade in the Pacific. All these states are mainly exporters of primary products, and except for foodstuffs, the Soviet Union already has most of what the neo-Europes have to offer. Equally depressing is the picture of Soviet exports. Soviet machinery is less sophisticated than that in the developed capitalist world and the West rarely trades such items with communist states.

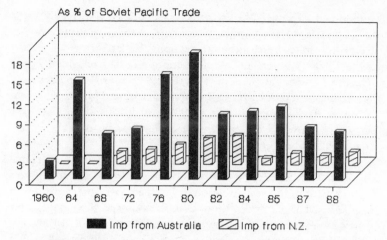

As % of Soviet Pacific Trade

■ Imp from Australia ▨ Imp from N.Z.

Figure 6.9 Trade with Australia/New Zealand: 1960–1988
Sources: UN and IMF trade statistics.

The Soviet Union accounted for 2 to 3 percent of Australian exports for much of the 1970s and 1980s, but by the 1980s China-Australia trade was nearly twice the level of Soviet-Australian trade. An even more dramatic reversal took place in Soviet-New Zealand trade. In both cases, the Soviet Union remained unable to export while China accounted for at least 1 percent of both Australian and New Zealand imports. Developing contacts at the scientific and research levels may be possible among the more developed resource exporters of the Pacific (Soviet Union, Canada, United States, Australia and New Zealand), but this is unlikely to provide a firm basis for large-scale trade.[73] There already has been limited cooperation in joint fishing companies with Canada, the United States and New Zealand.[74]

When Soviet fishing boats tried to gain greater access to Australian ports, the Australians tied the request to increased Soviet purchases of wheat, sugar and iron.[75] The tentative agreement reached in March 1989 did not allow for Soviet commercial fishing in Australian waters, but it did allow some so-called 'feasibility fishing'. The price Moscow paid was allowing long-term agreements for agricultural and mineral exports.[76]

On a calculation of per capita trade, the picture of Soviet trade with ASEAN states is even less impressive. Total trade with ASEAN was half that of Soviet-North Korean trade for most of the 1970s, and by the mid-1980s, after a brief rise, Soviet-ASEAN trade fell ever further to 25 percent of Soviet-North Korean trade. Malaysia was the Soviets' only significant trade partner, providing up to 22 percent of Soviet Pacific imports in 1970, although dropping back to around 4 percent in the 1980s (1.6 percent in 1988). Indonesia had provided 2 to 4 percent of Soviet Pacific imports in the 1960s but has slipped below 1 percent for the past 15 years. Singapore accounted for 2 to 4 percent of Soviet Pacific imports in the 1980s, as did Thailand. By 1988 Singapore provided 0.7 percent of Soviet Pacific imports, while Thailand did little better at 0.8 percent.

Trade with the Soviet Union has at best been of marginal importance to ASEAN states. Although 3 percent of Singapore's exports went to the Soviet Union in 1969, a mere 1 percent went in the 1980s. Malaysia ended up at a similar point to Singapore, after having sent 5 percent of its exports to the Soviet Union in 1969. By 1986, China accounted for some 2 percent of both total ASEAN imports and exports while by contrast even exports to the Soviet Union accounted for less than 1 percent of the ASEAN total. China had shown that increasing amounts of trade with ASEAN were possible even as the level of Soviet trade with these developing states declined.

The Soviet Union had hoped to import raw materials from ASEAN (for example, rubber) and export machinery.[77] However, despite lower prices for Soviet machinery, legendary problems with

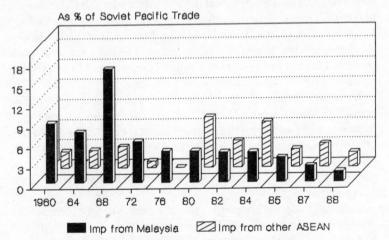

Figure 6.10 Trade with ASEAN: 1960–1988
Sources: UN and IMF trade statistics.

the quality of Soviet products and service made the equipment difficult to market. Unlike in its relations with Syria or even India, the Soviet Union has been unable to take advantage of the markets in the Pacific developing states because ASEAN states had much more ready access to goods from the NICs and the developed capitalist economies of the Pacific. As Soviet observers themselves are quick to point out, the nature of many ASEAN states' economies has changed, so that after rapid modernization they no longer fit the traditional image of Third-World states.[78]

The more subtle Soviet analysts have come to understand that the problems in Soviet-ASEAN trade have more to do with these structural elements than with ideological differences. Of course, they continue to argue that part of the blockage of trade comes from pressure from the United States, but most of that pressure flows from trade disputes rather than any particular concern with ASEAN's exports to the Soviet Union. Even Indonesia, nominally a non-aligned state, bends to US wishes and restricted the Soviet Union to the use of only four ports.

Among the structural problems is that few joint ventures in ASEAN involve the Soviet Union. Moscow lacks the capital and the will to integrate itself as closely with local markets as the multinational corporations in the capitalist economy have grown to expect.[79] The Soviets seem to be thinking, at least in the short term, that it will be easier for ASEAN states (usually poorer than the Soviet Union) to invest in the Soviet Far East. The prospect for much closer economic relations with ASEAN states seems dim, but there is increasing evidence that the new Soviet thinking at least recognizes the nature of the problem—a vital first step to expanding economic relations in the future.[80]

To some extent, if the Soviet Union felt it was a high political priority, it could increase its level of imports from ASEAN. It could focus a specific sector of its trade with the developing world on the region, even though this would harm relations with other developing states such as Sri Lanka. But the more realistic Soviet leadership seems to be interested in real and longer-lasting structural solutions. It recognizes that the deeper roots of the trade problem lie in the basic structure of the Soviet economy, particularly the part of it that faces the Pacific.

Trade figures can be a crude way of assessing relative economic importance, and this certainly is the case with Soviet-Singapore trade.

Singapore is increasingly seen as an NIC which can offer key services to assist Soviet trade in the region. Singapore may also play a crucial role in Soviet plans to develop participation in international shipping. Furthermore, considering the uncertain future of Hong Kong and the problems the Soviets have in dealing with that colony and with Taiwan, for fear of upsetting China, Singapore will probably become the focus of Soviet interest in ASEAN and possibly even among the NICs in general.

A characteristic of the new Soviet economic policy towards ASEAN is the recent focus on the richer parts of the region. Malaysia, as a proto-NIC, is more attractive to the new Soviet strategists. Agreements have already been reached that will facilitate Malaysian trade with the Uzbek SSR, as part of the new Soviet idea to encourage local links where more long-lasting agreements can be established.[81]

Fast-rising Thailand has most recently caught Soviet attention. Discussions have already begun on how to translate better political relations into new trade and investment. For the time being, most reports suggest more goodwill than good business.[82] Yet a joint Soviet-Japanese trading firm has already been set up to sell Soviet fertilizer, coal and machinery. This multilateral approach might offer a quicker path for closer Soviet integration into the regional economy.[83]

Similarly, but even more in the long-term Soviet perspective, there is potential for improved relations with the Philippines. A modest target of $200 million has been set for bilateral trade by 1992, and a joint commission was set up in December 1988 to help make it possible. The Soviet Union recognizes that in order to reach such a target, the balance of trade would have to be in favour of the Philippines. Soviet investment in a power plant in northern Luzon that would sell power to the local firms was only one of the more unorthodox measures devised to balance the trade. Yet even that target would require an eightfold increase in trade. In contrast to its dealings with other ASEAN states, the Soviet Union apparently hopes to achieve some of this increase by employing Filipinos in the Soviet Far East.[84] After a visit by the Philippine trade minister to Moscow in March 1989, it was announced that consideration was being given to opening a trade office in Vladivostok.[85]

The new focus on richer states, and the recognition of the new structural features of the developing world, are both particularly visible in the Soviet Union's relations with the NICs. Of course, this is a strange category of states for anyone to contemplate, let alone the Soviet Union, which has only begun its economic reforms at home. Like most countries, the Soviet Union has problems with the fact that the Newly Industrialized Countries are rarely countries in the full sense of the term. Only Singapore has full independence. Taiwan and Hong Kong are both claimed by China, and the Soviet's ally, North Korea, insists its friends maintain a solid front in not recognizing South Korea. It was only a pragmatic Soviet leadership that put aside these problems of diplomatic definition in order to get on with business.

The case of Singapore has already been discussed in the ASEAN context—it offers the fewest problems for Moscow. Hong Kong, especially following the 1984 Anglo-Chinese settlement, is returning to the Chinese fold in 1997, and the Soviet Union has therefore had only the most limited dealings with Hong Kong for fear of upsetting China. Although the Hong Kong authorities are mainly responsible for keeping Soviet contact with Hong Kong limited, and a Hong Kong trade seminar was held in Moscow in October 1989, there are few signs that the Soviet Union is deeply disturbed about being kept at bay.

The new Soviet interest in the NICs focuses on the untapped potential in relations with Taiwan and South Korea. Taiwan is, in many ways, more sensitive, because of the importance of Sino-Soviet detente. Yet China's own trade contacts with Taiwan have also increased in the 1980s and therefore it has become easier for other states, including the Soviet Union, to explore relations with this so-called province of China. To date, Soviet trade with Taiwan remains in the tens of millions of dollars and until 1990 is done through such third parties as Singapore.[86] Trade in 1989 was reportedly worth $127 million (nearly 4 times the 1988 figure), although total Taiwanese trade with Eastern Europe was valued at $350 million.[87] Contacts were managed on an 'interprovincial basis before 1990', with the Ukraine handling the Soviet side of the contacts. By 1989, the two sides were exploring the benefits of counter-trade deals with French middlemen helping swap personal computers for urea and scrap iron. Monthly trade was said to be approximately $10 million.[88]

Taiwan sent a large trade delegation to the Soviet Union in October 1988 after a major debate had been resolved in Taibei about whether such contacts should be explored at all.[89] They discussed the possibilities of investment in the timber, chemical and garment industries, and they optimistically suggested that there was good potential for trade. Unlike the ASEAN states, Taiwan has a capital surplus and therefore has the funds to invest in the Soviet Union.[90] Possible projects included the electronic industry, chemicals and the manufacture of machine tools. Taiwan was clearly interested in buying Soviet raw materials. When the Soviets announced changes in joint venture laws in 1988, such cooperation between the Soviet Union and Taiwan was becoming increasingly possible.

Taiwan remained cautious about trade with the Soviet Union, largely because of its reluctance to deal with China and communists in general. However, the Chinese were also part of the reason for delay because Beijing apparently tried to persuade its new friends in Eastern Europe and the Soviet Union that it should not open trade relations with Taiwan.[91] Taiwan nevertheless persevered in its new opening to the socialist world in 1989 and was making some progress. In contrast to South Korea, that other non–communist part of a divided country in East Asia, Taiwan was clearly slower in establishing trade with Moscow and Eastern Europe.

The real focus of the Soviet fascination with the NICs is South Korea. After years of neglect, the Soviet Union under Gorbachev began exploring the possibilities for trade with South Korea.[92] The timing was in part a function of the broader Soviet reform programme that took a more pragmatic look at the region, especially at the most vital Northeast Asian sector. South Korea was rapidly emerging as the most economically impressive NIC. Soviet officials recognized what they called 'structural compatibilities' between the economy of a NIC that would soon have capital to export, and the so far underdeveloped Soviet Far East. The Soviet Union saw South Korea as a newer version of Japan in the 1960s and 1970s.[93] Moscow could see greater scope for closer relations with South Korea than with the more modern, and more highly developed Japan of the 1980s. Moreover, China had shown throughout the 1980s that it was possible to expand trade with South Korea (to the value of $3 billion by 1988) without North Korea being able to do much about it. Given Sino-Soviet detente, Soviet contacts with South Korea became safer politically.

Of course, South Korea has its own motives, including the need for trade diversification, undermining support for North Korea, obtaining recognition through the 1988 Seoul Olympiad, and developing its eastern coastal region.[94] Thus, with all these factors coming together, 1988 was a striking year for Soviet-South Korean economic relations.[95]

In April 1989, the Soviet Union and South Korea exchanged 'trade offices' and agreement was soon reached on consular relations. The Soviet Chamber of Commerce in Seoul is reportedly staffed by officials on leave from the Ministry of Foreign Economic Relations.[96] Earlier in 1989, Hungary and South Korea upgraded their diplomatic missions to full embassy status, and Poland established full diplomatic relations on 1 November. With the spreading of democratic government in Eastern Europe in 1989, nearly all of the former communist states established official diplomatic relations with South Korea.[97]

As political reality caught up with economic desires, it became increasingly clear what kind of trade the Soviet Union could engage in with South Korea. Estimates on the 1987 trade ranged from $240 million to $1 billion.[98] Soviet officials said they only knew of $100 million trade in 1988, all of which was indirect,[99] although other estimates suggested the trade was in the region of $290 million. This was still much less than Soviet-North Korean trade, although the gap was apparently closing fast. As noted, serious problems prevent the rapid expansion of Soviet-North Korean trade. Much as Sino-South Korean trade has rapidly outstripped Chinese trade with North Korea, so the Soviet Union hopes to establish a major part of its Pacific trade with South Korea in the 1990s.

At this stage it is difficult to be sure what kind of trade will develop because so many ideas have been entertained by both sides. The mutual enthusiasm for expanded trade coupled with the secretive nature of the trade thus far make analysis particularly difficult.

There have reportedly already been agreements for the sale of South Korean electrical products, chemicals and machinery to the Soviet Union. The Soviet Union apparently asked South Korean *chaebols* to build new hotels and set up plants for construction materials. Soviet and South Korean banks have agreed to handle the financing for these and other agreements.[100] There have also been talks about links between shipping organizations—Soviet ships have already been repaired at Hyundai's shipyards. Talks in the spring of 1989 resulted in an agreement to establish a direct sea route between Pusan and the Soviet ports of Vostochny and Nakhodka. Both sides would divide evenly the transport of containerized cargo bound for the Middle East and Europe via the trans-Siberian railway.[101] South Korean ships were allowed to fish in Soviet waters in the sea of Okhotsk.[102] The new Soviet airline Avialat reportedly will handle the planned flights between the Soviet Union and South Korea.[103]

A steady stream of delegations has explored the new possibilities for economic cooperation. A delegation from Hyundai went to the Soviet Union in January 1989 to discuss the building of production facilities for aluminum, pulp, furniture and construction materials. The possibilities for coal mining have also been studied.[104] An agreement was signed with the Hyundai group in January 1989 for a joint venture to promote construction, manufacturing and fishery in the Siberian region.[105] This euphoria is so reminiscent of Japanese infatuation with Siberian prospects in the 1970s that it seems difficult to believe that the Koreans might commit the same mistakes of overexuberance. Deals have already been struck and the first joint venture was agreed to in early 1989; a South Korean firm will sell furs made of Soviet pelts.[106] Talks have also been conducted about cooperation in the fishery industry including fish catching, processing and even the manufacture of fish processing machinery in a special economic zone in the Soviet Union.[107] South Korean firms are apparently prepared to pay much higher rates for Soviet fish than are the Japanese.[108]

One of the most striking features of the new Soviet approach to South Korea is how Soviet observers have been sensitive to the new realities of the interdependent Pacific economy. One analyst suggested that joint ventures could be financed by complex deals involving export of Soviet coal, forestry concessions, income from running hotels for tourists or even the export of some Soviet aircraft such as the Yak–40.[109] There clearly is a new generation in the Soviet Union able to understand the basis of the Korean miracle and Pacific prosperity. Some Soviet observers are even suggesting that the East Europeans, and especially the Hungarians, be involved as possible multilateral partners in joint ventures in the Soviet Far East.[110]

Cooperation in the shipping sector also seems promising, and both sides now recognize the potential for involving third parties. Such wider, third-party issues initially caused problems in negotiations about direct access to each other's ports. The Soviet Union clearly wanted the right to transport third-party goods in order to enhance its role as the land bridge between East Asia and Europe. South Korea wanted reciprocal rights to carry third-party goods on the trans-Siberian railway, but that conflicted with an already existing

Japanese-Soviet arrangement for transhipment.[111] Yet it cannot be far from the Soviets' minds that the more successful the South Koreans are in doing business in the Soviet Far East, the sooner the Japanese will want to share in the profits, and even the Americans will grow concerned about breaches of Cocom regulations. The South Koreans, like the Japanese before them, quickly discovered that the real problems in relations with the Soviet Union were less political than economic. When the pace of Soviet reforms slowed, the fast-moving South Koreans experienced delays caused by the confusion in the Soviet marketplace.[112]

Thus Soviet-South Korean economic relations seemed relatively unhindered by political factors. The *de facto* cross-recognition that the Soviet Union has encouraged between the two Koreas will probably have to wait for formal endorsement after the death of Kim Il Sung and the assumption of power by a more pragmatic leader in North Korea.[113] By then, Soviet-South Korean trade should have emerged as Moscow's third or fourth largest trading relationship in the Pacific, leaving Soviet-North Korean relations far behind.

Farther afield in the south Pacific, the Soviet Union has begun to seek new friends. Trade with the tiny islands can never amount to much from an economic standpoint, and the existing patterns of trade dominated by Australia, New Zealand and Japan are unlikely to change. Yet because of the particular vulnerability of such small economies, the Soviet Union has been able to take advantage of some errors in Western policy and the generally hard-line bargaining, especially by the Japanese, on fees for fishing. Soviet fishing fees paid to Kiribati under a 1985 agreement doubled the US and Japanese offers and amounted to 15 percent of the Kiribati budget. When unable to renew this agreement at a lower price because of the unexpected small catches, the Soviet Union nevertheless made an even more generous offer to Vanuatu.[114]

For its highly developed long-range fishing fleet, the Soviet Union seeks reprovisioning facilities and friends, especially in the tuna-rich zone around Papua New Guinea, the Solomon islands and Vanuatu.[115] The Soviet Union has skills and expertise to offer in this area that are competitive with those on the international market. Western unwillingness to pay higher rates for local fishing, and the US rejection of the islanders' desires for greater control of their neighbouring waters under the UN Law of the Sea negotiations, have resulted in a partial reassessment of the islanders' position on dealing with the Soviet Union. The Soviet Union has the world's largest fishing fleet, and fish is a key part of the animal protein diet of Soviet citizens. Due to the new, more commercially oriented image of the Soviet Union under Gorbachev, more nations seem to be increasingly willing to deal with Moscow as a reasonable commercial partner.

The reasons for a Soviet economic interest in the region are obvious.[116] As a major fishing nation with a strong interest in oceanographic surveys, the Soviets find access to these vast waters useful. There is no Soviet commercial airline route in the region, and the area contains some of the largest underexploited fishing grounds in the world. Soviet trade with the Pacific islands is so small that it is not even recorded in official Soviet statistics. Existing trade is in such commodities as copra, coffee or tea, and the Soviets either trade through third countries or purchase the products on world markets.[117] Fishing grounds in the warmer waters are not nearly as productive as in the cooler waters off New Zealand, and New Zealand still provides the largest base for Soviet resupply of its fishing fleet.

Without a significant change in Soviet trade with the non-socialist Pacific, it is difficult to see a major Soviet economic presence in the region. Trade with ASEAN states or the neo-Europes suffer from different sorts of problems. In all the cases of Soviet imports and exports with Pacific states, the keys to change seem to lie in the reform of the Soviet economy and in the adaptation to new trends in the international, mostly capitalist, economy.

Multilateral economic relations

The Soviet Union has an unsatisfactory experience of participating in multilateral economic organizations. Even though the Pacific has no major regionwide economic organization, there has been much discussion, especially since the 1970s, about how to establish such multilateral cooperation. Efforts to shape such a Pacific community have, thus far, largely excluded the Soviet Union and its smaller allies. In the 1980s, as the Soviets acquired new attitudes towards cooperation with the organizations of the wider international capitalist economy (for example, GATT), the Soviet Union also began to take a more serious look at its possible role in multilateral organizations in the Pacific.[118] For instance, Moscow was impressed that China was making progress in its campaign to join these capitalist bodies. Yet tension remains in the Soviet position between developing relations between socialist states and integrating the Soviet Union into a global, capitalist-dominated economic world.

The Soviet Union is of course a member of the United Nations and as such is a member of the UN's Economic and Social Commission for Asia and the Pacific (ESCAP) as is the United States (but not the Latin American Pacific states or Canada). The Soviet Union has been active in ESCAP projects including major ones in the Mekong river, mineral prospecting and training of Asians to work in specialized bodies of ESCAP. Some ESCAP projects have operated on Soviet territory including training courses for planning of marine resources, prospecting techniques and railway transport. At a minimum, the cooperative attitude shown by the Soviet Union towards ESCAP strengthens its hand when seeking membership in the more important regional bodies.

However, the Soviet Union is not a member of any of the significant organizations that affect Pacific trade, such as the World Bank. Nor is the Soviet Union a member of the International Monetary Fund (IMF) or the Asian Development Bank (ADB), although Cambodia, Laos, Vietnam and, of course, China are ADB members. The United States and other leading capitalist economies are members of both. A Soviet representative attended the twentieth session of the ADB in April 1987, and the Soviet Union is still seeking full membership.

Nor is the Soviet Union a member of the Colombo plan for Cooperative Economic and Social Development in Asia and the Pacific. The United States now belongs to this body, founded by seven commonwealth countries in 1950. Also, Laos and Cambodia belong, although no other communist states are members.

Neither superpower is a member of the subregional organizations, ASEAN or the South Pacific Forum, although the United States is a member of the South Pacific Commission. Some Soviet reports suggest they would like to establish a formal dialogue with ASEAN on the model of the European Community's arrangement with ASEAN.[120] As the Indochinese war reaches settlement and the inclusion of Vietnam in ASEAN in the 1990s become increasingly possible, the Soviet Union may find its wishes fulfilled. Yet although the United States is a key participant in all attempts at establishing a Pacific-wide grouping, the Soviet Union is still usually excluded. The exceptions to this are the Pacific Economic Cooperation Conference (PECC) and the Pacific Basin Economic Council (PBEC)—and increasingly important exceptions these may be.

The PECC was founded in 1980, although it can trace its roots to various earlier Japanese-led attempts to organize regional trade and avoid trade friction.[121] It includes most Pacific states but excludes the Latin American and all communist states except China. It still is little more than a forum for academics and government and business officials to discuss mutual problems. Nevertheless, until 1986 the Soviet Union viewed this organization as yet another component in US-led attempts to build alliances against socialism.[122]

Since 1986, the issue of Soviet participation in the PECC has been placed on the agenda. The Soviet Union expressed an interest in joining the so-called PECC process and was allowed to sit as an observer at the 1986 meeting in Vancouver and as a 'guest' in Osaka in 1988. It has taken part in a number of the specific working groups as a sort of 'test of good intentions'. Chinese and even some Japanese officials have begun to take a more positive approach to future, full Soviet participation. In 1988, the Soviet National Committee on Asian Pacific Economic Cooperation was established in order to prepare the way for full Soviet participation in the PECC process.

The obstacles to Soviet participation in the PECC have been said to stem from Soviet military and political strategies in the Pacific and Soviet support for such states as Vietnam and North Korea. However, as some of these regional conflicts resolve, Sino-Soviet detente gathers momentum and the Soviet economy reforms, the newly stated Soviet desire to take part in the PECC process is being taken more seriously than before. Although the Soviet Union still makes a small contribution to overall Pacific trade, as noted previously, its contribution is not insignificant and is liable to increase.

In May 1989 the Soviet Union was allowed to attend a PBEC meeting as an observer. In the new mood of Pacific-wide pragmatism, the meeting was held in Taiwan, of all places. The Soviet Union is also seeking entry to the ADB, the IMF and GATT, and is changing its general approach to such capitalist-led international economic organizations. Certainly if the Soviet Union is serious about genuine integration with the Pacific economy, a place in the PECC, however ineffective the organization has so far been, will be useful.

Of course the Soviet Union is the leader of CMEA, which has two of its members in East Asia. But following the revolutions in Eastern Europe, the CMEA seems hardly likely to survive. But even before late 1989, serious problems of multilateral cooperation among socialist states in East Asia were plain to see.[123]

Vietnam's per capita national income was 7 percent of the average of the European CMEA in 1985, whereas Mongolia's was 40 percent. Few East Europeans wanted to import from Vietnam, and therefore Vietnam could afford few imports in return. The absence of reform in Vietnam was a major problem. Previous CMEA strategies of attempting to stimulate industrial development in Vietnam and Mongolia, bypassing pre-industrial stages, are now acknowledged to have been disastrous. As other developing states in the Pacific have shown, a better strategy is to support traditional economic sectors and pay more attention to small-scale production that has export potential.

CMEA aid to Vietnam and Mongolia was therefore often wasted. Because it was indiscriminate and not in touch with local conditions, CMEA's policies led to inefficiency and bureaucratic nonsense. New ideas now include more specific, small-scale direct links between enterprises. Joint ventures with more flexible types of management are urged as part of a general reform in management ideas. Specialized cooperatives rather than large-scale projects or general exchange of agricultural products are seen as likely to be more effective. Moreover, Vietnam in particular is seen as providing an avenue for wider Soviet participation in Pacific economic cooperation, especially if capitalist states become involved in cooperative ventures in a new, reformed Vietnam. The keys, as with much of Soviet economic policy in the region, are the pace and direction of the wider reforms in the socialist states.

The impetus for reform in Vietnam obviously comes from both domestic and foreign sources. From the Soviet perspective, the problem is how to encourage reform without risking the political and military gains already made. The answer has been in part a Soviet aid program that has risen to new high levels in the 1980s and that is increasingly accompanied by strings that tug Vietnam in the direction of reform. Aid to North Korea has declined and aid to Mongolia is stagnant; Vietnam has thus clearly taken the top spot among recipients of Soviet aid in East Asia. The aid to Vietnam is now twice the total of Soviet aid to Africa, surpassed only by the massive Soviet aid program to Cuba. Of course, the degree of Soviet aid to the socialist Pacific is still small in comparison to the sums spent by the United States in the Pacific.[124]

The Soviet Union has fewer formal economic friends in the Pacific. The socialist Pacific includes an independent and powerful China and a number of smaller, extremely weak economies badly in need of reform. The socialist economy cannot be compared to the strong and successful capitalist Pacific. Thus, although the Soviet Union will try to build better bridges to the socialist Pacific, it must also open new highways to the capitalist world.

New economic trends in the Pacific

The foregoing analysis of the previous patterns of Soviet economic relations in the Pacific may provide a good guide to what is to come. However, both Soviet domestic politics and the Pacific international system are undergoing major reforms, and at such times it is dangerous to argue that the future will probably be simply a continuation of the past. Certainly at the time of writing, the Soviet Union seems especially aware of the need for new thinking. Some major reforms are already underway. It is useful to identify several new trends that seem most essential to a proper reform of the Soviet economic position in the Pacific.

Domestic reform

Perhaps one of the clearest conclusions from previous Soviet attempts to improve its economic role in the Pacific is that the key to success lies in the Soviet domestic economy. In fact, this conclusion applies to Soviet foreign policy in general. Domestic reform has been at the heart of the new thinking of the late 1980s. Reform in foreign trade will only follow more basic reform of economics and politics within the Soviet Union. Indeed, in the short term, trade levels may fall (as they did for a time with China) in the transition period before reforms are fully implemented.

The general nature of the national economic reform has already been covered in a number of other sources. Of course many of the general components of domestic reform also apply to the Soviet Pacific region, which stands to benefit from possible improvements in management skills, industrial efficiency and a freer political system. Several possible reforms in the Pacific seem distinctive and require more detailed elaboration.[125]

First, the Soviet Pacific needs to be treated as a more autonomous region. The region has a tradition of distinctive development; its frontier spirit can be cultivated by an atmosphere of greater flexibility, more open to innovative reform. The Soviet Far East has lagged behind the rest of the already slowing Soviet economy and it needs a special effort at revitalization.

In December 1988, the Soviet Council of Ministers published new regulations on export-import operations and the convertibility of the rouble that indicated the Pacific region would be granted special status. For example, taxes for foreign trade ventures would be lower. The idea of granting special status to other regions had been abandoned because of the political fear generated by unrest in the Baltic area. The Far East was therefore benefiting by its isolation, which allowed it to become the testing ground for reforms.[126] But as the Baltics and other regions began to attempt to leave the Soviet Union in 1990, serious question marks were placed on the concessions already granted to the Soviet Far East.

The Soviets were clearly uncertain about how much leeway to give the Far Eastern area, although the debates were usually part of a wider debate about local self-management. At the time of writing, the issues were far from resolved and were being vociferously debated in the Politburo.[127] Conservatives called the more adventurous reforms 'economic romanticism' while the more forward thinking advocates spoke of 'a beneficial regime'. The debates are now quite public, and the battle between those seeking closer integration within the Soviet Union and those seeking greater local independence has now been joined.[128]

To some extent, the debate concerns the level at which decisions should be made in the reformed Soviet system. Unlike the Baltic region, which has a republican level of decision making that could direct greater regional autonomy or even lead to demands for independence, the Soviet Pacific has no obvious, existing political machinery. As has already been discussed, there is some confusion about the boundaries of the Soviet Pacific region, and certainly the leaders of the Soviet maritime territory are often the least likely candidates to lead a dynamic reform, even in that part of the Soviet Pacific.[129]

One discussion on Soviet television in March 1989 was unusually frank in airing a range of differences on the related matter of republican self-management.[130] All parties agreed this was a difficult period of transition, and there was much uncertainty about how much power the centre was actually relinquishing. Even if the centre gave up power, some observers remained concerned that local authorities could be even more shortsighted and wasteful than the centre had ever been. One wag even noted that it was peculiar for the Soviet Union to be considering decentralization when Western Europe was working to create a single, larger market. Academician Leonid Abalkin made especially scathing remarks about the trendiness of the self-management idea and warned that it was not a 'magic wand'. He also suggested that republican self-management would, at least in the short term, aggravate economic problems and might put some regions in even more dire straits. Indeed, many reformers were concerned that regionalism would only allow hard-core conservatives to entrench themselves and hold out against a nationally directed reform programme. Thus, giving the Soviet Far East more regional autonomy would not necessarily lead to more outward-looking reforms and integration with the Pacific.

Second, the Soviet Union cannot focus on all the problems of the Pacific at once. Priorities need to be set. As noted in chapter 3, Russian policy erred at various times in the past by not paying sufficient attention to the Amur basin and by stretching its resources too far in the Pacific. In modern times, concentration on the Amur basin means paying special attention to China and the possibilities of bilateral, and especially local, trade. Friendship with China continues to be the key to an improved Soviet position in the Pacific. The Sino-Soviet split, particularly as it concerned trade, accounted for much of the deterioration in the general Soviet position in the Pacific.

The Soviet Union is still not completely clear about the focus of its economic strategy in the Pacific. The debate concerning the location of the planned special economic zone in the Pacific region is part of the uncertainty. Some officials still speak of close cooperation with North Korea while others focus on China and/or South Korea. Other observers say some way should be found to incorporate Japan into the early stages of planning for special zones and joint ventures. The placement of the first special economic zone in Nakhodka suggests the focus will be on raw material exports to coastal East Asia.[131]

Third, there has ben a lopsided focus on the allure of the region's mineral wealth. V. Ivanov aptly described the past Soviet attitude as treating the Soviet Pacific as a 'huge mine or aquarium'.[132] The result has been a concentration on large-scale and expensive operations to dig out minerals and other natural resources under difficult climatic conditions. Certainly much more attention should be paid to the vast, relatively temperate parts of the Soviet Pacific, which could comfortably be home to a considerably larger population than lives there at present. Employment for newcomers, given the relative decline in demand around the Pacific for Soviet raw materials, could be provided by processing industries.

Yet it would be peculiar if the Soviet Union did not base its prosperity in the Pacific on its services as a mine and an aquarium.[133] A comparison with Australia is instructive. Calls for a shift away from a structure of foreign trade reminiscent of a developing economy are often heard in Australia. Yet the Australian mine and breadbasket for the Pacific has been an effective route to prosperity. Australia's currency reacts quickly to currency fluctuations and thereby minimizes the impact of rapidly changing commodity prices. Australia also has a reputation as a reliable supplier and has developed a sophisticated marketing and promotional organization.[134] All of these features, should they be developed in the Soviet Union, might make Soviet officials feel less embarrassed about relying on its mines and fish for prosperity. The booming Pacific economy certainly offers large scope for growth in mineral exports, and market projections for mineral consumption show a clear market niche for the Soviet Union.[135] Soviet observers are perfectly aware that some of Japan's sources of minerals— most notably South Africa—find their Japanese markets increasing rapidly.[136]

Fourth, without a large influx of people and a shift in the economic basis of the Soviet Pacific, contacts with other Pacific states cannot be expanded. Merely safeguarding Soviet territory from foreign encroachment, as understandable a policy as it might have been in previous generations, needs to give way to a more open attitude to the Pacific. The Soviet Pacific must be seen as part of the broader Pacific, in the same way that it is now seen as connected to European Russia. It has to be part of an integrated world, operating on the basis of a global economy, and it must establish its own special kinds of links with the region beyond.[137] Soviet sources speak of the need to build an 'eastern facade' much like the United States had a 'far western' consciousness. The Soviet region must genuinely begin to think Pacific, and the first attempts to do so have revealed just how far the Soviet economy has lagged. All the while, as the Soviet Union also acknowledges, the other economies of the Pacific are not going to stand still to let the Soviet Union catch up.

A number of more specific economic reforms have been suggested with a view to formulating a new conceptual idea of the Soviet Pacific and as a way of boosting the Soviet share of Pacific GDP. Soviet sources now accept that their Far Eastern territory actually produces less than 1 percent of Pacific output and that the root cause of this failure is to be found at home in the Soviet Union. For example, labour productivity is as much as 20 percent lower in the Soviet Far East than elsewhere in the already notoriously inefficient Soviet economy. The key to providing a modern manufacturing base is manpower, and some Soviet sources openly state that the stress of evening out social distinctions has to be abandoned in order to attract innovative and eager settlers. In other words, the rewards have to make the effort worthwhile. Furthermore, bureaucratic interference has to be minimized when the social experiment in the Soviet Pacific is undertaken. Both the positive and negative implications of the Chinese experience have been closely analysed in the Soviet Pacific.[138]

Improved productivity will come with a new influx of people who are enticed by big incentives. Such incentives can be developed in cooperation with Pacific neighbours and by adopting new ideas such as joint ventures and special processing zones. Joint ventures are already a controversial matter, and some leaders have voiced clear objections to them because of supposed limitations on sovereignty and control. Supporters of joint ventures emphasize that the booming economies of the Pacific have prospered by making extensive use of special zones. More sophisticated Soviet critics note that the other successful zones had cheap labour—certainly not available in the Soviet Far East. The supporters retort that raw materials will not have to be imported as in other zones, and so there is no particular problem as long as the projects are tailored accordingly.[139] But as of March 1990, there were 1,400 joint ventures with the Soviet Union, with no East Asian country in the top ten partners. As of October 1989 Japan had 21 joint ventures, Australia 15, China 14 and Singapore, which ranked twenty-fifth, had only 10 joint ventures. Of its 963 joint ventures by October 1989, barely 25 were in the Soviet Far East.[140]

Some suggest that the entire region might be considered such a special zone. Like China, vast areas can serve as laboratories for economic reform and, in case of problems, the new and potentially subversive economic ideas can be isolated from the rest of the Soviet economy. Yet giving the region special status is in conflict with the other Soviet drive for closer integration of the Soviet Far East and for large-scale domestic investment to solve its problems. Some Soviet sources see a need to take the 'far' out of 'Far East' and integrate its economy more closely into the rest of the Soviet Union, much as has been done in the United States.[141] However, the most innovative ideas remain those that encouraged broader integration of the region into the Pacific economies and investment in new kinds of enterprises from the region rather than from other Soviet sources. Here there is a genuine need for new ideas.

Important opportunities for regional development depend on a marked improvement in transport. However, the Soviets disagree among themselves. Some planners urge closer contacts with the rest of the Soviet Union (for example, via the Baikal-Amur railway and better air links), and other reformers prefer to develop better contacts with the wider Pacific by stressing shipping enterprises and exploitation of ocean resources. If the new policies are really to establish the Soviet Pacific as a more independent area with greater freedom to explore new economic styles, then huge communications projects like railways will be deemphasized in favor of maritime development. Vladivostok needs to be opened and developed much like the coastal cities in China. Closer contacts with the 'Pacific process' through the PECC, or even ASEAN, are essential to this more outward orientation.

Yet, almost perversely, the major investment plan announced in 1987 focused primarily on developing local manufacturing in order to establish, for example, a powerful metallurgical base, which would then process such products as steel for export. This basic tension between domestic- and foreign-led investment remains unresolved. The plan was sent back for redrafting and nothing new has yet emerged.

A host of other technical reforms are especially necessary in the Soviet Pacific. A freely convertible currency,[142] greater flexibility in establishing contacts with foreign firms and greater efficiency and quality of output are all essential to a successful reform package. Price reform and a reduction in bureaucratic interference are fundamental because lack of change has produced chronic problems limiting a more genuinely independent policy for the Soviet Pacific. Because unresolved conflicts remain in Soviet thinking about its own Pacific economy, and because the Soviet economic reform programme in general is a long-term venture, it is clear that at the start of the twenty-first century, the Soviet Pacific will, at best, only be beginning to meet the challenge. Needless to say, the rest of the Pacific economy will not have stood still while the Soviet Union decided how best to catch up. But as one Soviet analyst from IMEMO likes to put it, this problem is rather like trying to get olives out of American bottles. The biggest problem is getting the first olive out of the bottle, because once it is out of the way, then all the rest are easy to get at.[143]

Japan as number two

In addition to these changes in the Soviet domestic position in the Pacific, the Soviet Union has recognized major changes in the international politics of the Pacific. Foremost among the changes is the twin process of economic prosperity and closer integration of local economies. No country symbolizes this trend more than Japan, as it surpassed the Soviet Union in the mid-1980s to become the world's second largest economy.

The Soviet attitude towards Japan's economic growth has gradually become more sophisticated.[144] In the Gorbachev period, the Soviet Union has gone from merely being impressed with the importance of Japan as a trading power to recognizing that Japan is reshaping the economic relations of the Pacific. Gorbachev called Japan 'a power of front-rank significance' in his 1986 Vladivostok speech. Soviet officials are aware that Japan is not a conventional superpower if only because it is militarily vulnerable. However, they also realize that in many senses being an economic superpower is more important in the modern Pacific.

Japan is increasingly seen as taking the leading role in the economy of the Pacific.[145] Whereas previous Soviet analysis focused on the leading role of the United States, by the late 1980s Soviet analysts admitted the growing independence of the Japanese position and Tokyo's unwillingness to surrender its leading role to the United States.[146] Thus, the Soviet Union can seek a more direct route into Pacific economic cooperation by improving relations with Japan and appealing to the Japanese sense of independence. The Soviet Union is aware of the increasingly serious trade disputes between Japan and the United States and the debates in Japan about new directions in its foreign policy.

The Soviet Union has also grown more aware of the role Japan has played in invigorating the economy of the broader Pacific. As part of its leading role in the Pacific, Japan has both stimulated and led the NICs into their pattern of growth.[147] Not surprisingly, Japan is also seen as the key to the creation of a Pacific community and as the leading voice in deciding how such regionwide cooperation might be shaped.

Of some interest also are the new ideas in the Soviet Union about the reasons for Japan's economic success. The old line of attributing this mostly to US aid is being replaced by a more sophisticated analysis of the nature of Japanese political culture and the distinctive aspects of the state-directed Japanese economy.[148] At least one Soviet commentator in *Pravda* has made much of the advantages of large Japanese trading houses as a solution to the debate over decentralization in foreign trade. Citing the Japanese success in vertical integration and a sharper focus on the international market that comes from its large trading corporations (which account for 60 percent of Japan's trade turnover), it was noted that the supposed gap between the Soviet and Japanese systems would not be so great in an age of Soviet reform.[149]

The Soviet Union, of course, is also sharply critical of Japanese domestic politics. Nevertheless, greater realism in the Soviet view provides the basis for a more sensible relationship with Japan as well as a better understanding of the changes in the Japanese economy and the prospects for economic cooperation with the Soviet Union. If Japan becomes one of the models for a reformed Soviet economy, the potential for closer cooperation might be even greater than imagined.

The Chinese socialist mirror

As important as Japan may be in the Soviet view, it is not a socialist state. Soviet admiration for, and even learning from, Japan will be constrained for some time to come by the differences in ideology, culture and economic system. Thus, the Soviet Union has been (until June 1989 anyway) most impressed by the recent changes in China's role in the Pacific economy. In many important respects, China still remains closer to the Soviet Union's self-definition than does any other Pacific state.

What had impressed the Soviet Union most about Chinese socialism was how it adapted to the international economy. China went from being even more isolated that the Soviet Union to number five in terms of total Pacific trade.[150] Furthermore, China did this in less than a decade of sweeping economic reforms while retaining the basic socialist character of Chinese society.

China was therefore both a challenge and an inspiration to the Soviet Union. Although recognizing the limits of the comparisons between the Soviet and Chinese economies, Soviet observers have been quick to point to some obvious lessons. Not only is there clearly great potential in Sino-Soviet trade, but China can also serve as an example of how to deal with a basically capitalist-dominated international economy. The Soviet Union has no Hong Kong or overseas community to serve as its window on the Pacific, but it can learn from Chinese mistakes.

Even if the stalling of the Chinese reforms in mid-1989 means that China ceases to be a beacon for certain types of reforms, China nevertheless has achieved much in terms of the international economy that the Soviet Union would hope to emulate. Indeed, the extent to which the Soviet Union is prepared to study the Chinese mirror of socialism is already documented elsewhere.[151] The results are to be seen in great Soviet interest in joint ventures and export processing zones. The Soviet Union has learned the virtue of agricultural reform (at least in theory) and the necessity to pair political reform with economic reform. Above all, it has learned the need to adopt flexible systems of management, including price reform and an entirely new structure of foreign trade and practices and organizations.

On the other hand, China can also serve as a warning to the Soviet reformers about the problems of reform. In late 1988 when the Chinese economic reforms encountered inflation resulting from price reform, the tocsin was sounded for all communist reformers. The problems were clearly manifested in macroeconomic issues such as price reform and control of the money supply.

As Sino-Soviet relations crept towards normalization in 1989, and Chinese reforms slipped towards the disaster of Tiananmen in June 1989, the growing similarity of discussions on ideological matters was both a threat and a support for the reformers in both states. The fact that students, demonstrating in China in April and May 1989 for greater political reform, saw Gorbachev as a model to emulate suggested the importance of shared socialism and the challenge that could be seen in each other's socialist mirror. The failure of Chinese reforms signalled to Moscow that reform must be radical and swift, or else it was bound to fail. The close links between Chinese and Soviet reforms meant that the problems in China raised the stakes for reformers in the Soviet Union.

These lessons from, and interconnections with, China are gradually being understood in the Soviet Union. The evidence of what could be achieved remains a light for Soviet reformers and those people demanding far-reaching changes in the Soviet approach to the Pacific. It is not so much that the Chinese model has been a success—in some senses it clearly is not—but rather that China showed it is possible for a socialist state to have major reforms that enhance its international standing and permit greater integration with the global economy. The Soviet Union can substantially increase its trade with the capitalist world and obtain large amounts of modern technology. With the exception of Sino-Soviet trade, the role of the socialist world is marginal to this particular aspect of Soviet strategy. Yet the Soviet Union, like China, will most likely keep several different doors open to foreign trade.

NICs and other models of development

The meaning of socialism in foreign economic terms is clearly undergoing some revision in the Soviet Union. As Aleksandr Bovin noted in July 1988, 'Don't we deceive ourselves too often with debates about socialism and socialist orientation in Third World countries? . . . Pol Pot was also building socialism. Evidently it is necessary to distinguish more strictly between words, statements and assurances of friendship with the Soviet Union and the real state of affairs, real politics'.[152] This new realism, or what the Chinese reformers have called 'seeking truth from facts', has led the Soviet Union to reappraise the route to success in the developing world. When Pol Pot's or Enver Hoxa's socialism is juxtaposed with the state-directed capitalist success of Taiwan or South Korea, the Soviet reformers are challenged to rethink their ideas about the most successful strategy for development.[153]

Although the Soviet Union has taken longer to recognize the reasons and nature of the success of East Asian NICs than it did the capitalist trading partners of these states, the change in Soviet awareness is now clear. The implications are only now being fully understood in the Soviet Union.[154] First, the old image of Third World conflict pitting capitalism against communism in a zero-sum game has now been abandoned. Local problems require local solutions, and the NICs, even with their major aid from the United States, have now emerged in the Soviet world view as more independent and important actors.

Second, this independence is changing the global patterns of power. The Third World is no longer a unified bloc and therefore Third World solidarity is not a meaningful concept. Some states, such as the NICs, have clearly identified interests in the success of the international capitalist economy. They are so closely integrated with that system, as are the more developed states, that if the Soviet Union seeks the benefits of trade with these states, it must do so as part of the global capitalist-led economy.

Thus the third implication for the Soviet Union is the need to associate with these NICs in a more businesslike fashion, instead of sitting on the sidelines of success and carping about the origins of these states' economies. Soviet trade with South Korea, and even Taiwan, has therefore increased and is likely to continue to do so. Singapore has already shown signs of playing a more important role in Soviet trading patterns in the Pacific. These NICs need raw materials that the Soviet Union can provide. They have large amounts of capital to invest and they produce precisely the consumer goods that the Soviet Union must acquire if it is to raise the standard of living in the Soviet Pacific. These NICs are also experts at pragmatic and, if need be, secret international economic relations.

Fourth, the success of the NICs will limit how much the Soviet Union is willing to pay in order to rescue its socialist allies in the Pacific's developing world. The Soviet response, especially in the cases of Vietnam and North Korea, is to direct its socialist friends towards reform and the adoption of at least some of the economic tricks of the NICs. Just as Chinese export zones and certain cities have a per capita GDP approaching that of the capitalist NICs, so the Soviet Union seems to believe that socialist states can achieve similar levels of growth. North Korean determination no doubt matches South Korea's. However, it must be channeled more fully into economic rather than military competition. Vietnam has a low-wage work force with many of the advantages of a semi-Confucian political culture that has worked in Taiwan. At a minimum, the potential for minor economic miracles is present in Vietnam and North Korea.

In fact, taking all these changes together, the Soviet economic position in the Pacific clearly has great opportunities for reform.

Yet it is one thing to dream about what might be, and quite another to match the rhetoric to the reality. In the few years that Gorbachev has had to reshape the Soviet attitude and Soviet behaviour in the Pacific, some sweeping changes are already apparent. In the decade before the twenty-first century, the Soviet Union must take these reforms much further if it is to have an important place in the still growing Pacific economy that so captivates the minds of futurologists.

7

Looking Forward

Imagine if you will this scenario as the leadership of the Soviet Union wakes up on 1 January 2000 and gazes eastward from the Soviet Pacific coast.

- The domestic reforms have gone well and the massive investment plan in the Soviet Pacific has attracted a flood of new immigrants from European Russia.
- The storehouse of raw materials is being efficiently exploited and the processing of some of them is driving an export boom that has at least tripled Soviet trade with the Pacific.
- The Soviet Union has become a major market for other members of the Pacific as well as a major supplier of commodities, much like Australia and Canada.
- Light industrial products from China and the NICs have vastly improved the quality of life in the Soviet Pacific as the natural trade is unhindered by political divisions or military conflicts.
- Japan has joined in multilateral economic joint ventures with the communist states of Northeast Asia, and Japan has also begun investing large sums in joint ventures in the export processing zones in the Soviet Pacific.
- The NICs and ASEAN states are also buying Soviet commodities and investing in the dynamic new Soviet projects.
- Socialist East Asia has been revitalized, and Vietnam is beginning to undercut the price of Chinese light industrial products.
- The Soviet Union has new friends among Pacific islanders because of the Soviet Union's booming international mining and fishing industries.

- Soviet military power is still the second strongest in the Pacific, but it concentrates on naval operations close to home and on maintaining a skeleton force along the Sino–Soviet border.
- Confidence-building measures have been negotiated with China and Japan, and multilateral talks are under way with others in the region.
- The inhabitants of the Pacific now visit resorts on the Soviet Pacific coast, and Soviet airlines and trains serve as a bridge connecting East Asia and Europe.

Dream or nightmare? Impossible? Perhaps, but the possibility that the Soviet Union will finally fulfill its promise as a Pacific power is now more likely than ever. It is doubtful that the twenty-first century in the Soviet Pacific will be as fine as imagined here, but neither is a return to the Brezhnevian 1970s likely. Even if the full possibilities for the Soviet Union seem unobtainable by the twenty-first century, at least it is as unlikely that the nightmare of past Soviet policies will return.

Important changes in Soviet policy are already under way. A futurologist could take a conservative stance and dwell on all that has not changed in Soviet policy towards the Pacific. Given the present level of change and uncertainty in Eastern Europe and in the Soviet Union, it might be safer to suggest that Gorbachev has already taken enough gambles for any sensible politician. It is more revealing, however, to look at the margins of policy making where reform takes place and concentrate on what is likely to change. Formidable obstacles to reform remain, and the realities of the Pacific often change too fast for the Soviet Union to respond adequately. Yet we have already seen some sweeping and impressive changes (for example, Sino–Soviet detente). We therefore need to focus on what may follow. After all, so much of the discussion about the Pacific is speculative, that applying the same principles of positive thinking to Soviet policy in the region is only fair.

The enduring realities

The Soviet Union might like to change many things about its position in the Pacific, but some things are relatively fixed. In the 300 years since Russia gained its Pacific region (or, indeed, the 75 years of

Soviet control of the region), certain relatively consistent features have constrained the policy makers in Moscow. Some of these features are positive, some are negative and some have elements of both. Even though other things may change in Soviet policy towards the Pacific in the twenty-first century, these permanent features are likely to remain of vital importance.

Territory and population

The Soviet Union will continued as a north Pacific power stretching across a vast inhospitable territory. Despite being the largest country in Asia, its population will remain one of the smallest in the region. Even with rapid reforms, any likely influx of people will at best take the Soviet Union to the present-day level of the population of Taiwan (20 million). In the longer term, a cynical Soviet optimist might hope for serious deterioration caused by the greenhouse effect because global warming would greatly improve the prospects of developing the Soviet Far East.

In the near future, however, the people of the Soviet Pacific will, as in Canada, be spread mostly along the southern border—the frontier with China and especially where Japan, China, Korea and the Soviet Union come closest. Thus, the frontier spirit is likely to remain. If reform is successful, a positive spirit will encourage enterprise and experiment. If reform and opening up to the outside world fail, the frontier spirit will be in awe and fear of its surroundings.

China on the mind

For similar reasons of geography, the Soviet view of the Pacific will be dominated by China. The enduring lesson from the Russian experience in the Pacific is that failure to get along with China presents serious difficulties for Russian policy. Yet China poses a dilemma for Russia because although Russia must get along with China, China is also the Soviet Union's main rival in the region. Like the superpower relationship, the lesson is that mutual security is an imperative for both sides, and at best they can only have a stable relationship of competition and coexistence. Such uneasy detente will always be subject to the machinations of outsiders, but Moscow abandons detente with China at the peril of its entire Pacific prospects.

The elusive Japan

Japan has always been the second most important state in the Russian perspective of the Pacific. Given its continuing successes, Japan's offshore presence can only continue to complicate Soviet calculations. In the broad sweep of Russian experience in the Pacific, relations with Japan have rarely been warm. Despite the distinctive complementarity of the two countries' economies, it is difficult to see why the two should get along especially well. The enduring Soviet priority given to China and the clear orientation of Japan towards the global capitalist economy mean there are few avenues for close collaboration. As in Anglo-Soviet relations, the reasons for poor cooperation between Japan and the Soviet Union are not due entirely to the Soviets. The upshot is that Japan is likely to remain the most difficult major power for the Soviet Union to deal with in the Pacific.

An outsider in the global economy

Although Russia was occasionally more closely involved in the Pacific economy, its reach has rarely been a long one. The problems do not stem only from the continental Russian tendency to underestimate naval power. They are also now aggravated by the fact that the Soviet Union's adopted political and economic system has kept it out of the mainstream of success that has so transformed the Pacific. Insofar as the Soviet Union ever had a role in the regional division of labour, this role was largely focused on bilateral relations with China. Trade patterns are difficult to shape and sustain in a region divided among several competing centres of influence, especially when other states, such as Canada or Australia, have similar products to sell and much closer political affiliations with the intended markets.

The not-so-hidden powerhouse in this global economy remains the United States. For all the talk of the decline of the superpowers, the United States remains the most powerful economy in the region as well as the primary reason people 'think Pacific' at all rather than simply in East Asian terms. For long periods of Pacific history, Russia and the United States have made common cause. Although conditions have changed since 1945, the enduring lesson for the Soviet Union is that good relations with the United States may be an easier way to ensure an active part in the Pacific system than is struggling to forge a warm relationship with Japan.

Regional diversity

One enduring difference between the Atlantic and Pacific worlds is the much more diverse political world in the Pacific. From the Soviet point of view, this diversity is both a problem and an opportunity. If Moscow is intent on building regionwide cooperation or formulating a similarly general strategy for the Pacific, this will likely be wrecked on the rocks of diversity. The opportunity in the diversity is that for a country seeking entry into an otherwise successful international system, diversity allows the Soviet Union to select its opportunities with less fear of making a fatal blunder. Most states in the Pacific system of international relations have not seen Russia as a major actor in the past because they have focused on the capitalist world. However, due to the very diversity and rivalry within the region, many states, such as China or Indonesia, will welcome a new Soviet player as an excuse for reshuffling the deck.

Reforms in Soviet foreign policy

Of course, change in the post-1945 international system must always be on the margins because that great facilitator of past change, major war, is clearly not a useful instrument of policy. As a result, real change is more difficult to spot because it happens in the margins of the old system. Some smaller wars, and some striking personalities, help mark the transformations. Yet as interdependence increases and states lose their sovereignty, the more far-reaching changes often take place because of simultaneous reforms in the domestic politics of several states. Recent events in Eastern Europe are striking examples of such change in communist systems. The changes in Soviet policy in the Pacific are less striking examples of domestic reform driving foreign policy reform, and then domestic politics in turn being affected by the international system.

Confusion about socialism

Whether Mikhail Gorbachev's reforms in the Soviet Pacific were inspired by the example of successful competitors like Japan, or whether they are driven by the stalling of the Soviet economy and society, reform was urgent. For a one-party state with a supposedly guiding ideology, the first reform had to be the acknowledgment that past strategies were wrong. Socialist hubris has been consigned to the background as the leadership experiments with reform. Although it is claimed that no matter what the reform the essential character of the Soviet Union will remain socialist, such claims grow harder to sustain.

Given the death of communism in most of Eastern Europe in 1989, it is increasingly likely that the Soviet Union will also cease to be ruled by a communist party. But it is far from clear that the state we still call the Soviet Union will be socialist in the twenty-first century. All one can say in the unstable time of early 1990 is that present signs suggest is that a fairly authoritarian regime is likely to be in power, even if it is not a communist party. It also seems more likely than not that some degree of socialist principles will be retained.

It is clear that the new, reformed socialism has already begun to change the domestic base of the Soviet Pacific. The Soviets have already decided to play a greater role in the international division of labour. Also, they are implementing the decisions to open a special economic zone and to encourage joint ventures, particularly in the Pacific. These major reforms have come about faster than most people thought possible. To be sure, much work remains in terms of how these reforms will develop in practice, but the Soviets are clearly determined to reform their home base and to join the Pacific economy.

Detente with China

Sino-Soviet detente began before Gorbachev came to power, and, at least in the early stages, it was as much a Chinese reform as a Soviet one. After only five years in power, Mikhail Gorbachev achieved the normalization of Sino-Soviet relations that had eluded his predecessors. It is not an exaggeration to suggest that no single improvement to the postwar strategic position of the Soviet Union is as important as Sino-Soviet detente. If Gorbachev achieves nothing else, he will have taken the most important step in transforming the Soviet position in the Pacific.

Of course, this detente will remain a mix of competition and coexistence. It makes possible the revitalization of the domestic Soviet economy in the Pacific. The target of tripling trade with other Pacific states by the year 2000 also suddenly becomes attainable.

Sino-Soviet detente sets a new agenda for Soviet policy in the Pacific, and it also sets a new agenda for the region as a whole. It is the most important shift in the regional strategic balance since the US detente with China in 1972.

Declining use of military force

The withdrawal of the Soviet Union from more direct involvement in regional conflict has taken place both inside and outside the Pacific. The specific changes in the Pacific—including troop cuts, less out-of-area naval operations and pressure on allies to lower regional tension—have been made quickly. These changes will eventually save the Soviets money and therefore will affect domestic reform. Yet their main purpose is to improve political relations in the Pacific.

Although the political impact has been uneven, these changes in Soviet policy have already had a positive effect. Soviet relations with ASEAN are improved by pressure on Vietnam to end the Cambodian conflict, much as relations with Japan are improved by pressure on North Korea and troop cuts in Northeast Asia. Although none of these changes is irreversible, any decision to undertake such a reversal would need to justify why the benefits should be lost.

Of course, if the Soviet Union puts less emphasis on military power, admits to having made ideological mistakes and does not develop a strong economic presence in the Pacific, there will be less reason to consider the Soviet Union as a superpower in the Pacific. In that case, would we be witnessing the slimming down of the Soviet Union into the mere shadow of a great power? That implication alone might lead the Soviets to reevaluate their lower military profile.

Dealing with the NICs

Nothing illustrates the new Soviet pragmatism in the Pacific as well as Moscow's improved relations with the NICs. Singapore has always had the best economic relations with the Soviet Union and will be the key to Soviet plans to establish a presence in Southeast Asia. Taiwan is likely to increase in importance as a Soviet trade partner, but political relations with Taiwan will be limited by the much more important detente with China.

Detente with South Korea is of greatest importance. Not only does South Korea sit in the more vital Northeast Asian region, but its larger population and rapid repeat of the Japanese miracle also make it a more important trade partner. Even though successful detente with China will account for the largest part of the improvement in the Soviet position in the Pacific economy, improved relations with South Korea might be the next most important reform for the Soviet Union. Moscow expects that once South Korea becomes involved with the Soviet Union, Japan will not be far behind.

Accepting the United States

A major reform of Soviet policy towards Western Europe was Moscow's acceptance that the United States could not be excluded from discussions of European security. The ensuing arms control and confidence-building measures were built on the implicit recognition of the variety of US links with allies far from its shores. Similarly, the acceptance of the United States as a Pacific power in Gorbachev's Vladivostok speech of 1986 marked the maturity of the Soviet view of the Pacific. Although periodic Soviet attempts to make mischief in the United States' relations with its allies can be expected, a more stable security in the Pacific, including arms control agreements, is now easier to negotiate.

Continuing debates[1]

Reform, especially at the pace and scope now underway in the Soviet Union, inevitably results from and encourages further debate. All of the changes already discussed could be reversed by still other changes in domestic and international politics. In many cases, it is still hard to distinguish between the reality and rhetoric of reform. Because the reforms are happening so fast and are so far-reaching, some regression, however temporary, seems likely. Therefore it is well to consider the consequences of those debates and the implications of the likely outcomes.

The speed of the general domestic reform

The debates in the Soviet Union about reforms are too numerous and complex to be recounted here. Almost all the debates relate in some way to the Soviet Pacific. Without macroeconomic reform as well as resolution of such microeconomic problems as a convertible rouble, real interchange with the Pacific will be restrained. Without new ideas about management, no joint venture will succeed. Without rethinking the role of military power as part of a reassessment of military doctrine, the temptation to intervene in regional conflict will remain. The list is seemingly endless. But the main point is that an understanding of the success of Soviet policy in the Pacific requires an appreciation of the struggles in Moscow and, indeed, in the towns and villages of European Russia.

Maritime or continental

Perhaps the most vociferous debate at present in the Soviet Union is between the inward-lookers and those urging a genuinely more international development strategy. In the Soviet Pacific, as indeed elsewhere in the Soviet Union, there is a serious need to look towards the outside world for finance, ideas and even people to make the Soviet Pacific flourish. In China this more outgoing strategy was described as the open door strategy, which in 1989 clearly encountered its biggest crisis in its 10 years of operation. In the Soviet Pacific such a strategy is best described as a maritime orientation. Its supporters call for greater freedom in the region to experiment with new ideas, rates of pay, systems of management, types of investment and types of partners. However, as downtown Moscow sees itself as the arbiter of reforms in the Soviet Pacific, it is not surprising that bureaucrats often stifle local initiative. The absence of a powerful, regional decision-making apparatus means such problems are likely to persist for some time. Therefore it becomes clear why, as one Soviet observer notes, there is a freshly painted 'welcome' sign put up in the Soviet Pacific, but the old 'keep out' sign is still visible beneath it.[2]

The more conservative, continental school urges less regional differentiation, more balanced growth and less reliance on the outside world. There is even a so-called green, or ecological, strand to the argument that stresses the perils of rapid development. So far, the maritime school is in charge, but their ability to remain in control depends on successful reforms at home and on interest from the outside. It also depends on how the various subcategories of the maritime school (with some supporting emphasis on opening to Europe rather than Asia) manage to resolve their differences. So far, those officials who emphasize paying attention to the Pacific have apparently held their own. Hence, the Vladivostok initiative, detente with China, openness towards the NICs and a form of Soviet military retreat.

A Pacific aquarium or a processing zone

The factions are complex, and even within the maritime school there are differences of opinion. The strategy for the Soviet Pacific in the 1970s was to draw foreign finance and technology to aid an essentially Soviet programme of exploiting the raw materials in the region for export. Since then, the reformers have argued that the plan to wait for investment from European Russia to stimulate the Soviet Pacific economy—the continental approach—will not work. The maritime school, however, has not yet agreed on exactly how much it can open to the outside world without relying on the old strategy of raw material extraction and selling fish. One reformer notes the similarity between today's cautious stance and that in the period before Peter the Great when Russia thought only of 'timber, hemp and blubber-oil'.

The more radical reformers are convinced that the service sector can, as in the case of China, provide vital experience and finance for other industries—for example by providing tourist facilities. The intention would be to take advantage of the better trained Soviet labour force in order to produce light industrial and even electrical goods with foreign investment in export processing zones. Soviet raw materials would be extracted, but they would be processed first in the Soviet Pacific territory and then exported to Pacific markets. This argument is probably still too extreme for even the main group of reformers, but it may provide the most successful long-term basis for growth of the Soviet Pacific.

Northeast Asia or the wider Pacific

When the Soviet Union thinks Pacific, what does it see? As suggested, China and Japan dominate the view. Because of the diversity of the Pacific, it is more difficult to invest time and thought in other parts of the Pacific, especially at the early stages of reform. Thus, the emphasis has so far been on Northeast Asia, including the Koreas, and tacitly even the United States. The Soviet Union has thus tended to see the Pacific as the north Pacific.

However, some thinkers—curiously, those mostly associated with a less ambitious idea of the Pacific—would concentrate on a socialist base. This school of thought looks to Vietnam, the third most populous communist state, as a vital part of the Soviet strategy in the Pacific. Its proponents see Laos and Cambodia as additional elements to be developed. Some of them also realize China is larger than just the Amur basin and see possibilities in wider contacts with the parts of China in the heartland that have not had the benefit of coastal contacts with the West.

These divisions within factions are often thin and even overlapping. Other observers also look beyond Northeast Asia but are attracted by the ASEAN states. Still others continue to think more in Asian than in Pacific terms. Many of these differences stem from regional specialization—the country an expert knows well often determines what is thought to be important. The main point is that the diversity of the region may distract the Soviet Union from the northern Pacific, where it can achieve the easiest and most important gains.

Territorial concession

A much more specific debate (which may be over by the time this book is published) concerns the vexed question of territorial concessions. The agreements with China on settling border disputes have yet to be completed or published. However, they seem to include the Soviet Union's return to an earlier position that recognized some Chinese claims, especially along the river border. Little, if any, territory is expected actually to change hands. By all accounts, some officials argued that even such a limited shift in the Soviet position should not have been made for fear of leading other states to believe that they could reclaim territory from the Soviet Union. The 1975 Helsinki agreement in Europe, in the old Soviet perspective at least, codified the principle of no change in postwar borders.

In the early 1990s, the major Pacific territorial debate in the Soviet Union will concern Japan's claim to what it calls the Northern Territories. As is already evident, some leaders are willing to return some islands and are prepared to honour the compromise of 1956. Less ambitious leaders do not want to do anything. The outcome may depend on how much Japan is prepared to compromise, for the

Japanese rejected these terms in 1956. The outcome may also depend on whether other territories, for example in the Baltics, are allowed to break away. Without some arrangement on the territorial issues, Soviet-Chinese and Soviet-Japanese relations will certainly be worse than they need to be. The apparent Sino-Soviet deal suggests that leaders willing to trade territory for peace and prosperity are taking charge of Soviet policy.

What is to be done

As one Soviet specialist described the challenge facing the Soviet Union in the Pacific, 'The dilemma before us is that either we will adopt radical structural decisions for our ship to gather headway, or the pace of growth will remain slow. . . . time is no ally of [our] country.'[3] Under such time pressure, we will probably not have to wait long to see how successful the Soviet Union will be in transforming its position in the Pacific.

In the decade before the millennium, there is increasing evidence that the Soviet Union has already begun to improve its standing in the Pacific. However it is not yet clear whether, like an energetic acrobat having performed a somersault, the Soviet Union will end facing the same direction and problems as when it started. It seems likely that the Soviet Union will reach its modest targets of tripling foreign trade, improving the standard of living in the Soviet Pacific, attracting more immigrants to the region and becoming more integrated into the prosperous pattern of international relations in the Pacific. Unless it does most of these things, it will not have moved forward very far.

Thus, the future of the Soviet Union in the Pacific depends on the type and depth of reforms that the Soviet Union chooses to adopt. The reaction of other states is important—for example, China may change its policies and worsen relations with the Soviet Union—but the primary variable for Soviet success is its own responsibility.

Perhaps the worst of the most likely outcomes for the Soviet Union would be its gradual decline as a superpower. This might result from half-hearted reforms that produce little real change in the Soviet domestic scene and therefore less change in its international economic position. If the Soviets have retreated militarily and continue to tinker with an obsolete ideology, there will be less reason than before to take the Soviet Union seriously. Like the Turkish empire, the Soviet Union might gradually crack apart, with all the destabilizing consequences for international security that surrounded the death of the Turkish empire.

Indeed, at the time of writing, when so much of the European and even Central Asian parts of the Russian empire seem to be in revolt and/or drifting away, the Turkish empire model seems less far-fetched. While there seems little prospect that the Soviet Pacific territory is also likely to spin-off, it must be true that its eastern fringes will feature far less on Moscow's agenda than the western and southern borders. In the short-term, the risks of instability must increase and the prospects for reform must fade. But it may be one of the great paradoxes of modern Soviet policy in the Pacific that a great shock, such as the disintegration of the eastern and southern parts of the empire, might well make Moscow more willing to invest in its far east and seek closer relations with neighbours in the region.

A more likely, but still less than satisfactory, scenario would be that significant success in Soviet reforms would result in more efficiency in the present system rather than in any systemic change. The Soviet Union might then be a poorer version of Canada or even possibly Australia, a hewer of wood for the resource-poor economies of the Pacific, yet having a decent standard of living. Assuming, as one must in the short term of any of the positive scenarios, that the Soviet Union will deemphasize its military power in the Pacific, it will nevertheless still be better armed than Canada or Australia but not much more influential.

The best scenario would depend on massive reform along the lines of the maritime strategy outlined above. At best, the Soviet Union would be wealthier (more like Canada and Australia) and more integrated into the Pacific region. Yet it is difficult to imagine this taking place with a growing Soviet military presence in the Pacific. Integration into a booming Pacific economy seems to require a less threatening posture. If the United States is satisfied with this stage of affairs, and other powers such as China and Japan do not try to take advantage of the new balance of power, then the Soviet military weakness might not be a problem.

If the Soviet Union does become an Australia with atomic weapons (and this is not meant to be pejorative), it will not have reached this status by the year 2000. The task facing the Soviet Union is enormous. Yet it is in the interest of other states in the Pacific that the

Soviet Union and its friends do become more integrated into the Pacific. Because the Soviet Union is likely to remain the second largest military power in the Pacific for the foreseeable future, it is in the interest of all those who want to have a prosperous international economy, that, at a minimum, the normalization of Soviet power in the Pacific be managed peacefully.

Irrespective of which scenario eventually comes to pass, it is no exaggeration to note that with less than ten years to go to the year 2000, the Soviet Union's position in the Pacific is probably better than at any time in its past. Moreover, this improvement has been attained remarkably rapidly in a five-year period. Of course, as they say, 'that was the easy bit'. In order for the Soviet Union to keep pace with the change in the Pacific then the past reforms will only have been a warm-up for the bigger game to come.

Notes

Chapter 1

1 Soviet official comments in 'The Vladivostok Initiatives: Two Years On' in *International Affairs* (Moscow, August 1988).
2 The definition of the Pacific is far from agreed. For a general discussion of the name and its different uses, see Gerald Segal, *Rethinking the Pacific* (Oxford: Oxford University Press, 1990). For the purpose of this study, the Pacific refers to the countries around and inside the geographic feature of the Pacific ocean. Thus, it includes the Pacific coast of the Americas and excludes Burma and points west outside the region. It includes the immediate hinterland states of Laos and Mongolia. The definition of Soviet Pacific territory is discussed below.
3 The Soviet Union tends to think of Asia-Pacific as a region stretching from Kabul to California. In practice, however, the Soviet Union has now begun to distinguish between South Asia (from Afghanistan to Burma) and the Pacific (as designated in this study). At the first Soviet-run international conference on Asia-Pacific in Vladivostok, even the map symbol for the conference left South Asia out and included the Americas. Thus, the analysis that follows takes up what might be called the hidden agenda in Soviet views of Asia-Pacific because it is increasingly clear that the Soviet Union distinguishes between South Asia and the Pacific and is primarily interested in, and intrigued by, the latter.

Chapter 2

1 From the Soviet Academy of Sciences (SAS) (Moscow), 'Maritime Territory: Past, Present and Future' (Mimeo for the SAS conference in Vladivostok, September 1988).
2 See the discussion in Allen Whiting, *Siberian Development and East Asia* (Stanford, Calif.: Stanford University Press, 1981) and Paul Dibb, *Siberia and the Pacific* (London: Praeger, 1972). Robert Manning, in one of the most recent books on the Soviet Union and the region, uses a title of *Asian Policy* but a subtitle of *The New Soviet Challenge in the Pacific* (New York: Priority Press, 1989).
3 The border between east and west Siberia can be taken to be roughly the same line of longitude as the western border of Mongolia, Han China and Southeast Asia. See a similar Soviet designation in the 1987

plan for development of the Soviet Pacific, noted by I. Ivanov on Soviet television on 7 February 1989 in British Broadcasting Corporation, Summary of World Broadcasts (henceforth BBC, SWB) SU,0386,A3,1.

4   Details cited in James Hoare and Susan Pares, *Korea: An Introduction* (London: Kegan Paul, 1988), pp. 200–201.

5   E. Stuart Kirby, *The Soviet Far East* (London: Macmillan, 1971), p. 11.

6   Violet Conolly, *Siberia, Today and Tomorrow* (London: Collins, 1975).

7   Dibb, *Siberia*, ch. 1.

8   Stuart Kirby, 'The USSR in Asia', in *Australasian Yearbook 1988* (London: Europa, 1988) and Whiting, *Siberian Development*, p. 35.

9   E.B. Kovrigin, 'The Soviet Far East', John J. Stephan and V.P. Chichkanov, eds., *Soviet-American Horizons on the Pacific* (Honolulu: University of Hawaii Press, 1986), pp. 1, 13.

10   Conolly, *Siberia*, ch. 9.

11   Dibb, *Siberia*, ch. 2.

12   Victor Mote, 'The Communications Infrastructure' in Rodger Swearingen, ed., *Siberia and the Soviet Far East* (Stanford, Calif.: Hoover Institution, 1987).

13   Ibid., p. 65.

14   Conolly, *Siberia*, ch. 4.

15   Such criticisms have long been made in Western assessments but Soviet sources are now going even further. This discussion of problems in the Soviet Far East is based on discussions in Moscow and Vladivostok in September 1988 as well as on Yu Skorokhodov, 'The Soviet Far East: Problems and Prospects', *Far Eastern Affairs*, no. 3, 1988 and 'Vladivostok Initiatives'.

16   Cited in Violet Conolly, 'Siberia: Yesterday, Today and Tomorrow' in Swearingen, *Siberia*, p. 16.

17   V.P. Chichkanov and P.A. Minakir, 'Economic Development of the Soviet Far East' in Stephan and Chichkanov, *Soviet-American Horizons*.

18   Swearingen, *Siberia*.

19   Thane Gustafson, 'The Energy Scene' in Swearingen, *Siberia*.

20   Skorokhodov, 'Soviet Far East', p. 6.

21   Ibid., pp. 8–9, and see the more detailed analysis in Jonathan Schiffer, *Soviet Regional Economic Policy* (London: Macmillan, 1989).

22   Kirby, '*Soviet Far East*'.

23   See the speech by V.I. Ilychev to the 1988 Vladivostok meeting. This point is also based on discussions in Vladivostok and Moscow.

Chapter 3

1   Hugh Thomas, *An Unfinished History of the World* (London: Pan, 1979).

2   C.P. Fitzgerald, *A Concise History of East Asia* (London: Penguin, 1966).

3   Alan Wood, 'From Conquest to Revolution' in Alan Wood, ed., *Siberia* (London: Croom Helm, 1987).

4   W. Gordon East, 'Asiatic USSR and the MPR' in W. Gordon East, O. H. K. Spate and Charles Fisher, *The Changing Map of Asia* (London: Methuen, 1971), p. 563.
5   Samuel Eliot Morisson, *The Great Explorers* (Oxford: Oxford University Press, 1978).
6   Terence Armstrong, *Russian Settlement in the North* (Cambridge: Cambridge University Press, 1965), p. 18.
7   B.N. Slavinskii, 'Russia and the Pacific to 1917' in Stephan and Chichkanov, *Soviet-American Horizons*, p. 32.
8   Ibid., p. 33.
9   East, 'Asiatic USSR', pp. 574–6.
10 Morisson, *Great Explorers*.
11 Glyn Barratt, *Russia in Pacific Waters, 1715–1825* (Vancouver: University of British Columbia Press, 1981), pp. 42–74.
12 Slavinskii, 'Russia and the Pacific', pp. 35–6.
13 Walter Kolarz, *The Peoples of the Soviet Far East* (London: George Philip, 1954), p. 22.
14 Ernest Dodge, *Beyond the Capes* (Oxford: Oxford University Press, 1976), ch. 12.
15 Slavinskii, 'Russia and the Pacific', p. 37.
16 John J. Stephan, 'Russian-American Economic Relations in the Pacific' in Stephan and Chichkanov, *Soviet-American Horizons*, p. 63.
17 Armstrong, *Russian Settlement*, p. 30.
18 Stephan, 'Russian-American', p. 63 and Franklin C.L. Ng, 'American Economic Interests in the Pacific to 1945' in Stephan and Chichkanov, *Soviet-American Horizons*, p. 52.
19 Richard Batman, *Outer Coast* (New York: Harcourt Brace Jovanovich, 1985).
20 Curiously for such an important Pacific venture, Perry sailed from Newport and went east to Japan. The Pacific had yet to obtain a natural American presence.
21 Slavinskii, 'Russia and the Pacific'.
22 John Stephan, *Sakhalin: A History* (Oxford: Oxford University Press, 1971).
23 H.F. McNair and Donald Lasch, *Modern Far Eastern International Relations* (London: D. Van Nostrand, 1950), pp. 54–5. See generally Ian Nish, *Japanese Foreign Policy, 1869–1942* (London: Routledge and Kegan Paul, 1977).
24 Ian Nish, *The Origins of the Russo-Japanese War* (London: Longman, 1985), pp. 2–17.
25 Richard Storry, *Japan and the Decline of the West in Asia, 1894–1943* (London: Macmillan, 1979), pp. 44–51.
26 Raymond Esthus, *Double Eagle and Rising Son* (London: Duke University Press, 1988).
27 Ibid., p. 202.
28 G.A. Lensen, *Balance of Intrigue* (Tallahassee: University of Florida, 1982).
29 Kolarz, *Soviet Far East*, pp. 2–22.

30   As discussed in Elie Kedourie, 'A New International Disorder' in Hedley Bull and Adam Watson, eds., *The Expansion of International Society* (Oxford: Clarendon Press, 1984).

31   Akira Iriye, *The Origins of the Second World War in Asia and the Pacific* (London: Longman, 1987).

32   Akira Iriye, 'Japanese Aggression and China's International Position, 1931–1949' in J.K. Fairbank and Albert Fuerwerker, eds., *The Cambridge History of China*, vol. 13, pt. 2 (Cambridge: Cambridge University Press, 1986), p. 497.

33   Storry, *Decline of the West*, p. 129.

34   The thesis is fully developed and the causes of war fully covered by Christopher Thorne, *The Limits of Foreign Policy* (London: Hamish Hamilton, 1972), pp. 39–126.

35   Akira Iriye, *Power and Culture* (Cambridge: Harvard University Press, 1981), pp. 3–4.

36   Donald Macintyre, *Sea Power in the Pacific* (New York: Crane and Russak, 1972), p. 196.

37   Cited in Thorne, *The Issues of War* (London: Hamish Hamilton, 1985), p. 25.

38   Thorne, *Allies of a Kind* (Oxford: Oxford University Press, 1979), p. 135.

39   Ibid., pp. 296, 407, 526.

40   Stephan, 'Russian-American', pp. 75–80.

41   J. Arthur Lower, *Ocean of Destiny* (Vancouver: University of British Columbia Press, 1978), p. 145.

42   Gabriel Kolko, *The Politics of War* (New York: Random House, 1968) generally and p. 535.

43   Iriye, *Power and Culture*, pp. 230–2.

44   These issues are discussed in Kolko, *Politics of War* and Herbert Feis, *The Atomic Bomb and the End of World War Two* (Princeton: Princeton University Press, 1970). See also Thorne, *Allies* for a careful discussion.

45   Cited in Thorne, *Issues of War*, p. 206.

Chapter 4

1   Gerald Segal, *Rethinking the Pacific* (Oxford: Oxford University Press, 1990).

2   For the purposes of this section, and unless otherwise noted, the term 'The Soviet Union' refers to the Soviet Pacific territory as outlined in chapter 1. Despite its total population of just under 17 million in 1986, its size would make it the largest country, so to speak, in the Pacific.

3   Figures in this section are calculated from the appendix of David Crystal, *The Cambridge Encyclopedia of Language* (Cambridge: Cambridge University Press, 1987).

4   *The Economist*, 20 December 1986 and Robert McCrum, William Cran, Robert MacNeil, *The Story of English* (London: Faber and Faber, 1986).

5   See, for example, Xinhua's reports on unrest in Georgia on 18 April 1989 in FE,0441,A2,1.
6   Details reported by Kyodo on 18 March 1989 in FE,0415,A2,2 and 10 April in FE,0432,i.
7   Soviet radio on 5 August 1988 in BBC,SBW,SU,0222,i.
8   For the last mention of this issue see Kyodo 19 March 1989 in FE,0414,A2,1.
9   Figures in this section are from the annual statistical compendium of the World Tourist Organization (Madrid).
10 See *International Herald Tribune*, 23 February 1989 for examples of such contacts.
11 On contract labour in the Soviet Union, see a Chinese report of 30 September 1988 in FE,W0050,A2,1.
12 For example, *Socialist Industry*, 27 September 1988 in FBIS,SOV, 88–189, pp. 17–19 and *Beijing Review*, 10 October 1988, p. 27.
13 Noted in 'Vladivostok Initiatives'.
14 For a possible harbinger of change for meetings on the environment and energy, see Moscow radio 25 February 1989 in SU,W0066,A11.
15 'World Broadcasting', *The Economist*, 6 June 1987.
16 See a report on Soviet aid to Cambodia on 30 November 1988 in FE,W0054,i.
17 Of course, China and the Soviet Union tend to see eye to eye on such issues anyway. For a recent example, see *Beijing Review*, 10 April 1989.
18 These details, and most others in this section, are drawn from 'The USSR and Asian Pacific Countries: Cultural Contacts', a document produced for the Vladivostok conference in October 1988.
19 See, for example, Moscow Home Service's report of the visit of Chinese journalists on 30 March 1989 in SU,0432,A3,1.
20 Moscow radio on 7 March 1989 in SU,W0068,A16.
21 *The Economist*, 6 May 1989.
22 Gilbert Rozman, 'Moscow's Japan-Watchers in the First Years of the Gorbachev Era', *The Pacific Review*, no. 3, 1988.
23 *Asiaweek*, 3 February 1989, p. 40.
24 Some South Europeans did drift in and out of democracy during this period. For a more complete discussion of these patterns see Segal, *Rethinking*, section 2.
25 Gerald Segal, *Sino-Soviet Relations after Mao* (London: International Institute for Strategic Studies [or IISS], Adelphi Paper No. 202, 1985).
26 Gilbert Rozman, *A Mirror for Socialism* (London: I.B. Tauris, 1985).
27 Details of the summit that normalized relations are in SWB,FE,0459 and 0460 on 17 and 18 May 1989.
28 See Deng Xiaoping's use of the term as reported by Kyodo on 22 October 1988 in FE,0293,A2,3.
29 For discussion of the presummit rationalization of the decision, see Li Peng on 14 April 1989 in FE,0431,A3,3,7–8 and Zhongguo Xinwen She 15 March 1989 in 0411,A2,1. Details of the summit that normalized relations are in SWB,FE,0459 and 0460 on 17 and 18 May 1989.

30   See for example, 'Moscow Plugs New Eastern Europe Deal' by Song Yubo in *Beijing Review*, 24 April 1989.

31   For discussion of the Soviet debate see, for example, Nikolai Anin, 'What We Wish the Chinese People', *New Times*, no. 25, 1989; Albert Vlasov, 'After Liberating Tiananmen', *Moscow News*, no. 24, 1989 and Fedor Burlatsky, 28 June 1989, reported on Moscow radio in SU,0497,A3,1. Burlatsky and a Moscow World Service commentary on 5 June 1989 made explicit comparison to killings in Georgia. See SU,0476,A3,1. See the more careful official reaction on Soviet television on 21 May in SU,0466,A3,3 and, of course, the Soviet delegation to the summit, which regularly refused comment on events on the streets.

32   Soviet television, 2 July 1989 in SU,0513,A3,5–6; Moscow radio in standard Chinese, 9 October 1989 in SU,0598,A3,1–2; 'The Echo of Tiananmen Square', *Moscow News*, no. 44 1989 and 'The Arduous Path of Socialism', *New Times*, no. 40 1989.

33   Dae-Sook Suh, *The Korean Communist Movement* (Princeton: Princeton University Press, 1967).

34   Robert Scalapino and Chong-Sik Lee, *Communism in Korea* (Berkeley: University of California Press, 1972), vol. 1.

35   Chin Chung, *Pyongyang between Peking and Moscow* (Tuscaloosa: University of Alabama Press, 1978).

36   Robert Simmons, *The Strained Alliance* (New York: Free Press, 1975).

37   Gerald Segal, *Defending China* (Oxford: Oxford University Press, 1985).

38   Chung, *Pyongyang*, ch. 2.

39   Scalapino and Lee, *Communism*, vol. 2, ch. 15.

40   Reports in 1988 in FE,0325,i and 0319,A2,1.

41   Moscow radio in Korean, 11 January 1990 in SU,0673,A3,1–2.

42   Alan Sanders, *Mongolia* (London: Frances Pinter, 1987), ch. 1.

43   Robert Rupen, *How Mongolia Is Really Ruled* (Stanford: Hoover Institution, 1979).

44   Segal, *Sino-Soviet Relations after Mao* and Alan Sanders, 'Sino-Soviet Detente and Mongolia', *The Pacific Review*, vol. 1, no. 2, 1988.

45   Rupen, *Mongolia Is Ruled*, ch. 8 and Soviet discussion in *History of the Mongolian People's Republic* (Moscow: Nauka, 1973).

46   Discussed by Alan Sanders in 'Avoiding Extremes', *The Far Eastern Economic Review*, 6 July 1989.

47   Melanie Beresford, *Vietnam* (London: Frances Pinter, 1988), ch. 1.

48   William Duiker, *The Communist Road to Power in Vietnam* (Boulder, Colo.: Westview, 1981).

49   James Harrison, *The Endless War* (New York: Free Press, 1982).

50   Beresford, *Vietnam*, ch. 11.

51   Adam Fforde and Suzanne Paine, *The Limits of National Liberation* (London: Croom Helm, 1987).

52   See, generally, Michael Vickery, *Kampuchea* (London: Frances Pinter, 1986) and Martin Stuart-Fox, *Laos* (London: Frances Pinter, 1987).

53   Gerald Curtis, *The Japanese Way of Politics* (New York: Columbia University Press, 1988), pp. 27–30.

54   *Pravda*, 21 October 1988 in FBIS-SOV,88,209,21.

Chapter 5

1 See comments by Vladimir Lukin in 'The Vladivostok Initiatives: Two Years On', *International Affairs*, August 1988, p. 146.

2 J. D. B. Miller, *Asia and the Pacific* (New York: Institute for East-West Security, Occasional Paper No. 4, 1985); Seizaboro Sato and Kenneth Hunt, 'Convergence and Divergence in East Asian and Western Security Interests', both in IISS, *Adelphi Paper* No. 216, Spring 1987 and Michael Leifer, ed., *The Balance of Power in East Asia* (London: Macmillan 1986).

3 Donald and Janet Zagoria, 'Crises on the Korean Peninsula' in Stephan Kaplan, ed., *Force Without War* (Washington, D.C.: Brookings, 1981).

4 J. H. Kalicki, *The Pattern of Sino-American Crisis* (London: Cambridge University Press, 1975); Alexander George and Richard Smoke, *Deterrence in American Foreign Policy* (New York: Columbia University Press, 1974); and Gerald Segal, *Defending China* (Oxford: Oxford University Press, 1985), ch. 7.

5 This process is best documented in Henry Kissinger, *The White House Years* (London: Weidenfeld, 1979) and Seymour Hersh, *The Price of Peace* (London: Faber and Faber, 1981).

6 Gerald Segal, *The Great Power Triangle* (London: Macmillan, 1982).

7 Thailand is, of course, a US ally on the mainland, and Malaysia leans to the US side and has both continental and island parts. Korea, with its US forces, is also on the mainland.

8 Barry Blechman and Robert Berman, *Guide to Far East Navies* (Annapolis, Md.: Naval Institute Press, 1983).

9 Malcolm McIntosh, *Arms across the Pacific* (London: Frances Pinter, 1987) presents one distinctive view. For a partisan Soviet assessment, see Vyacheslav Bunin, *Asia-Pacific Region* (Moscow: Novosti, 1988) and Yuri Vinogradov, *Asia-Pacific Security and Regional Organizations* (New Delhi: Allied Publishers, 1988). The US view is available in a number of government publications, but a particularly succinct presentation of the line is available in two articles by Lieutenant Commander G. S. Thomas in *Naval Forces*, nos. 3 and 4, 1988.

10 Robert Berman and John Baker, *Soviet Strategic Forces* (Washington, D.C.: Brookings, 1982).

11 Harry Gelman, 'The Soviet Far East Military Buildup' and J. J. Martin, 'Thinking about the Nuclear Balance in Asia', both in Richard Solomon and Masataka Kosaka, eds., *The Soviet Far East Military Buildup* (London: Croom Helm, 1986).

12 Full text in FE,0460,C1.

13 See comments by Major General G. V. Batenin on Soviet television on 7 February 1989 in SU,0386,A3,1 and Bunin, *Asia-Pacific*, p. 17.

14 For a recent statement of the Soviet view, see a paper by V. Lukin, 'Southeast Asia and Pacific Asia Security in the Final Decade of the 20th Century' presented to a conference in Kuala Lumpur organized by the Malaysian International Affairs Forum, March 1988.

15 Interviewed in *New Times*, September 1988.

16   R. A. Wolff, *Changes in the Soviet Far East Forces Command* (Royal Military Academy Sandhurst, Soviet Studies Research Centre, 1987) and Ichiro Takizawa, 'Soviet Military Forces', *Soviet Studies*, no. 7, October 1988, p. 117.

17   Derek da Cunha, 'The Growth of the Soviet Pacific Fleet's Submarine Force', *International Defense Review*, February 1988.

18   For details see Peter Hayes, et al., *American Lake* (London: Penguin, 1987).

19   Statistics from the IISS, *Military Balance* (London: International Institute for Strategic Studies, various years).

20   John Collins, *U.S.-Soviet Military Balance, 1980–1985* (Oxford: Pergamon, 1985), p. 144.

21   See various issues of the 1980s of the IISS' annual publication, *Strategic Survey*.

22   For details, see Peter Hayes, et al., *American Lake*, appendix E.

23   Anthony Preston, 'The Changing Balance in the Pacific', *Jane's Defence Weekly*, 20 September 1984 and 'The Pacific Still America's Lake?', *East-West Papers*, no. 8, July 1987. Other Soviet figures are cited in Soviet sources in chapter 5, note 13.

24   Francis Fukayama, *Soviet Civil-Military Relations and the Power Projection Mission* (Santa Monica, Calif.: RAND, April 1987) and *Far Eastern Economic Review*, 12 May 1988, p. 20 and *International Herald Tribune*, 23 October 1987.

25   *International Herald Tribune*, 13 April 1988.

26   In the journal *Red Star* and noted by Lukin in 'Pacific Asia Security', p. 27.

27   Soviet television on 7 February 1989 in SU,0386,A3,1 and Kuzmin on Moscow radio in Japanese, 6 February 1989, p. 8.

28   Data are derived from the IISS, *Military Balance* for the relevant years. See also continuing analysis in *Pacific Research*, no. 2, November 1988. For Kuzmin, see SU,0386,A3,8. *Pacific Research* in February 1988, p. 15, points out that there has been a reported increase in the number of Soviet intelligence-gathering ships in the vicinity of Hawaii since 1986.

29   Tass military analyst on 19 May 1989 in SU,0466,A3,3–4.

30   Bunin, *Asia-Pacific*, pp. 26–7.

31   *Pravda*, 28 May 1989 in SU,0468,C3,1–2.

32   See General Moiseyev in *Pravda* on 4 May 1989 in SU,0453,A3,7–9.

33   *International Herald Tribune*, 11 March 1989.

34   Robert O'Neill, 'The Balance of Naval Power in the Pacific', *The Pacific Review*, vol. 1, no. 2, 1988.

35   See for example Richard Solomon in June 1989 reported in *Far Eastern Economic Review*, 6 July 1989, p. 23.

36   *Far Eastern Economic Review*, 18 June 1987.

37   *International Herald Tribune*, 23 October 1988.

38   Anthony Cordesman, 'The Western Naval Threat to the Soviet Military Presence in Asia', *Armed Forces Journal*, April 1983.

39   Ibid., ch. 16.

40   Michael Leifer, *Malaysia, Singapore and Indonesia* (Alphen ann den Rijin: Sijthoff and Noordhoff, 1978).

41 Allen Whiting, *Siberian Development and East Asia* (Stanford, Calif.: Stanford University Press, 1981).

42 Ibid., and Michael Leifer, *Indonesia's Foreign Policy* (London: Allen & Unwin, 1983). Yaacov Vertzberger, *The Malacca-Singapore Straits* (London: Institute for the Study of Conflict, Conflict Paper No. 140).

43 *International Herald Tribune*, 3–4 May 1986.

44 *The Economist*, 14 November 1987.

45 William Feeney, 'The Pacific Basing System and United States Security', William Tow and William Feeney, eds., *U.S. Foreign Policy and Asian-Pacific Security* (Boulder, Colo.: Westview Press, 1982).

46 William Arkin and David Chappell, 'Forward Offensive Strategy', *World Policy Journal*, Summer 1985, and William Arkin and Richard Fieldhouse, *Nuclear Battlefields* (Cambridge, Mass.: Ballinger, 1985), ch. 7.

47 *International Herald Tribune*, 21 January 1987; W. T. Roy, 'The Soviets and the South Pacific', *Asia-Pacific Defense Forum*, Winter 1985–6. See more generally the regular updates in *Pacific Research*.

48 Malcolm McIntosh, 'Fish Bone of Contention', *The Guardian*, 12 June 1987, and *Asiaweek*, 24 August 1986.

49 *Jane's Defence Weekly*, 23 May 1987.

50 Coral Bell, 'The Security of Pacific Ministates', *Asia-Pacific Defense Forum*, Winter 1985–6.

51 The discussion of this and the following territorial disputes depends heavily on Alan Day, ed., *Border and Territorial Disputes* (London: Longman, 1982) and Henry Degenhardt, *Maritime Affairs—A World Handbook* (London: Longman, 1985).

52 The idea is developed in the IMEMO Yearbook, 1986, *Disarmament and Security* (Moscow: 1987) and is discussed in Bunin, *Asia-Pacific*.

53 See, generally, Marc Gallicchio, *The Cold War Begins in Asia* (New York: Columbia University Press, 1988) and John Garver, *Chinese-Soviet Relations 1937–1945* (Oxford: Oxford University Press, 1988).

54 Donald Zagoria, *The Sino-Soviet Conflict* (Princeton: Princeton University Press, 1962) and John Gittings, *Survey of the Sino-Soviet Dispute* (Oxford: Oxford University Press, 1969).

55 For example, A. Bovin in *Izvestiya* on 8 February in SU,0386,A3,4. See also the comments by Soviet television's political observer, Vladimir Tsvetov, on 7 February in SU,0386,A3,2.

56 William Griffiths, *Sino-Soviet Relations* (Cambridge, Mass.: MIT Press, 1967) and Segal, *Great Power Triangle*.

57 Philip Karber, 'The Military Impact of the Gorbachev Reductions', *Armed Forces Journal*, January 1989.

58 Thomas Robinson, *The Sino-Soviet Border Dispute* (Santa Monica, Calif.: The Rand Corporation, 1970).

59 Segal, *Defending China*, ch. 10.

60 Alan Day, *China and the Soviet Union* (London: Longman, 1985).

61 Richard Wich, *Sino-Soviet Crisis Politics* (Cambridge, Mass: Harvard University Press, 1980).

62 Kissinger, *White House Years*.

63 Details from Segal, *Sino-Soviet Relations after Mao* and Gerald Segal, ed., *The China Factor* (London: Croom Helm, 1982).

64 Segal, *Sino-Soviet Relations after Mao*; 'Sino-Soviet Detente', *The World Today*, May 1987 and 'Sino-Soviet Relations: The New Agenda', June 1988.

65 Yazov on 28 May 1989 in SU,0468,C3,1–2. Gorbachev clarified the nature of the cuts on 18 January 1989 reported in SU,0363,A1,2. For analysis, see Gerald Segal, 'Sino-Soviet Relations', *The Washington Quarterly*, June 1989.

66 *Far Eastern Economic Review*, 16 March 1989 and 31 August 1989.

67 *The Economist*, 24 October 1987.

68 For some of the details see 4 November 1988 in SU,0300,i, Moscow radio 27 October in SU,0303,A3,2, Peking Home Service 28 November in 0321,A3,6, Sovetskaya Rossiya 18 November in FE,0313,A2,2, Ulan Bator on 10 December in FE,0333,A3,1, Tass in Russian on 21 January 1989 in FE,0366,A2,1; *Beijing Review*, 2 January 1989 and more generally Erkin Alptekin, 'Relations between Eastern and Western Turkestan', *Radio Free Europe*, RL 548/88, 30 November 1988. See also *Far Eastern Economic Review*, 22 December 1988, p. 18.

69 See, for example, a Chinese report on March 1989 in FE,0423,i and Kyodo on 24 February 1990, in FBIS-CHI-90-039-5.

70 Robert Scalapino, 'Asia in a Global Context', Gelman, 'Soviet Military Buildup' and Martin, 'Thinking about the Nuclear Balance in Asia', all in Solomon and Kosaka, *Military Buildup*.

71 Ellis Joffe, *The Chinese Army after Mao* (London: Weidenfeld, 1987), and Ellis Joffe and Gerald Segal, 'The PLA under Modern Conditions', *Survival*, August 1985.

72 Harry Gelman, *The Soviet Far East Buildup and Soviet Risk-Taking Against China* (Santa Monica, Calif.: The Rand Corporation, 1982).

73 'People's Daily', 9 March 1989 in FE,0408,A2,1 and Gerald Segal, 'Chinese Strategy to the Year 2000', *The Yearbook of PLA Affairs, 1989* (Kaohsiung, Taiwan: Sun Yat Sen University, 1989).

74 Chinese Foreign Ministry official on 20 April 1989 in FE,0444,i.

75 See, for example, a series of articles in *Beijing Review*, 27 February and 6 March 1989. Of course, in the longer term, Sino-Soviet detente may lead to less Japanese defence spending.

76 See US public opinion polls reported in *Financial Times*, 23 February 1989.

77 Brian Bridges, *Korea and the West* (London: Chatham House Paper No. 33, 1986).

78 Peter Lowe, *The Origins of the Korean War* (London: Longman, 1986), ch. 1 and Gallicchio, *Cold War in Asia*.

79 Ibid., both Lowe and Gallicchio, and especially Bruce Cummings, *The Origins of the Korean War* (Guildford, 1981) and Callum MacDonald, *Korea: The War Before Vietnam* (London: Macmillan, 1986).

80 Allen Whiting, *China Crosses the Yalu* (Stanford: Stanford University Press, 1960) and Robert Simmons, *The Strained Alliance* (New York: Free Press, 1975).

81 Robert O'Neil, in *Australia in the Korean War* (Canberra: Australian National University, 1981), who notes the following states that were involved in the Korean conflict: Australia, Belgium, Canada, Colombia, Ethiopia, France, Greece, Luxembourg, The Netherlands, New Zealand, Philippines, Thailand, Turkey, South Africa and the United Kingdom. Denmark, Italy, India, Norway and Sweden sent medical units. Of the total casualties, some 1.3 million were suffered by South Korea, 42,091 by the United States and 17,260 by other United Nation troops. Total communist casualties were estimated at from 1.5 to 2 million. David Rees, *Korea: The Limited War* (London: Macmillan, 1964).

82 Lowe, *Korean War*, ch. 7.

83 Rosemary Foot, *The Wrong War* (London: Cornell University Press, 1985) and Segal, *Defending China*, ch. 6.

84 Roger Dingman, 'Atomic Diplomacy during the Korean War' and Rosemary Foot, 'Nuclear Coercion and the Ending of the Korea Conflict', both in *International Security*, no. 3, Winter 1988–9.

85 Zagoria and Zagoria, 'Crises on the Korean Peninsula'.

86 The question of the military balance is tackled in a number of ways by different analysts. For a sampling, see Georges Tan Eng Bok, 'Arms Control in Korea' in Gerald Segal, ed., *Arms Control in Asia* (London: Macmillan, 1987) and various chapters in Douglas Stuart, ed., *East Asian Security* (London: Gower, 1987).

87 Statistics from the IISS, *Military Balance*.

88 Gerald Segal, 'The Soviet Union and Korea' in Gerald Segal, ed., *The Soviet Union and East Asia* (London: Heinemann, for the RIIA, 1983) and Ralph Clough, 'The Soviet Union and the Two Koreas' in Donald Zagoria, ed., *Soviet Policy in East Asia* (New Haven: Yale University Press, 1983).

89 Moscow radio in Japanese on 6 February 1989 in SU,0386,A3,9.

90 *New Times*, No. 25, 1989.

91 Harold Hinton, *Korea under New Leadership* (New York: Praeger, 1983).

92 Gerald Segal, 'Sino–Soviet Detente: How Far How Fast', *The World Today*, May 1987 and Segal, 'Taking Sino-Soviet Detente Seriously', *The Washington Quarterly*, Summer 1989.

93 Leon Sigal, *Fighting to a Finish* (Ithaca, N.Y.: Cornell University Press, 1988).

94 Wolf Mendl, 'The Soviet Union and Japan' in Segal, *Soviet Union and East Asia*.

95 Furthermore, to call the disputed islands 'the Kurile islands' is tacitly to support the Soviet position.

96 Donald Hellmann, *Japanese Foreign Policy and Domestic Politics* (Berkeley: University of California Press, 1969).

97 Gregory Clark, 'The Cold War Goes On and On for Tokyo and Moscow', *International Herald Tribune*, 12 June 1986.

98 *Far Eastern Economic Review*, 10 September 1987.

99   See the argument below. Also, an implicit Soviet recognition of the need to return to the 1956 deal is presented in the detailed legal arguments of Y. Prokhorov and L. Shevchuk, 'Japan's Territorial Claims to the USSR', *International Affairs*, February 1989.

100   For a good background, see Wolf Mendl, 'Japan's Northern Territories: An Asian Falklands?', *The World Today*, June 1987.

101   This is a vastly complex story, but see some of the Soviet proposals in Kyodo, 7 September 1988 in SOV,88,174,20–21. On the Soviet view of talks about the islands as 'a concession', see Moscow radio commentary on 22 December in SU,0347,A3,1–2. Other signs of change are in the various reports on the visit in the FE and SU series from numbers 0340–0343. See general reports on the visit in *The Financial Times*, 17 and 20 December 1988 and *Far Eastern Economic Review*, 22 and 29 December 1988. On continuing Soviet debates, see the saga of Yury Afanasyev in October 1989 in SU,0595,i.

102   Alexei Bogaturov and Mikhail Nosov, 'How to Even Out the Lop-Sided "Triangle" ', *New Times*, no. 18, 1989.

103   See the Soviet publication of an article by the noted Japanese scholar Hiroshi Kimura in *New Times*, no. 23, 1989 entitled 'Impatience Only Spoils Things', dealing with the territorial issue.

104   See Kyodo on 24 March 1989 in FE,0418,A2,1.

105   Karel van Wolferen, *The Enigma of Japanese Power* (London: Macmillan, 1989).

106   Major General Batenin on 7 February in SU,0286,A3,3–4.

107   Gilbert Rozman's two articles on Soviet-Japanese relations in the age of realism and respect, both in *The Pacific Review*, nos. 3 and 4, 1988.

108   See the visit of the Japanese foreign minister to Moscow in November 1988 to discuss Korean matters in FE,0304,i.

109   Cited in FE,0402,A2,1.

110   Discussed by Rozman as noted in note 107.

111   Martin Stuart-Fox, *Laos*, ch. 1.

112   Arthur Dommen, *Laos* (Boulder: Westview, 1985).

113   Ben Kiernan and Boua Chantou, *Peasants and Politics in Kampuchea, 1941–1981* (London: Zed Press, 1982) and Ben Kiernan, *How Pol Pot Came to Power* (London: Verso, 1984).

114   Michael Vickery, *Kampuchea* (London: Frances Pinter, 1986), ch. 3.

115   Ibid.

116   Segal, *Great Power Triangle*, ch. 4.

117   The literature on the war is vast. For a range of analyses, see Stanley Karnow, *Vietnam: A History* (New York: Viking, 1983); R. B. Smith, *An International History of the Vietnam War*, vols. 1 and 2 (London: Macmillan, 1985); George Kahin, *Intervention* (New York: Alfred Knopf, 1986) and Gabriel Kolko, *Anatomy of War* (Toronto: Pantheon Books, 1985).

118   Allen Whiting, *The Chinese Calculus of Deterrence* (Ann Arbor: University of Michigan, 1975) and Segal, *Defending China*.

119 Robert Ross, 'Indochina's Continuing Tragedy', in *Problems of Communism*, November 1986 and Ross, *Indochina Tangle* (New York: Columbia University Press, 1988).

120 Kiernan, *Pol Pot* and Elizabeth Becker, *When the War Was Over* (New York: Simon and Schuster, 1986).

121 Nayan Chanda, *Brother Enemy* (New York: Harcourt, Brace, Jovanovich, 1986).

122 See several essays in David Elliot, ed., *The Third Indochina Conflict* (Boulder, Colo.: Westview, 1981).

123 Evelyn Colbert cited in Ross, 'Indochina Tragedy'.

124 William Duiker, *Vietnam Since the Fall of Saigon* (Athens, Ohio: Ohio University Press, 1985).

125 Leszek Buszynski, *Soviet Foreign Policy and Southeast Asia* (London: Croom Helm, 1986), ch. 4.

126 Chanda, *Brother Enemy*, p. 397.

127 Ibid., ch. 8.

128 Charles McGregor, *The Sino-Vietnamese Relationship and the Soviet Union* (London: IISS, Adelphi Paper No. 232, 1988).

129 Chang Pao-Min, *Kampuchea between China and Vietnam* (Singapore: Singapore University Press, 1985).

130 Segal, *Sino-Soviet Relations after Mao*.

131 Segal, *Defending China*, ch. 12.

132 Chanda, *Brother Enemy*, chs. 5, 9.

133 Zbigniew Brzezinski, *Power and Principle* (New York: Farrar, Straus and Giroux, 1983); Jimmy Carter, *Keeping Faith* (London: Collins, 1982) and Cyrus Vance, *Hard Choices* (New York: Simon and Schuster, 1983).

134 Bruce Burton, 'Contending Explanations of the 1979 Sino-Vietnamese War', *International Journal*, vol. 34, no. 4, Autumn 1979; Daniel Tretiak, 'China's Vietnam War and Its Consequences', *The China Quarterly*, no. 80, December 1979; Harlan Jencks, 'China's "Punitive" War on Vietnam', *Asian Survey*, vol. 19, no. 8, December 1979; King Chen, 'China's War against Vietnam, 1979', *The Journal of Northeast Asian Affairs*, vol. 3, no. 1, Spring/Summer 1983 and Segal, *Defending China*, ch. 12.

135 Segal, *Defending China* and Jencks, 'China's "Punitive" War'.

136 Joffe, *Chinese Army* and David Goodman, et al., *The China Challenge* (London: Royal Institute of International Affairs, Chatham House Paper No. 32, 1986).

137 Segal, 'Sino-Soviet Detente'.

138 Donald Zagoria, ed., *Soviet Policy in East Asia* (London: Yale University Press, 1982), Segal, *Soviet Union in East Asia;* Georges Tan Eng Bok, *The USSR in East Asia* (Paris: Atlantic Institute Papers No. 59–60, 1986) and Gerald Segal, 'The Soviet Union and the Pacific Century', *The Journal of Communist Studies*, December 1987.

139 Xinhua 5 February 1989 in FE,0378,C2,1.

140 See reports of Moscow radio on 3 April 1989 in SU,3430,A3,3 and, more generally, *Far Eastern Economic Review*, 30 March 1989.

141   For example, Tass on 30 November in SU,047,A3,3.
142   *The Economist*, 17 December 1988.
143   Tass in Russian 21 December 1988 in FE,0342,A2,2–4. See also Tass on 17 January 1989 in 0366,A2,1 and, generally, *Far Eastern Economic Review*, 5 January 1989.
144   Marwyn Samuels, *Contest for the South China Sea* (London: Methuen, 1982) and Chi-kin Lo, *China's Policy towards Territorial Disputes* (London: Routledge, 1989).
145   Details in Segal, *Defending China*, ch. 11. Also Ronald Keith, ed., *Energy, Security and Economic Development in East Asia* (London: Croom Helm, 1986).
146   Gerald Segal, 'As China Grows Strong', *International Affairs*, March 1988.
147   Gerald Segal, *Defending China*.
148   Mark Valencia, 'Troubled Waters', *Far Eastern Economic Review*, 31 March 1988.
149   For example, the Japan–South Korea disputes over Takeshima (Tokdo) and Danjo islands, the former held by South Korea and the latter by Japan, but both disputed.
150   Sir Anthony Parsons, *Antarctica: The Next Decade* (Cambridge, U.K.: Cambridge University Press, 1987) and *Far Eastern Economic Review*, 11 February 1988.
151   Robert O'Neill and D. M. Horner, eds., *Australian Defence Policy for the 1980s* (London: University of Queensland Press, 1982) and Ramesh Thakur, *In Defence of New Zealand* (Boulder, Colo.: Westview, 1986).
152   Ross Babbage, 'Australian Defence Policy', *The Pacific Review*, no. 1, 1988.
153   Paul Dibb, 'Soviet Strategy towards Australia, New Zealand and the South-West Pacific', *Australian Outlook*, August 1985.
154   Ibid., ch. 4. Defence Minister Kim Beazley said in 1988 that no Soviet surface warship has been sighted in the south Pacific since World War II. *Pacific Research*, August 1988, p. 10.
155   John Bowan, 'Australia's Relations with the Soviet Bloc' in Paul Dibb, ed., *Australia's External Relations in the 1980s* (London: Croom Helm, 1983).
156   Tass on 2 November 1988 in FBIS-SOV,88,217,31.
157   A series of Tass reports in November 1988 in FBIS-SOV,88,222,15–17.
158   Daniel Tumarkin, 'USSR: The Unknown Northern Neighbour', in R. Crocombe and A. Ali, eds., *Foreign Forces in Pacific Politics* (Fiji: University of South Pacific, 1983).
159   Paul Gardner, 'Tuna Poaching and Nuclear Testing in the South Pacific', *Orbis*, Spring 1988.
160   Dibb, 'Soviet Strategy', p. 72.
161   12 October 1988 in FE,0280,i.
162   4 November 1988 in FE,0300,i.
163   Dibb, 'Soviet Strategy' and *International Herald Tribune*, 7 July 1988.
164   Wider issues are discussed in Segal, *Arms Control in Asia*; Gerald Segal, 'Soviet Arms Control and the Pacific', *Council for Arms Control*, 1989 and Tsuyoshi Hasegawa, 'Soviet Arms Control Policy in Asia and the

US-Japan Alliance', *Japan Review of International Affairs*, vol. 2, no. 2, 1988.

165   Reinhard Drifte, 'China and the NPT' in Joseph Goldblatt, ed., *Non-Proliferation* (London: Taylor and Francis, 1985), pp. 45–55 and Gerald Segal, 'China and Arms Control', *The World Today*, August 1985.

166   *International Herald Tribune*, 30 May 1986.

167   F. A. Mediansky, 'The South Pacific Nuclear Free Zone', *Asian-Pacific Defense Forum*, Winter 1985–6.

168   *Far Eastern Economic Review*, 15 May 1986.

169   Bridges, *Korea and the West*.

170   Bok, 'Arms Control in Korea'.

171   Details on the balance of forces in Segal, *Sino-Soviet Relations after Mao*. The precise number of troops in the Soviet divisions is a matter of much controversy, but the facts that the number of Soviet divisions has remained constant and that their state of readiness has been reduced are relatively uncontested. Basic figures are in the IISS, *Military Balance*.

172   For the moves in May 1989, see SU and FE, 0469,1.

173   For two reports of talks in June 1989 see SU,0497,A3,2.

174   See Part 8 of the Institute of World Economy and International Relations, *Disarmament and Security Yearbook 1987* (Moscow: Novosti, 1988).

175   Gerald Segal, 'Introduction' in Segal, *Arms Control in Asia*.

176   Masashi Nishihara, *East Asian Security* (London: Trilateral Commission Triangle Paper No. 30, 1985).

177   Institute of World Economy *Yearbook 1987*, p. 425. See also Institute of World Economy and International Relations, *Disarmament and Security Yearbook 1986* (Moscow: Novosti, 1987), vol. 2, sec. 4, ch. 6.

178   Gerald Segal, 'Defence Culture and Sino-Soviet Relations', *Journal of Strategic Studies*, June 1985.

179   For an early statement before Gorbachev, see Soviet Government Statement, 23 April 1986 in BBC,SWB,SU,8242,A3,1–3 and *Pravda*, 12 May 1986 in No. 8263,A3,1–2.

180   Tass, 2 February 1989 in FE,0376,A2,2.

181   E. Shevardnadze on 2 February in FE,0376,A2,4.

182   V. Ovchinnikov in *Pravda* on 28 January, SU,0374,A3,6.

183   Ibid., p. 429.

184   On Korea, see *New Times*, no. 23, 1989.

185   Ken Booth, *Law, Force and Diplomacy at Sea* (London: Allen and Unwin, 1985).

186   L. Ngok, 'The Pacific Ocean Region', *Naval Forces*, no. 2, 1988.

187   These issues are discussed in Segal, *The China Factor*.

188   On these treaties see Lawrence Freedman, *The Evolution of Nuclear Strategy* (London: Macmillan, 1980).

189   Solomon and Kosaka, *Military Buildup*; and Hiroshi Kimura, 'Arms Control in East Asia' in Adam Garfinkle, ed., *Global Perspectives on Arms Control* (New York: Praeger, 1984).

190   Institute of World Economy, *Yearbook 1987*, ch. 21.

191   Paul Bracken, 'Crises and Northeast Asia', *The Washington Quarterly*, Autumn 1988.

192   See some Soviet proposals by Vladimir Ivanov, 'Soviet–US Face-off Must End', *The Far Eastern Economic Review*, 12 January 1989, p. 19.
193   Ivanov again, this time in *New Times*, no. 40, September 1988 and Admiral G. Khatov to the Vladivostok conference on 1 October 1988.

Chapter 6

1   These figures, and those following, are based on figures used in the International Monetary Fund's *Direction of Trade* annual volumes and on the trade figures from the United Nations's annual yearbook. Trade figures are both unreliable and imprecise, despite the illusion of precision generated by easy use of decimal points and detailed charts. The figures used in this chapter are usually stated in percentages and should be treated with care. The intention is to identify trends. Numerous sources have commented on how trade data are increasingly less precise because of the difficulty of accounting for trade in services, not to mention intercompany trade. See also *The Economist*, 20 August 1988, and DeAnne Julius and Stephen E. Thomsen, 'Inward Investment and Foreign-owned Firms in the G–5' (London: RIIA, Discussion Paper No. 12, 1989).
2   A. B. Parkanskii, 'Soviet–American Trade in the Pacific' in John J. Stephan and V. P. Chichkanov, eds., *Soviet–American Horizons on the Pacific* (Honolulu: University of Hawaii Press, 1986).
3   John Gittings, *Survey of the Sino-Soviet Dispute* (Oxford: Oxford University Press, 1969).
4   Mineo Nakajima, 'Foreign Relations from the Korean War to the Bandung Line' in Roderick MacFarquhar, ed., *The Cambridge History of China*, vol. 14 (Cambridge: Cambridge University Press, 1987).
5   Ibid., pp. 282–3.
6   See various reports in discussions and an article by Bovin in February 1989 in SU,0386,A3.
7   Donald Zagoria, *The Sino-Soviet Conflict* (Princeton: Princeton University Press, 1962) and William Griffiths, *Sino-Soviet Rift* (London: Allen & Unwin, 1964).
8   Roderick MacFarquhar, *The Origins of the Cultural Revolution*, vol. 2 (Oxford: Oxford University Press, 1983).
9   Gerald Segal, *Sino-Soviet Relations after Mao* (London: IISS, Adelphi Paper No. 202, 1985).
10   Donald Zagoria, ed., *The Soviet Union in East Asia* (London: Yale University Press, 1982); Gerald Segal, ed., *The Soviet Union in East Asia* (London: Heinemann, 1983) and Rodger Swearingen, ed., *Siberia and the Soviet Far East* (Stanford, Calif.: Hoover Institution, 1987).
11   Swearingen, *Soviet Far East* and Allen Whiting, *Siberian Development and East Asia* (Stanford, Calif.: Stanford University Press, 1981).
12   Michael Kaser, 'Reforms in the Soviet Union and China', *The Pacific Review*, vol. 1, no. 2, Summer 1988.

13   Tass on 19 January 1989 in SU,W0061,A,3.
14   *The Economist*, September 1987.
15   *Beijing Review*, 30 January 1989, p. 30.
16   *Socialist Industry* in BBC,SWB,SU,W0026,A1.
17   Tass, 3 March 1989 in SU,W0067,A,3 and *Beijing Review*, 11 September 1989, p. 29.
18   *Financial Times*, 15 March 1989.
19   Although trade between Heilongjiang and the USSR in 1988 was contracted to reach 688 million Swiss francs, owing to transport problems, deliveries amounted to only 196 million Swiss francs. See Xinhua, 13 April 1989 in FE,W0074,A,5. On the Soviet side, see *Sovetskaya Rossiya* on 12 July 1989 in SU,W0087,A1–3.
20   Gilbert Rozman, *A Mirror for Socialism* (London: I. B. Tauris, 1985) and *The Chinese Debates about Soviet Socialism* (London: I. B. Tauris, 1987).
21   See, for example, a Soviet panel discussion on Soviet television, 30 January 1989 in SU,0376,A3,1–4 and *Pravda* 5 June 1989 in SU,W0081,A,4.
22   Xinhua on 23 January 1989 in FE,0368,C1,4 and on 14 March in W0069,A,6. See also Tass, 24 March in FE,0418,A2,2 and *Beijing Review*, 5 June 1989, p. 22.
23   Khabarovsk radio on 25 April 1989 in SU,W0083,A,3, various reports from May SU,W0078,A,7 and W0080,A,2. One Chinese report suggested that up to one million workers could soon be sent to the Soviet Union. *China Daily* cited in *Beijing Review*, 24 July 1989, p. 30.
24   Peking radio in Russian on 17 March 1989 in FE,W0070,A,3 and *Financial Times*, 7 March 1989.
25   There is a mass of such details, but for a sampling see a Soviet report on 21 September 1988 in SU,W0045,A,2; Soviet radio on 9 November 1988 in SU,W0051,A,10 and 18 November in W0058,A,1; Tass, 26 November 1988 in FE,W0055,A,8; Moscow radio, 25 December 1988 in FE,W0058,A,12; Moscow World Service, 11 January 1989 in SU,0356,i; Soviet television, 16 January 1989 in SU,0376,A3,4. More generally, see *The Economist*, 4 February 1989, p. 57.
26   Gerald Segal, 'Sino-Soviet Detente: How Far How Fast', *The World Today*, May 1987.
27   *Far Eastern Economic Review*, 15 December 1988, p. 13.
28   For example, see reports in January 1989 in FE,0366,i and *Beijing Review*, 12 December 1988, p. 11.
29   Chinese Ministry of Foreign Economic Relations and Trade, *Almanac of China's Foreign Economic Relations and Trade, 1986* cited in an unpublished paper by Gaye Christoffersen, 'The Economic Reforms in Northeast China'.
30   See Christoffersen, 'Economic Reforms', for the Chinese view. A Soviet report is in 4 November 1988, SU,W0050,A,5.
31   Tatsuo Kaneda, 'The New Soviet Economic Policy and Asia', *Japan Review of International Affairs*, no. 2, Fall/Winter 1988.

32   Kazuyuki Kinbara, 'The Economic Dimension' (London: Heinemann for the RIIA, 1983).
33   Whiting, *Siberian Development*.
34   Gerald Segal, 'The Soviet Union and the Pacific Century', *The Journal of Communist Studies*, vol. 3, no. 4, December 1987.
35   Y. Balakh in *Pravda*, 30 March 1989 in SU, W0073, A1–2.
36   *Far Eastern Economic Review*, 12 June 1986. A Soviet view is in 'Exploring
      Ways of Cooperation', *Far Eastern Affairs*, no. 3, 1989.
37   Tanjug, 20 April 1989 in SU, W0074, A, 2; *Financial Times*, 26 April 1989. See also 'Exploring Ways'.
38   'Exploring Ways' and R. S. H. Aliev, 'Polemic Notes of a Japanese Affairs Specialist', *Far Eastern Affairs*, no. 3, 1989.
39   See the comprehensive analysis in Leonard Geron, *Joint Ventures in the USSR: Data Base* (London: Chatham House Special Paper, 1989).
40   *Japan Economic Journal*, 22 April 1989.
41   *International Herald Tribune*, 14 July 1989. More curiously, the Soviet Union is now exporting Sakhalin peat moss to Japan for packing orchids and tulips (noted in *Asiaweek*, 23 June 1989). This might give a whole new twist to the idea of territorial readjustments in the region.
42   *New York Times*, 9 November 1988 and *International Herald Tribune*, 14 November 1988.
43   Moscow radio on 2 May 1989 in SU, W0076, A, 1 and *Far Eastern Economic Review*, 20 July 1989, p. 32.
44   On these ideas see *Japan Economic Journal*, 24 December 1988; Tass, 20 December 1988 in SU, W0058, A, 9 and Kyodo, 12 December in FE, W0056, i. Also see the *Financial Times*, 25 November 1988.
45   *International Herald Tribune*, 9 December 1988.
46   *Financial Times*, 25 November 1988.
47   For one of many reports on these problems, see *Pravda*, 10 October 1988 in SU, W0061, A, 3.
48   Alan Sanders, *Mongolia* (London: Frances Pinter, 1987).
49   Quintin Bach, *Soviet Economic Assistance to the Less Developed Countries* (Oxford: Clarendon Press, 1987).
50   M. Trigubenko, 'Soviet Far East and Asian Socialist Countries', *Far Eastern Affairs*, no. 5, 1987.
51   Yu Stolyarov, 'Soviet Trade and Economic Relations with APR Countries', *Far Eastern Affairs*, no. 4, 1988.
52   *Izvestiya*, 16 April 1989 in SU, W0074, A, 2–3.
53   Bach, *Soviet Economic Assistance*.
54   See some sparse but still useful comparative trade data for all Indochinese states in *Asian Economic Handbook* (London: Euromonitor Publications, 1987).
55   *Far Eastern Economic Review*, 23 July 1987.
56   M. Trigubenko, 'Cooperation between CMEA and Vietnam', *Far Eastern Affairs*, no. 4, 1988.
57   Ibid., p. 67; Hanoi radio, 4 November 1988 in FE, W0052, A, 9 and *Far Eastern Economic Review*, 10 November 1988.
58   Trigubenko, 'Soviet Far East', p. 25.

59   VNA on 1 March 1989 in FE,0402,A2,3; *Far Eastern Economic Review*, 20 April 1989, p. 8.
60   *Far Eastern Economic Review*, 11 May 1989.
61   Yonhap, 8 June 1989 in FE,W0081,i.
62   Ibid. and George Ginsburgs, 'The Case of Vietnamese *Gastarbeiters* in the Soviet Union' (unpublished paper, 1988). See also more current reports in 'Maritime Territory: Past, Present and Future', a background brief issued by the hosts of the Vladivostok conference, October 1988.
63   Details from V. Mikheyev, 'The DPRK's Regional Economic Relations', *Far Eastern Affairs*, no. 2, 1989.
64   Ginsburgs, 'Vietnamese *Gastarbeiters*'.
65   *Far Eastern Economic Review*, 27 April 1989, p. 33. Cites CIA figures.
66   Mikheyev, 'DPRK's Regional Economic Relations'.
67   Trigubenko, 'Soviet Far East', pp. 25–7.
68   Radio Peace and Progress in Chinese on 16 February 1989, SU,0402,A3,2 and *New Times*, no. 8, 1989.
69   Xinhua on 4 March 1989 in FE,0404,A2,1.
70   *Asian Economic Handbook*, p. 167.
71   *Far Eastern Economic Review*, 16 February 1989, p. 23.
72   One Soviet source put Soviet Pacific trade with California at merely $121 million in 1980. See Parkanskii, 'Soviet-American'.
73   See some evidence of such discussions in Soviet television, 1 December 1988, on a Siberia-Alaska project in SU,W0055,A,14 and a deal with Australia on Moscow World Service in December 1988 in SU,0330,i.
74   Cited in 'Maritime Territory: Past, Present and Future', a background brief issued by the hosts of the Vladivostok conference, October 1988.
75   7 July 1988 in FE,0197,i.
76   Reports in SU,W0067,A2 and *Financial Times*, 3 March 1989.
77   Buszynski, *Soviet Foreign Policy*, appendix.
78   G. Chufrin in *Izvestiya*, 6 October 1988 in SOV,88,195,13–15.
79   Ibid.
80   For a particularly pessimistic view see Graeme Gill, 'The Soviet Union and Southeast Asia: A New Beginning', *Contemporary Southeast Asia*, no. 1, June 1988. See more optimism in reports of Indonesian President Suharto's visit to Moscow in September 1989 in *Izvestiya*, 30 August 1989 in SU,0549,A3,1–2 and *Far Eastern Economic Review*, 21 September 1989, pp. 10–12.
81   Tass on 5 December 1988 in FE,0328,A2,3.
82   Moscow World Service on 6 September 1988 in FBIS-SOV,88,173, 25–6 and Moscow Home Service, 16 May 1989 in SU,0497,A3,3.
83   Moscow World Service, 19 July 1988 in SU,W0036,A,2.
84   See the Soviet-Filipino statement on 22 December 1988 in FE,0343,A2,1–2, and Radio Veritas on 9 January 1989 in FE,0356,A2,2.
85   Details in *Far Eastern Economic Review*, 30 March 1989 and Moscow radio in Tagalog, 1 October 1989 in SU,0589,A3,2.
86   Agence France Press on 10 October 1988 in SOV,88,197,19 and the *Free China Journal*, 30 October 1989, p. 8.
87   CNA in January 1990 in FE,W0111,1.

88   *Far Eastern Economic Review*, 20 July 1989, p. 67.
89   *Far Eastern Economic Review*, 3 November 1988 and *Financial Times*, 25 November 1988.
90   See also China News Agency on 5 October 1988 in SU,W0048,A3.
91   China News Agency, 24 March 1989 in FE,0421,A2,2. See also FE,0424,i and W0071,i.
92   James Riordan, 'Korea-Soviet Union Relations', *Korea and World Affairs*, vol. 12, no. 4, Winter 1988.
93   Alexei Bogaturov and Mikhail Nosov, 'The Korean Aspect', *New Times*, no. 23, 1989.
94   For background see Roy Kim, 'Gorbachev and the Korean Peninsula', *The Third World Quarterly*, July 1988 and *Far Eastern Economic Review*, 18 May and 28 September 1989.
95   *Far Eastern Economic Review*, 8 December 1988.
96   Ibid., p. 22. See Yonhap on 5 April in FE,0435,A2,1.
97   *Far Eastern Economic Review*, 22 March 1990, pp. 22–3 and *Billion*, February 1990, p. 48.
98   *New York Times*, 5 February 1988 and other notes in Kim, 'Gorbachev and Korea', p. 1293.
99   V. Golanov, deputy chairman of the Presidium of the USSR Chamber of Trade and Industry, on 10 February quoted by Tass in SU,W0065,A,3. The USSR reportedly supplied coal, sawn timber and fish products.
100 Xinhua, 26 December 1988 in SU,W0058,A,9.
101 Yonhap, 3 April 1989 in FE,W0071,i.
102 Yonhap, 23 February 1989 in FE,0402,A2,3.
103 *Izvestiya*, 5 January 1989 in SU,W0060,A,2–3 and Yonhap, 20 January 1989 in FE,W0062,A,9. Also on the Avialat link, see Yonhap on 10 February 1989 in FE,0382,i. Avialat will handle some domestic Soviet flights and flights to countries with which the Soviet Union has no official diplomatic relations.
104 *Izvestiya*, 12 January 1989 in SU,W0061,A,4.
105 Yonhap, 24 January 1989 in FE,0369,A2,1 and 23 March 1989 in 0418,A2,3.
106 Yonhap, 9 March 1989 in SU,W0068,A,3.
107 *Izvestiya*, 5 January 1989 in SU,W0060,A,2–3 and Yonhap, 22 December 1988 in FE,03433,A2,5.
108 Soviet television on 30 March 1989 in SU,W0072,A5–6.
109 V. Shipayev in *Komsomolskaya Pravda*, 25 October 1988 in SOV,88,209,17–19 and F. I. Shabshina in *Izvestiya* reported in SU,0564,A3,1–2, 18 September 1989.
110 Moscow Home Service, 9 February 1989 in SU,0384,i and see more generally S. Shilovtsev, 'Economic Modernization in South Korea', *Far Eastern Affairs*, no. 5, 1989.
111 Yonhap, 23 January 1989 in FE,0366,A2,2 and 25 January in 0369,A2,1.
112 For a sample problem, see Moscow television on 30 March 1989 in SU,W0072,A,6.
113 See a comment by Bovin as well as by a leading East German official, quoted in Yutaka Akino, 'The Soviet Asian Policy in a New

Perspective', unpublished paper presented to a Chatham House conference in December 1988. See a more modern German solution in Jin Park, 'Korean Reunification and the New German Question', *The Pacific Review*, no. 1, 1990.

114 Paul Gardner, 'Tuna Poaching and Nuclear Testing in the South Pacific', *Orbis*, Spring 1988.

115 *Far Eastern Economic Review*, 27 April 1989, p. 31.

116 Paul Dibb, 'Soviet Strategy towards Australia, New Zealand and the South-West Pacific', *Australian Outlook*, August 1985.

117 D. D. Tumarkin, 'USSR—The Unknown Northern Neighbour' in R. Crocombe and A. Ali, eds., *Foreign Forces in Pacific Politics* (Fiji: University of South Pacific, 1983).

118 'Foreign Trade Reform' issued by the organizers of the Vladivostok conference in October 1988.

119 'USSR for Trade and Economic Cooperation in Asia and the Pacific', issued by the organizers of the Vladivostok conference, October 1988.

120 G. Chufrin in *Izvestiya*, 6 October 1988 in SOV,88,195,13–14.

121 David Arase, 'Pacific Economic Cooperation', *The Pacific Review*, vol. 1, no. 2.

122 Segal, 'Pacific Century'.

123 Trigubenko, 'Cooperation between CMEA and Vietnam'.

124 Central Intelligence Agency, *Handbook of Economic Statistics*, 1987.

125 B. Klyuchnikov, 'The Soviet Far East in the Pacific Century' and Stolyarov, 'Soviet Trade', both in *Far Eastern Affairs*, no. 4, 1988 and 'The Soviet Far East and the Asian Pacific Region', *Far Eastern Affairs*, no. 4, 1989.

126 10 December 1988 in SU,0336,C2 and SU,W0058,A,1–8.

127 See Politburo discussions assessed on Moscow Home Service, 17 February 1989 in SU,0390,B,1–2 and Soviet television on 13 April in 0436,B,6–7. For background see the excellent Jonathan Shiffer, *Soviet Regional Economic Policy* (London: Macmillan, 1989).

128 The controversy was most apparent during the October 1988 Vladivostok conference and in the pages of *International Affairs*, August 1988 and *Far Eastern Affairs*, no. 4, 1989. More specific evidence is in Tass, 15 December 1988 in FE,W0057,A,4. Most surprising of all, the head of the Soviet PECC committee, Y. Primakov, argued the conservative case in *Pravda*, 7 December 1988 in SU,W0057,A,6–8. See Tass, 25 January 1989 for another conservative comment by I. Ivanov in SU,W0062,A,1. Note also that the Vladivostok first party secretary was fired in January 1989 in SU,0359,i, and the commander of the Far Eastern military district was defeated in the elections in March 1989. See SU,0428,B,5–6 for the commander's explanation.

129 See the discussion in *International Herald Tribune*, 13 May 1989.

130 29 March 1989 in SU,0439,C1–4 and Academician Abalkin on 3 April 1989 on p. 4.

131 Based on discussion in Vladivostok, but see also I. Ivanov on 25 January 1989 in SU,W0062,A,1, and again on Soviet television, 7 February 1989 in SU,0386,A3,3; *Far Eastern Economic Review*, 2 February 1989, p. 54

and *Izvestiya*, 18 June 1989 in SU, W0083, A, 1–2. See an interview with Ivanov in *Argumenty i Fakty*, no. 32, 12–18 August 1989 in SU, W0091, A, 1. Also see the views of Vladimir Golanov in Novosti Press Agency Bulletin No. 14, August 1989.

132   Noted in *International Affairs*, August 1988, p. 150.

133   See a useful survey by James Dorian and Helen Caldwell, *Soviet-Asian Minerals Cooperation* (Honolulu: East-West Center Working Paper, April 1989).

134   *The Economist*, 6 May 1989, p. 16 of Australia survey.

135   *Far Eastern Economic Review*, 11 May 1989, p. 76, notes that growth in demand for metals is higher in Asia than anywhere else except Japan.

136   'Exploring Ways'.

137   This is the theme of much of the evidence in *International Affairs*, August 1988 and the Vladivostok meeting in general.

138   See, for example, *Izvestiya* roundtable on 14 August 1988 in SU, W0042, A, 11; Tass 15 December 1988 in SU, W0057, A, 4–5 and also the proceedings of the Vladivostok meeting.

139   *Pravda*, 12 February 1989 in SU, W0065, A, 4.

140   See Leonard Geron, 'Joint ventures in the Soviet Union and Eastern Europe', *Global Finance Forum* (forthcoming) and 'Joint Ventures' in *Vestnik*, March 1990.

141   See a report on Vladivostok in *Moscow News*, no. 41, 1988 and 'USSR Far East' issued by Novosti in September 1988 for the Vladivostok conference.

142   Discussed in detail in *The Economist*, 14 January 1989, pp. 70–71.

143   A member of IMEMO speaking at Chatham House, 16 February 1989.

144   Gilbert Rozman, 'Moscow's Japan-Watchers in the First Years of the Gorbachev Era', *The Pacific Review*, no. 3, 1988.

145   Klyuchnikov, 'Soviet Far East', p. 8.

146   These discussions are detailed in Segal, 'Pacific Century' and in issue no. 3 of *The Pacific Review* in 1988.

147   For example, M. Senina and A. Solovyova, 'The Struggle for the Computer Markets in the APR', *Far Eastern Affairs*, no. 4, 1988.

148   Rozman, 'Moscow's Japan-Watchers'.

149   For this fascinating argument, which holds Sweden up as a positive example of reformed socialism, see *Pravda*, 30 March 1989 in SU, W0073, A, 1–2.

150   For a fuller analysis of these Pacific trends see Gerald Segal, *Rethinking the Pacific* (Oxford: Oxford University Press, 1990).

151   The image and the detailed analysis are in the twin volumes by Gilbert Rozman, *A Mirror for Socialism* (London: I. B. Tauris, 1985) and *The Chinese Debate about Soviet Socialism* (London: I. B. Tauris, 1987).

152   31 July 1988, cited in SWB, SU, 0233, A3, 2.

153   For some useful background to these issues see Galia Golan, *The Soviet Union and National Liberation Movements in the Third World* (London: Unwin Hyman, 1988) and Stephen Shenfield, 'The Long and Winding Road' in Stephen White and Alex Pravda, eds., *Ideology and Soviet Politics* (London: Macmillan, 1988).

154 These issues are documented in several articles in *The Pacific Review*, no. 3, 1988 and Segal, 'The Soviet Union'.

Chapter 7

1 Descriptions of these debates are based on material presented in earlier chapters and on informal discussions with Soviet officials and scholars during a trip to Moscow and Vladivostok in September–October 1988.
2 Konstantin Pleshakov, 'Citadel or Harbour?', *New Times*, no. 20, 1989.
3 A. Nagorny, 'The Vladivostok Initiative: Two Years On', *International Affairs*, August 1988, p. 152.

Bibliographical Note

When, in 1983, the Royal Institute of International Affairs asked me to edit a volume on the Soviet Union's role in East Asia, I began the analysis by suggesting that the Soviet Union was a power in East Asia but not an East Asian power (Gerald Segal, ed., *The Soviet Union and East Asia*, London: Heinemann, 1983). Six years later, after much change in Soviet and East Asian politics, it is time to look at the subject again, but this time—in keeping with the trend to analyse broader, Pacific-wide international relations—to consider the Soviet Union as a Pacific power.

To help the reader understand the reasons for adopting a wider scope, as well as to avoid the usual undifferentiated bibliography, I offer a brief, annotated bibliography.

The existing literature can be categorized in several ways. First, because of the complexity of the subject, there has been a tendency to write article-length analyses, which are then gathered up in an edited volume. *The Soviet Union in East Asia* (New Haven: Yale University Press, 1982), edited by Donald Zagoria, falls into this category, as does my own *The Soviet Union and East Asia*, mentioned above. However, as any honest editor knows, contributors never quite write the chapters that fit with all the rest, and such volumes tend to lack coherence. More recent attempts to look at Soviet policy in the region have suffered from similar problems, despite the presence of fine individual chapters. Ramesh Thakur and Carlyle Thayer, eds., *The Soviet Union as an Asian Pacific Power* (London: Westview, 1987); Georges Tan Eng Bok, *The USSR in East Asia* (Paris: Atlantic Institute Papers Nos. 59–60, 1986); and Richard Solomon and Masataka Kosaka, eds., *The Soviet Far East Military Buildup* (London: Croom Helm, 1986) are examples. For a brief, but more innovative, analysis, see Tsuyoshi Hasegawa, ed., *The Soviet Union Faces Asia* (Sapporo: Slavic Research Centre, 1987).

Second, certain countries have been more important for Soviet policy in the region and have therefore drawn the attention of analysts. Relations with China and Japan are obvious cases in point, but recently there have also been some studies of Soviet relations with Southeast Asia: e.g., Myles Robertson, *The Soviet Union and Japan*

(Cambridge: Cambridge University Press, 1988), Tom Hart, *Sino-Soviet Relations* (London: Gower, 1987), and the fine analyses in Gilbert Rozman's two studies, *A Mirror for Socialism* (London: I. B. Tauris, 1985) and *The Chinese Debates about Soviet Socialism* (London: I. B. Tauris, 1987). See also Harry Gelman, *The Soviet Far East Buildup and Soviet Risk-Taking against China* (Santa Monica, Calif.: Rand R–2943–AF, 1982); John J. Stephan and V. P. Chichkanov, eds., *Soviet American Horizons on the Pacific* (Honolulu: University of Hawaii Press, 1986); R. A. Longmire, *Soviet Relations with South East Asia* (London: Kegan Paul International, 1989); and Leszek Buszynski, *Soviet Foreign Policy and Southeast Asia* (London: Croom Helm, 1986). These studies are useful in providing detail about specific aspects of Soviet policy in the region, but by definition they are not intended to provide an overview of the Soviet role.

Third, most studies have concentrated on Soviet policy rather than on the more complex question of Soviet interaction with the region. See, for instance, Robert Manning, *Asian Policy* (New York: Priority Press, 1989). Inevitably, studies that approach the subject from the perspective of a single country tend to be unduly concerned with the perceptions of the state concerned and less careful to assess the international relations dimensions. This was a particular problem in many analyses of Sino–Soviet relations, whether from the Soviet or the Chinese side. See a discussion in Gerald Segal, *Sino-Soviet Relations after Mao* (London: IISS, Adelphi Papers No. 202, 1985). Of course, due attention must be paid to the Soviet perspective on Pacific issues, but especially at a time when Soviet officials are admitting their previous misperceptions of the region, it is important for outsiders to take a broader look at the place of the Soviet Union in the Pacific.

Fourth, there has been a problem in integrating aspects of Soviet domestic and foreign policy. Of course, this is a problem in the analyses of most states' foreign relations, and there have been a few serious efforts in the case of Soviet policy towards East Asia. See Paul Dibb, *Siberia and the Pacific* (London: Praeger, 1972); E. Stuart Kirby, *The Soviet Far East* (London: Macmillan, 1971); Violet Conolly, *Siberia, Today and Tomorrow* (London: Collins, 1975); Allen Whiting, *Siberian Development and East Asia* (Stanford: Stanford University Press, 1981); Rodger Swearingen, ed., *Siberia and the Soviet Far East* (Stanford: Hoover Institution, 1987), which has a superb bibliography on Soviet sources; and Jonathan Schiffer, *Soviet Regional Economic Policy* (London: Macmillan, 1989). Yet as the Soviet Union undertakes major reform, these previous analyses are inevitably dated or avowedly do not deal with current issues under debate in the Soviet Union.

Fifth, few of the books already noted focus on Soviet policy in the Pacific. Rather, most authors are interested in the Soviet Union as an East Asian power. It is true, if only for reasons of demography, that the Soviet Union is not an East Asian power. Yet, like the United States, it does have a claim to be a Pacific power—especially now, when the new Soviet orientation is to take the notion of Pacific cooperation more seriously, so that the focus of analysis must change from the narrower East Asian to the broader Pacific-wide view.

Finally, many of the books already listed take some note of the history of Russian approaches to the region. In addition, see Allen Wood, ed., *Siberia* (London: Croom Helm, 1987); Glyn Barratt, *Russia in Pacific Waters* (Vancouver: University of British Columbia Press, 1981); or even Walter Kolarz, *The Peoples of the Soviet Far East* (London: George Philip, 1954). Most recent analyses seem much less interested in the legacy of the past. In view of the depth of the challenges facing the Soviet Union, it is important not to lose sight of previous Russian experiences in the area. Similarly, matters of ideology used to loom large in studies of Soviet policy, but most were concerned primarily with communist politics. In the new age of reform in the Soviet Union, it is clear that ideological questions are broader and deserve a wide treatment that covers aspects of culture.

Index